THE POEMS OF ARCHIBALD LAMPMAN

Literature of Canada

Poetry and Prose in Reprint

Douglas Lochhead, General Editor

The Poems of Archibald Lampman

(including At the Long Sault)

Introduction by Margaret Coulby Whitridge

UNIVERSITY OF TORONTO PRESS

© University of Toronto Press 1974
Toronto and Buffalo
Printed in Canada
ISBN (casebound) 0-8020-2074-7
ISBN (paperback) 0-8020-6204-0
LC 73-92517

819.1
L238p

Literature of Canada Series 12
This reprint includes the following two volumes: *The Poems of Archibald Lampman* (Morang 1900) and *At the Long Sault and Other New Poems* (Ryerson 1943).

This book has been published with the assistance of a grant from the Ontario Arts Council.

189686

Preface

Yes, there is a Canadian literature. It does exist. Part of the evidence to support these statements is presented in the form of reprints of the poetry and prose of the authors included in this series. Much of this literature has been long out of print. If the country's culture and traditions are to be sampled and measured, both in terms of past and present-day conditions, then the major works of both our well-known and our lesser-known writers should be available for all to buy and read. The Literature of Canada series aims to meet this need. It shares with its companion series, The Social History of Canada, the purpose of making the documents of the country's heritage accessible to an increasingly large national and international public, a public which is anxious to acquaint itself with Canadian literature — the writing itself — and also to become intimate with the times in which it grew.

DL

Archibald Lampman, 1861-99

Margaret Coulby Whitridge

Introduction

Canadian literature, in terms of its distinctive identity, dates from about 1870. One of the most exciting periods of its development occurred in the period from 1880 to 1900, when there was an outburst of intellectual, political, social, and economic activity as the new generation of young men and women, bred from determined pioneer stock, was inspired to seek creative fulfilment in the image of nationhood. Much of their interest focused on Ottawa.

The small nucleus of writers who banded together to found a national literature during this period is known as the Confederation Group or the Group of '61, since most of its members were born in that year. The group included three poets living in Ottawa: Duncan Campbell Scott, William Wilfred Campbell, and the most original talent of the three, Archibald Lampman. They were described, not altogether accurately, as nature poets, although their interests encompassed politics, science, and the arts, allied with their strong regional orientation. All three were the sons of clergymen, Lampman and Campbell having been destined for the Anglican ministry until they turned their backs on formal religion at the conclusion of their university days. These were acts of personal rebellion which took considerable courage and caused much regret to their families. The three young men entered the government of Canada as clerks in the civil service. Scott, the only one without a university education, rose to become deputy minister for Indian Affairs and Campbell achieved some advancement through the influence of his close friend, William Lyon Mackenzie King, but Lampman remained a poorly paid clerk at the time of his death in 1899.

Closely allied with the Ottawa poets were their friends Bliss Carman and Charles G.D. Roberts. Indeed, Lampman claimed that Roberts inspired him to become a poet and enlisted his support to help establish a national literature. The two Maritime poets, who commenced writing in their native New Brunswick, later moved to the United States where they achieved a recognition denied to them at home. They continued, however, to encourage Lampman and were able, in their editorial capacities, to arrange for publication of his work in leading American periodicals.

The depth of the lasting friendship which united Lampman, Carman, and Roberts can best be grasped from their letters. In 1882 Lampman graduated from the University of Toronto with honours in languages — he was fluent in German, French, and English and competent in Greek, Latin, and Hebrew. He then embarked upon a brief, disastrous career as a schoolmaster in Orangeville, Ontario. On 23 September of that year Roberts, who was teaching school in Fredericton, wrote to his friend commiserating with him over their unfortunate lot as teachers:

> It is a costly profession for the literary man ... As for British Columbia, I should be sorry to see you, even for a very short time, remove yourself so far from the centres of Canadian life and thought ... I suppose, from your intimacy with Collins, that you are one of us right through, a Canadian republican![1] We want to get together literary and independent young Canada, and to spread our doctrine with untiring hands.

He added sage criticism:

> I suppose he told you what I thought of the last two poems of yours. There was still, I think, an evidence of haste, and too

little of determined perplexing and polishing; but there appeared a marked increase of flesh and blood, a warmer beating of the pulse of humanity. At the same time, your spontaneity, the indubitable lyric grace and flavor of detached lines was not less apparent, and in the battle verses there was a very fine swing and lilt. I hope soon to see some more of your work.

The two poems were 'The Last Sortie' and 'Derelict,' which were published in the Trinity College review, *Rouge et Noir*, in September 1882. They have not since been reprinted and are chiefly of interest as examples of the Germanic influence evident in Lampman's early work. Lampman sent copies to several friends during July and August, admitting that he already suffered from a sense of defeat as the result of their rejection by American journals.

Six years later, on 18 December 1888, when he was teaching at King's College in Windsor, Nova Scotia, Roberts wrote to Lampman congratulating him on the publication of his first volume of poetry, *Among the Millet:*

I have read it nearly all and am filled with enthusiastic delight and pride. It seems to me one of the finest first volumes ever issued by a poet. The genius of it is utterly beyond question. Among the poets across the line there are none of the like age to compare at all with you and Carman. We will make this a glorious epoch in our country's history, I do from the bottom of my soul believe. Your sonnets are exquisite, your lyrics not less admirable. Shall particularize later on — and in public shall speak with no uncertain note. Carman is staying with me, and has been parading up and down the room raving on your verses. Send him a copy (to Fredericton, N.B.) and he will give it a long and glowing review in the *Boston Advertiser!*[2]

ix

Such sincere praise and interested criticism from his fellow poets provided a continuing stimulus for Lampman, who was locked by illness and insecurity into a life which seemed to him both narrow and provincial.

Similarly, Lampman's correspondence with Bliss Carman spanned a number of years commencing with an admiring letter from Carman late in 1888. The three friends met as frequently as possible and shared their mutual theories on politics, philosophy, and poetry. Happy hours were spent drinking beer and talking late over their pipes when they met in Quebec City in 1890. They wrote each other humorous verses on scraps of paper; signed copies may still be found in Lampman's manuscript notebooks of Roberts' poem, 'Remember One Day in Quebec,' and of Carman's less aptly titled verse, 'On a Ball Programme.'[3] They furthered each other's career whenever possible in published reviews and they enjoyed their rare holidays together while Lampman's wife was tucked away with the children in a small cottage on the bank of Lac Deschênes near Ottawa.

In Toronto, Lampman could also count on the support of literary friends. J.E. Collins was a minor novelist, journalist, and historian with a discriminating sensitivity who believed that Lampman was Canada's most outstanding poet. Collins also appreciated Lampman's ability as a prose writer and during the winter of 1883-4 he commissioned his young friend to collaborate anonymously in his second historical work, *Canada under the Administration of Lord Lorne*. There is evidence that Lampman was responsible for the natural descriptions of Ontario and Quebec in the book.

Another of Lampman's friends in Toronto was Edward William Thomson, editor of *The Globe*. This 'prince of friends,' a man of distinction and power, moved to Boston in 1891 to become editor of the *Youth's Companion*, but he remained Lampman's closest friend and real confidant. They visited each other and corresponded frequently during the last decade of the century, sharing mutual aspirations and problems, frustrations and triumphs. Their correspondence, which was witty as well as intellectual, adds greatly to any understanding of Lampman's beliefs and personality. It was published, with some interesting deletions, by Arthur Bourinot of Ottawa in 1956 and 1957.[4]

Lampman was fortunate in numbering among his friends a literate and encouraging circle of intellectual acquaintances in Montreal which included the doctor-poet, William Henry Drummond; Dr Tait McKenzie, physician, sculptor, and writer; William Douw Lighthall, lawyer and writer; and the fascinating French-Canadian portrait painter, Edmond Dyonnet, whose Dorchester Street apartment was a favourite haunt during Lampman's visits to Montreal. It was here that Dyonnet painted what is reputedly the best likeness of Lampman, a three-quarter portrait, which cannot now be traced.

On various occasions, Lampman travelled to Montreal, Boston, Quebec City, and as far east as Digby, Nova Scotia. He visited Chicago and Philadelphia but he never saw western Canada nor did he travel abroad. On his trips he often stopped to visit friends en route and of one such visit to Montreal, Arthur Stringer in 1941 wrote an intriguing reminiscence which appeared in *Saturday Night*.[5] He recounted the circumstances surrounding his only meeting with Lampman in June 1898 at Dr Drummond's home on Sherbrooke Street, during the poet's last trip to Montreal.

That Lampman was by then highly reputed can be learned from Stringer's description of the 'uncrowned poet laureate of

Canada.' Stringer saw the poet as a man

> slight of frame, with a pendant forelock and a smallish yellow-brown beard. His neatly chiselled face was long and thin and touched with melancholy. The almost womanly delicacy of moulding and the large gentleness of the meditative eyes at once reminded me of earlier suggestions that so many of this earth's men of genius carried with them a mysterious touch of the feminine.

But Stringer recognized the sensitivity of spirit, the immediate response to beauty, and above all, the outward shyness that sheathed the inner courage of the true creator. 'The carelessly dressed figure before me looked frail. But from it I harvested an impression of some stubborn inner strength that would mock and defy the outer fragility of the flesh.' The talk that night was about Canadian poets – the writing of poetry as a vocation in Canada and the themes available to the poet.

Stringer was, at the time, a young reporter on the *Montreal Herald*, and it is remarkable that, towards the end of his long career, he could still vividly recall his encounter with the two poets and describe Lampman in such human and accurate terms. For Lampman's outstanding characteristics were stubborness and inner courage. They were at the same time his strength and his greatest weakness. To the end of his life, in spite of suffering from heart disease, he courageously carried on punishing physical activities – fishing, hiking, canoeing and portaging, swimming in icy waters, and farming, during the summers, on rented properties near Wakefield, Quebec. He worked as a civil servant and played active roles in the Fabian Society, the Progressive Club, the Debating Society, the Ottawa Literary and Scientific Society, the

Social Science Club, and the Royal Society of Canada, where he presented papers or gave poetry readings. And always, he continued to write.

Through his work for these societies, Lampman made several friends in Ottawa who appreciated his ability as a poet. An example of their devotion may still be seen in Ottawa where, for almost seventy years, a yellowing government memorandum has hung on a wall of the Ottawa Public Library. It is addressed to W.A. Code of the Post Office Department and is signed simply with the initials 'A.L.' The text is brief:

Date of birth 1861 — Place: Thorold, County of Kent, Ontario — of German stock on both sides — father a clergyman of the Church of England — educated at Trinity University, Toronto — graduated B.A. 1882 — entered Civil Service 1883.

As to the circumstances that first caused me to think of writing verse, it is not an easy thing to talk about, and I really do not know what there is to say. I have occupied and amused myself with verse writing for fourteen or fifteen years. I took to it, I suppose, because I found it a fine intellectual exercise, and also because it was a method of self-expression which brought me peace and serenity.

On the back of the framed memorandum is a note by the recipient, Mr Code, who noted:

The attached was given to me by the poet A. Lampman in response to a request made of him as to the circumstances that caused him to write verse. Mr Lampman and the undersigned were fellow civil servants in the Post Office Department, Langevin Block, for many years and during two years of the period ... I was president of the Y.M.C.A. Library and Debating

Society. 'An Evening with Lampman' was on the programme one winter and the accompanying paper signed 'A.L.' formed part of the evening's entertainment...

Lampman's note, far from reflecting his complex personality, classical education, and powerful intellect, is the statement of a shy, introverted, and modest young man. However, he was well understood and his literary merit appreciated by close friends and colleagues, including Mr Code, who carefully preserved the note for many years before presenting it to the Ottawa Public Library.

Other enduring friendships were made in Ottawa by Scott, Lampman and Campbell because of their memberships in the Royal Society of Canada, although Lampman almost despaired of being admitted by the time of his election to its ranks in 1895, through the offices of John G. Bourinot and George Stewart, the latter then secretary of the Society. It was an honour Lampman had long desired and felt he deserved, particularly since Scott and Campbell were already members.

James Fletcher, the Dominion entomologist, and John Macoun, assistant director and naturalist of the Geological Survey of Canada, who became friends and admirers of Lampman, were members of the biological sciences section of the society. Both were brilliant natural scientists who appreciated Lampman's love of nature and his sensitive, accurate descriptions of Canada's flora and fauna, which gave his poems a striking originality and national character rarely found in Canadian poetry. Macoun's two sons, also noted scientists, shared the poet's interest in political and social causes. These friends often accompanied Scott and Lampman on long hikes through the Gatineau Hills or up the Lièvre River, sixty miles north of Ottawa. The trips were celebrated by Lampman in poems such as the beautiful sonnet 'A

Dawn on the Lièvre' and the brilliant stanzas of 'Morning on the Lièvre.' The latter was in 1961 translated into a prize-winning film produced by David Bairstow of the National Film Board.

Lampman's poetry has also, in several instances, been set to music, partly because of its lyrical qualities noted earlier by Roberts. 'A Summer Evening,' arranged by Keith Bissell in 1967, is a good example. Music is a major subject in Lampman's work, as may be seen in poems such as 'The Child's Music Lesson,' 'The Organist,' 'Music,' 'The Minstrel,' 'The Piano,' and 'Even beyond Music.' Both his family and his wife were greatly interested in music, his mother and his youngest sister Annie having studied music in Europe and been concert performers and professional musicians in Ottawa for many years. Many of Lampman's poems are described by him as songs and given titles to that effect, including 'The Song of Pan,' 'The Song of the Stream-drops,' and 'The Poet's Song.'

Music was for Lampman an intensely personal experience. For example, in 'The Child's Music Lesson,' an early poem, the wavering piano notes played by the little girl remind the poet of his own, happier youth, which is also recalled by the beauty of the kitchen garden where he sits and dreams, surrounded by yellow, bell-like pumpkin flowers, while listening to the music through an open window. He compares the girl's distress with his own pain and the frustration of his narrow existence since, he realizes: 'My heart, a garden in a hidden place/Is full of folded buds of memories.' Against the pattern of music, interwoven with the earthy beauty of nature, is pitted Lampman's enemy, the city: 'Yet even here the voices of hard life go by;/Outside the city strains with its eternal cry.'

Another poem having music as a subject, 'Even beyond Music,' was written in January 1899, three weeks prior to his death, worn out at the age of thirty-seven by the encroachments of heart disease and pneumonia. It is not a brilliant poem but it is a strong, final personal expression, clearly delineating Lampman's understanding of his failing physical condition and the threat of death. It was first published in *At the Long Sault and Other New Poems* in 1943, having been chosen by E.K. Brown from Lampman's last pencilled manuscript notebook.[6] Lampman and his wife apparently separated for a brief period, but were reunited during the severe illness of his last two years, and it is presumably to her that the verses were addressed:

Touch not the ivory keys again
No music tonight, my dear.
The rhythmic sound is too full of pain
I cannot bear to hear.

The music reminded Lampman of his restricted world and pointed 'To the beautiful things we sought in vain/And the things we loved and lost.' He concluded intuitively:

Then touch the ivory keys no more,
Nay, let them be, I cried,
For my heart tonight is bleeding and sore
And all its wounds are wide.

Whatever his mood, Lampman often used music to bare his feelings, weaving them compellingly into an unusual natural setting, juxtaposing the pumpkin blossoms, for example, with the almost visible music notes of the child's piano. Again, he might interlock a romantic musical theme with a pattern of lacy green, spring-leaved trees or with a flower-laden lovers' arbour.

Lampman was also interested in art. His manuscript notebooks are bordered with sketches of cats and trees, friends and enemies, flowers and mountains. The effect of his knowledge and love of art on his writing was noted early by his admirers. In 1894, writing in the *Canadian Magazine*, Arthur Stringer shrewdly estimated the poet's place among the founders of what he hoped would develop into a national literature:

> Of the group of Canadian poets who have obtained a recognized standing — Roberts, Lampman, Carman, Campbell and Scott — probably Lampman is the most thoroughly Canadian and in Canada the most popular. He is not as scholarly as Roberts; he has not the strong imaginative power of Campbell; he may not have the mysterious melody of language peculiar to Carman nor the pleasing daintiness and occasional felicitousness of Scott; but he is the strongest and broadest poet of the group, possessing what Landor has called 'substantiality.' He has an artist's eye for color, and the quiet thoughtfulness of a student of scenery ... No one has written more happily of our seasons and landscapes, of the long, white, silent winter; of the warm, melodious awakening spring, of the hot, parched Canadian midsummer days, with their dust and drought, and of the reddening and yellowing leaves of autumn ... Lampman sees nature in a peculiarly simple light; there is little of the transforming fancy in his word-painted scenes. They are more than ideal ... graphic and impressive.[7]

Lampman used colour masterfully in his poetry and if, in his later work, gray became a favourite adjective, it was accurately and deliberately chosen to reflect his state of mind.

There were two other vital influences discernible in Lampman's art. Upon his death on 10 February 1899, he was eulogized in the *Ottawa Journal* as 'one of the leading socialists in the city.' This description is in contrast to the misapprehension of his only biographer, Carl Connor, who asserted in *Archibald Lampman: Canadian Poet of Nature* that the poet merely flirted briefly with socialist ideology.[8] The same belief was erroneously shared by Lampman's close friend and literary executor, Duncan Campbell Scott, who explained why he deliberately omitted 'The Land of Pallas' from his 1925 selection of Lampman's poems, *Lyrics of Earth: Sonnets and Ballads:* 'This poem is a trace of the thinking in which Lampman indulged in 1894-1895 when he belonged to a group of friends who were playing lightly with socialistic ideas which he translated into poetry.'[9] Scott appears to have never fully recognized the extent of his friend's involvement with socialism, which was outlined in definite and unmistakable terms in Lampman's unpublished paper, 'Essay on Socialism,' written between 1895 and 1898.

The anonymous tribute in the *Ottawa Journal* revealed a better grasp of the poet's ideals:

Mr Lampman was quiet and gentle in manner, slightly built but of fine form and feature. He was a man of strong views upon almost every subject. Although his writings deal to a large extent with nature, it will be found that, in the main, they have a greater reference to human life and its many interests. He was particularly interested in all social and economic questions and was a member of the Social Science Club. He was formerly a member of the Fabian Society of Ottawa and was one of the leading socialists in the city. One of the last views Mr Lampman expressed with reference to Canadian

nationality and the purpose of a national life was that 'Canada
has an opportunity of giving the world an object lesson in the
adoption of socialism as a form of government which would
not only make us a nation, but give us a unique place in the
world's history. But,' he remarked, with a shrewdness which
characterized him, 'there is probably no country under heaven
in which it would be more difficult to convince the people of
the desirability of such a form of government.'[10]

In his 'Essay on Socialism' Lampman passionately spoke out
against the ills of society:

> The cause of Socialism is the cause of love and hope and
> humanity: the cause of competition is the cause of anarchy,
> pessimism and disbelief in a possible manhood for human
> nature just emerging from its barbarous infancy ... There is a
> wrong and inhuman principle at the bottom of our whole
> industrial system; the principle that the private individual may
> take possession of the common earth and use it in any way he
> will for his own advantage ... The man who has money takes
> possession of the strength and intelligence of men who have
> none and sets them to labour ... The people who carp at
> Socialism seem to be immensely taken up with that profundity
> which is apparently so prevalent in human nature, the golden
> game, the desire of material splendour, the love of the pomp
> and circumstance attending the possession of wealth and power ...
> Many people are frightened at Socialism because they think
> of tumult and insurrection, of mob violence and the tyranny
> of the masses that have risen and got power with their hands.[11]

However, Lampman believed in 'quiet' revolution. Man, he
thought, had developed a safety valve after the horrors of the

French Revolution. Never again would the streets run with blood in a civilized country. The feudal chains had been broken and liberty won long ago in the streets of Paris. The change to socialism would, he concluded, 'work itself out gradually and intelligently from possibility to possibility.' This commitment to the ideals of socialism, including the 'liberation' of women, was typical of Lampman's modernism. It was one of the strongest motivating forces during the last ten years of his life, when he was most active and renowned, and left an indelible stamp upon his art.

Although he is chiefly remembered as a poet, Lampman was also a distinguished essayist, critic, and litterateur. He aired his views, with wit and intelligence, in the weekly column, 'At the Mermaid Inn,' which appeared in the Toronto *Globe* from 6 February 1892 to 1 July 1893 and which was conducted by himself, Scott, and Campbell. 'At the Mermaid Inn. was characterized by, and eventually gained notoriety for, the outspoken opinions on current life, literature, art, and religion expressed by its authors. It occasionally carried new poems, lengthy essays, or reviews. Lampman's verse in 'At the Mermaid Inn' was often experimental and important in revealing the trends which he was exploring in the 1890s.

Among the twenty essays written by Lampman during his lifetime were papers on subjects as diverse as 'Fishing in Rice Lake,' 'German Patriotic Poetry,' 'George F. Cameron,' 'The Modern School of Poetry in England,' 'Keats,' 'Happiness,' and 'The Poetry of Byron.' His only novel, a Spanish romance, was left unfinished.

The one force more influential than socialism on Lampman's work during the last decade of his life was also unrecognized by

Scott, who always believed that he had known the poet more intimately than any other man. After an ardent courtship, enlivened by parental opposition on the part of the bride's family, Lampman quietly married Maud Playter in Ottawa on 3 September 1887, shortly after her eighteenth birthday. Lampman had known Maud, the daughter of physician Dr Edward Playter, for about two years and was particularly attracted by her musical ability and a certain ethereal reserve. Several of his love sonnets to her were included in his first volume of poetry, *Among the Millet*, which was published privately with a legacy inherited by Maud about the time of the marriage. However, disillusioned by the poet's lack of financial success either as a writer or a civil servant and alienated by his lack of interest in the social activities which appealed to her, Maud rapidly lost her initial sympathy with Lampman's poetic aspirations. Their growing separation was widened and crystallized permanently when Lampman fell in love with a young Ottawa schoolteacher, Katherine Waddell, whom he idolized as his true spiritual mate.

Kate Waddell gave up her profession and entered the Post Office Department as a clerk in the same branch as Lampman. His love poems, written to her from 1889 until the end of his life, have never been fully published and, indeed, none was printed until 1943 when E.K. Brown insisted, over the objections of his co-editor, Scott, on publishing 'A Portrait in Six Sonnets,' describing Lampman's lady, in *At the Long Sault and Other New Poems*. With considerable irony, they appear in that volume immediately following the sonnet sequence, 'The Growth of Love,' written before his marriage.

In 1889, shortly after meeting Kate Waddell, Lampman began a beautifully penned, green leather volume of poems, which he presented to Kate in the summer of 1895 when he finally realized, after a period of heart-breaking indecision and crisis, that their permanent union was impossible. His bitter attitude and broken spirit, from which he never recovered, were communicated only to his close friend Edward William Thomson through urgent letters and several hurried trips to Boston. Passages of these letters were deleted before they were returned to Lampman's estate.

Thomson, who had a similar problem, provided constant support and counsel. However, nothing could be accomplished after Lampman's wife apparently refused the divorce he sought and Kate was unwilling to share what would have been a scandalous liaison with the postal clerk who was also Canada's most renowned poet. They remained close friends to the end. Kate Waddell never married, and after her death the manuscript volume of poems given to her by Lampman passed to a niece in Ottawa and then to the library of the University of Toronto. A plaque, to the poet's memory, believed to have been donated by Kate Waddell and her family, may be found in St Margaret's Anglican Church on the Montreal Road in Vanier, an Ottawa suburb where Lampman frequently stopped to rest during his long walks through the outlying areas of Ottawa. Kate's influence on the poet's work has never been fully understood or adequately evaluated, but the deeply felt personal bitterness, which leaps out of otherwise unrelated poems, is an indication of his stress and later his resignation, as are the love poems, many of which exist only in the manuscript notebooks. There they eloquently express his doubts, his passion, and the depth of their relationship.

Lampman's social ideas were obviously in advance of his age. More than any other poet writing in Canada before 1900, he belongs to the twentieth century. Several critics, including Louis Dudek in his article, 'The Significance of Lampman,' and John Sutherland in a witty review entitled 'Edgar Allan Poe in Canada,' have compared Lampman's art with that of twentieth-century writers and with certain English poets of the late nineteenth century.[12] Lampman was one of the first Canadian poets to be obsessed by the theme of man's isolation and alienation from society. There is a tension in his work resulting from the uneasy balance between fear and resignation; between his two great enemies, the towering city and the lightless north; between delight and the pain of loss; and even between heat and cold. The lushness of nature, which is essentially cruel, is pitted against the desolation of industrial society as shown in such poems as 'Avarice,' 'To a Modern Politician,' 'At the Railway Station,' and 'To a Millionaire.' Finally, there is a tension born out of Lampman's will to live and the inevitability of an early death. Youthful idealism, dreams, and nature gave way, in his later work, to social criticism and melancholy. In the end, Lampman appeared to believe only in socialism and science as the hope of civilization.

In one respect above all Lampman differs from every other Canadian poet of the nineteenth century. He struck the first authentic note of fear in Canadian literature, a fear stripped bare of Victorian dream-garden mysticism and expressed in poems about politicians and money lenders, towering, impersonal city buildings and solitary, homeless figures prowling the city streets, seen from behind drawn curtains late at night. Dogs are run over and left to die, children are kicked, trains thunder from the station like iron monsters leaving tearful women crumpled on hard, wooden, waiting-room seats, factories endlessly chew out their mechanically produced pieces. In the eery light of blast furnaces

xxiii

men wear their lives away like robots and the poet sits helpless in Ottawa facing 'the lightless north' with a growing sense of horror and a rapidly developing social conscience.

More than any other poem, 'The City of the End of Things' incorporates most fully the mature ideas of the poet. It has been widely anthologized during the past thirty years, although while Lampman was alive it received only fugitive publication, first in the March 1894 *Atlantic Monthly* and then in Edmund C. Stedman's *A Victorian Anthology* in 1895. It was included in Lampman's third, posthumous collection of poetry, *Alcyone*, which forms part of *The Poems of Archibald Lampman*, and has lately been reissued by Michael Gnarowski.[13] The poem was assigned various titles by Lampman, including: 'The Issue of Things That Are,' 'The City of Machinery,' and 'The Nameless City.' It was written on 3 June 1892, when Lampman was thirty-one.

A city of industrial death is foreseen, where vulgarity and vice will overcome civilization and men become robots, unless socialist ideals can be achieved. The poem is derivative; its roots can be traced to Poe's 'The City in the Sea' published in 1831 and also to James Thomson's 'The City of Dreadful Night' published in 1874. A secondary influence on Lampman in depicting the nameless fear of men stripped of humanity is Coleridge's 'The Ancient Mariner.' It is scarcely surprising to find Lampman moving away from the influences of Keats and Arnold, Wordsworth and Tennyson, to which he and most other Victorian poets originally succumbed. Lotus-land was left far behind when the poet faced reality with a sense of impending terror and tried to depict the coming age.

In 'The City of the End of Things' an inhuman society is described where creatures live in multi-storied skyscrapers and work ceaselessly night and day in response to unspoken commands, while functioning in a monotonous routine that would 'shrivel the soul' of more sensitive people. Of the human race only four monstrous men survive, including a guardian, 'looking toward the lightless north,/Beyond the reach of memories.' When the monsters die the poet predicts that 'The silence of eternal night/Shall gather close and settle down.' The grim grandeur of the city's towers 'Shall be abandoned utterly/And into rust and dust shall fall/From century to century.' The poem possesses an integrity lacking in some of Lampman's earlier work and the imagery exhibits a gripping power beyond the dream-like sentiment of his love poetry or the heat and colour of the nature poems.

Two other poems particularly reflect Lampman's final position. 'Easter Eve,' written in December 1886 and published in *Among the Millet*, and 'A Vision of Twilight' written on 19 September 1895 and published in *Alcyone*. Like many of Lampman's poems, these bear more than one manuscript title. In an unpublished version, 'Easter Eve' exists as 'Alexis'; 'A Vision of Twilight' was also called 'The City of the Spirit.'

Lampman's poetry centres on about a dozen topics — nature, the poet, music, night, the city, war, socialism, despair, love, eternity, birth, and death. Death was usually depicted in legendary or symbolic terms. Consequently, a single idea may evolve through several stages, each developed as an individual poem. An example of this technique may be seen by comparing 'The City,' which was originally published in *The Week* on 1 July 1892, with 'The City of the End of Things' and 'A Vision of Twilight' (See pp 215, 179, and 195 in *The Poems of Archibald Lampman*.)

During his lifetime Lampman published only two volumes of poetry and some fugitive verse, in all just over one hundred and twenty poems. He arranged privately for the publication of his first book, *Among the Millet*, which contains seventy-one poems and was printed in Ottawa in 1888 by J. Durie and Son, and in 1895 Copeland and Day of Boston agreed to publish five hundred copies of a small volume containing twenty-nine poems, *Lyrics of Earth*. Upon those one hundred poems, together with the fugitive verse which appeared chiefly in American periodicals, his considerable poetic reputation rested. He experienced great difficulty in finding a publisher and during the final months of his life decided once again to finance publication himself. He accordingly arranged with T. and A. Constable of Edinburgh to produce for him a volume of thirty-nine poems under the title *Alcyone*. This volume was in press at the time of his death and Scott, acting as literary executor for his estate, ordered that only twelve copies should be printed, by James Ogilvy of Ottawa. Fortunately for Lampman's claim to modern attention, since it contains his late, socially oriented work, the contents were included in the memorial volume, *The Poems of Archibald Lampman*, edited by Scott and published in 1900 and reproduced in this reprint.

With the exception of a single poem, 'Impromptu,' included by Scott in his 1925 selection, *Lyrics of Earth: Sonnets and Ballads*, and two or three poems chosen by periodicals for memorial publication, no new poetry by Lampman was published until the Ryerson Press issued *At the Long Sault and Other New Poems* in 1943, which is also reprinted here. This last book contains twenty-six poems chosen by E.K. Brown and Duncan Campbell Scott from the poet's manuscripts, including a late narrative poem, 'At the Long Sault,' considered by some critics to represent a completely new direction which Lampman had decided to follow shortly before his death. Lampman commenced writing the poem in August 1898 when he knew that he was gravely ill with heart disease and had not long to live. He left it unfinished for some months but resumed work upon it sometime in January 1899, a few weeks before his death. 'At the Long Sault' remained in a comparatively unpolished form in two different manuscript versions when the poet died. Brown noted that in his later years Lampman's conception of life was much more comprehensive than his readers and interpreters have generally supposed, and Scott acknowledged that, while it was impossible to conjecture what his course of development might have been, it appeared that Lampman would have tended 'towards the drama of life and away from the picture of nature.'

In the title poem, Lampman broke completely away from the ballad and sonnet forms of which he was a master and from the stereotyped romantic concept of some of his earlier work. With ease and a dramatic sense of balance he described the massacre of Daulac and his comrades by Indians in May 1660 at the Long Sault Rapids. The siege is delineated by the use of expanded lines and onomatopoeia, by accumulated adjectives, and by the contrast of images such as 'the waters glitter and leap' while 'the grey hawk soars' and 'the plunging stream' foretells 'ruin and murder impending.' The 'innocent flowers' are symbolic of the innocent 'maiden and matron and child,' just as the grey hawk precedes the arrival of 'foes, not men but devils, panting for prey.' The juxtaposition of natural images against the pattern of the human action which develops inevitably heightens the sense of dramatic irony and reveals the brilliant power which was at the heart of Lampman's mature artistry. The poem is not so much a new, experimental technique which Lampman was adopting but is, rather, the culmination of his poetic development. With the failure of his marriage and his approaching death, his morbid sensitivity sharpened and he wrote with an intensity not hitherto expressed in Canadian literature.

The last poem, and one of the finest sonnets written by Lampman, was 'Winter Uplands,' which he dated '30-1-99' and penned carefully in his final manuscript notebook. It is included in *The Poems of Archibald Lampman* and the theme is a familiar one, that of the poet's isolation from 'The far off city, towered and roofed in blue,' balanced against his fear of nature which he depicts as 'The loneliness of this forsaken ground.' Perhaps he derives some slight comfort from the frost, the stars, 'and beauty everywhere.' This poem, ostensibly a description of a winter night in Ottawa, actually contains an intensely personal expression of self, superimposed upon the natural scene. The sonnet gains in power from the impending sense of death, for nature 'stings like fire upon my cheek' while the poet stoically awaits his fate, sitting 'in the great silence as one bound.'

During fifteen years in Ottawa, Lampman produced some of the most memorable poetry written in Canada during the nineteenth century. His influence is evident today in the social and literary advances made in twentieth-century Canada. His reputation as a founder of Canadian literature is assured.

NOTES

1 J.E. Collins (1855-92), city editor of *The Globe*, Toronto
2 Charles G.D. Roberts to Archibald Lampman, 23 September 1882 (incomplete) and 18 December 1888, Melvin Hammond Papers, Toronto Public Library
3 Most of Lampman's mss are now located in the Public Archives of Canada.
4 Arthur S. Bourinot, editor, *Archibald Lampman's Letters to Edward William Thomson (1890-1898)* (Montreal 1956) and *The Letters of Edward William Thomson to Archibald Lampman (1891-1897)* (Montreal 1957)
5 Arthur Stringer, 'Wild Poets I've Known: Archibald Lampman,' *Saturday Night* LVI (24 May 1941) 29
6 Public Archives of Canada
7 Stringer, 'A Glance at Lampman,' *Canadian Magazine* II (April 1894) 545-6
8 Carl Y. Connor, *Archibald Lampman: Canadian Poet of Nature* (Montreal 1929) 84
9 Duncan Campbell Scott, editor, Archibald Lampman, *Lyrics of Earth: Sonnets and Ballads* (Toronto 1925) 41
10 *Ottawa Journal* (10 February 1899) 3
11 Public Archives of Canada
12 Louis Dudek, 'The Significance of Lampman,' *Culture* XVIII (September 1957) 277-9 and John Sutherland, 'Edgar Allan Poe in Canada,' *Northern Review* IV (February-March 1951) 29-31
13 Lampman, *Alcyone* (Ottawa 1899) 5-8

Bibliographical Note

Although Lampman published just over one hundred poems during his lifetime and an additional thirty-nine appeared in the posthumous volume, *Alcyone*, his manuscripts contain over four hundred poems. Duncan Campbell Scott became literary executor after his death and, with the assistance of two friends, S.E. Dawson and William D. LeSeur, arranged for the publication of *The Poems of Archibald Lampman.*

This volume, containing two hundred and thirty-seven poems, was published in 1900 by George N. Morang and Company of Toronto and the first edition was soon exhausted as the result of a letter requesting subscriptions which was sent out on 1 June 1899 by the friends. Almost five thousand dollars were obtained for Lampman's family, acknowledged by Scott, Dawson, and LeSueur in a note of thanks on the final page of the edition.

The quality of some of the poems was questionable, as Scott acknowledged in his introduction to *Lyrics of Earth: Sonnets and Ballads* in 1925: 'In this book almost everything that he had written was included. The critical faculty was in suspension. The aim was to produce a book attractive from its bulk, and considering the prime object of the publication, that idea was laudable enough...' The letter seeking advance orders for the collected poems explained the purpose of the volume and contained an interesting tribute to Lampman:

Ottawa, 1st June, 1899

Dear Sir or Madam:

You have no doubt heard of the death of Archibald Lampman for it was very widely noticed by the press, and the leading

xxx

newspapers in all parts of Canada gave expression in their editorial columns to the prevailing feeling of regret and sympathy — of regret that the country has lost one in the very foremost rank of her men of letters, and sympathy for the young widow and children so sadly bereaved. Mr Lampman's position as a junior official in the Civil Service of the Dominion did not permit much provision to be made against his early death, and it is needless to dwell upon the trite observation that the pursuit of literature in Canada is not remunerative in a pecuniary sense. Nevertheless, the born poet is like a song bird and must utter his melody whether listened to or not. In reality, we all profit by every true poetic utterance, for it is through the works of poets and other literary men that the community gains its rank in the world of letters; and when they demonstrate abroad the ability of Canadians to wield with power the resources of their mother tongue, every Canadian shares the lustre of their labours and their triumph.

We have had, and we still have, writers who have brought to us from the motherland results of training acquired there, and of natural gifts, which are the outcome of different conditions. For these writers, and for their labours among us, we ought to be, and we are, sincerely grateful. But Archibald Lampman is one of our very own, born among us, trained in our schools, familiar with our ways, and intimate with every aspect of our skies, weeds and waters. The historic land of his forefathers he never saw with his outward eyes, but this, our own land, he knew by heart in all its marvellous variety of changing moods. In his poems he had described it with vivid and loving appreciation in every phase, from its resting time under the white coverlet faintly tinted with reflections of blue and rosy skies, through the brilliant outburst of spring and the sultry summer, to the dreamy autumn.

Lampman's reputation as a writer was not merely local. Many probably, who are not otherwise familiar with his work, have from time to time seen and admired his contributions to such magazines as *The Atlantic Monthly, The Century, Scribner's, Harper's, Blackwood's* etcetera. Out of a large number of notices of his work, which have appeared in English and American journals, a few are subjoined.

It is not possible now to do anything for him whom we have lost. In his life he was simple and unobtrusive, but his gentle presence and quiet voice will be only the more missed by his intimate friends. To borrow a poet's word on a like occasion:

> He is a portion of the loveliness
> Which once he made more lovely. He doth bear
> His part, while the One Spirit's plastic stress
> Sweeps through the dull, dense world.

We still, however, possess the poems which express his quiet, meditative soul; and it is open to us to express our appreciation of his work and testify our sympathy with those who have been deprived of his support, by adding to our libraries a copy of the memorial edition of his collected poems. The object of this letter is to explain what is being done for the production of such an edition, and to bespeak the interest of all cultivated readers.

There is now being prepared, and will be published for the sole benefit of the widow, a collected edition of Archibald Lampman's poems. It will be one volume of four hundred to five hundred pages, and will be printed in excellent style on good paper. The volume will be edited by the late poet's most intimate friend, Mr Duncan Campbell Scott and will contain a portrait of Lampman and also a short biographical sketch. It will include, in addition to the work which Mr Lampman had published in his lifetime, a careful selection from a quantity of unpublished work, all in fact, which there is reason to believe he would himself have eventually published. A facsimile of a sonnet in his own hand will also be included. The price of the volume has been fixed at $2.25.

This somewhat unusual method of direct application has been adopted in order to secure to the widow the full and entire return without deduction or discount of any kind whatever. The undersigned are attending to this work solely as a tribute to the memory of a departed friend and in aid of his family. There are friends also concerned who wish to be nameless, but it is necessary that some names should appear as responsible for the undertaking. It will not be possible to employ canvassers to solicit subscriptions. Those who have taken the initiative in the matter feel confident that there are many who 'strictly meditate the thankless muse' who will assist in sending in subscribers' names and they believe that there are many men busily engaged in important undertakings and reaping the well-earned rewards of many remunerative callings, who have the love of letters at heart, and will not grudge the few moments necessary to fill up the enclosed form for copies, not only for themselves but for their friends.

In this hope we make our appeal, trusting that the response will be prompt and generous and that a lasting memorial may be established for one whose name, highly honoured as it is today, is destined, we believe, to greater honour in the future.

    With great respect, we are,
Yours truly,

S.E. Dawson, Lit.D., F.R.S.C.
William D. LeSeur, B.A.
Duncan C. Scott, F.R.S.C.

Morang brought out a two-volume Holiday Edition in 1901 with the following note:

> The universal attention which was aroused by the publication of the memorial edition of Archibald Lampman's poems was an indication of the esteem in which he was held as a poet and a man; and the large advance subscription sale for the work comprised residents in nearly every part of Canada and in places very distant from the somewhat small sphere in which the poet's life was spent. In placing before the public this second edition of the Poems, the publishers are obeying numerous and earnest requests, and they feel sure that the book will be prized by an ever-widening circle of appreciative and cultured readers.
> Toronto, September, 1900.

This note was included in all later editions.

    The Holiday Edition was succeeded by the third edition published by Morang in 1905. A fourth and final edition was published by the Musson Book Company Limited about 1915. All four editions contain identical texts. Variations in the four editions are minimal; for this reprint the first edition of 1900 has been reproduced.

Scott edited several new editions of Lampman's poetry, and in 1925 the Musson Book Company published *Lyrics of Earth: Sonnets and Ballads*, which contains one hitherto unpublished poem, 'Impromptu,' and an evaluation by Scott of Lampman's work. In 1943, Scott and E.K. Brown edited *At the Long Sault and Other New Poems*, with a foreword by Scott and an introduction by Brown. The final collection of Lampman's poetry, *Selected Poems*, chosen by Scott, was published by the Ryerson Press in 1947. It contains no new work but is a judicious selection of the best of Lampman's poems. Scott wisely dropped the lengthy narrative poems, which add little to the poet's lustre and represent an outmoded literary convention. The measure of Lampman's art depends, therefore, upon two volumes, *The Poems of Archibald Lampman* and the later selection from his manuscripts, *At the Long Sault and Other New Poems*.

Lampman had a distressing habit of using titles more than once. The collected poems contain two poems entitled 'In November,' two named 'Song,' and two versions of 'The City.' In his 1925 selection, Scott retitled 'In November,' on page 117, 'Late November.' Lampman also published two versions of 'Dead Cities,' 'Passion,' 'Sleep,' 'Music,' 'Winter Evening,' and 'New Year's Eve,' as well as a third poem entitled 'Song.' These poems may be differentiated by the date on which each was written, given in Lampman's manuscripts and letters, by the first lines and, in some cases, by the form used. The notes below are offered as a guide to duplicate titles in *The Poems of Archibald Lampman*.

PAGE

40 Song
First line 'Songs that could span the earth.' Five stanzas of four lines (1886)

Select Bibliography

PRIMARY SOURCES

Bourinot, Arthur Stanley *Archibald Lampman's Letters to Edward William Thomson (1890-1898)* Montreal: Quality Press 1956, 74p
- *At the Mermaid Inn* Montreal: Quality Press 1958, 96p
Lampman, Archibald *Alcyone* Edinburgh: T. & A. Constable 1899, 110p
- *Among the Millet* Ottawa: John Durie & Son 1888, 151p
- *Lyrics of Earth: Sonnets and Ballads* Boston, Copeland & Day 1895, 56p
Scott, Duncan Campbell & Edward Killoran Brown *At the Long Sault and Other New Poems* Toronto: Ryerson 1943, 45p

SECONDARY SOURCES

Bourinot, Arthur Stanley *Five Canadian Poets* Montreal: Quality Press 1954, pp 4-7
- *The Letters of Edward William Thomson to Archibald Lampman (1891-1897)* Montreal: Quality Press 1957, 49p
Brown, Edward Killoran *On Canadian Poetry* Toronto: Ryerson 1943, pp 80-108
Collin, W.E. 'Natural Landscape,' in *The White Savannahs* Toronto: Macmillan 1936, pp 3-40 (forthcoming in the Literature of Canada: Prose and Poetry in Reprint Series)
Connor, Carl Y. *Archibald Lampman: Canadian Poet of Nature* Montreal: Carrier 1929, 210p
Dudek, Louis 'The Significance of Lampman,' in *Culture* XVIII (September 1957) 277-90

Gnarowski, Michael *Archibald Lampman: The City of the End of Things* Montreal: The Golden Dog Press 1972, unpaged

Kennedy, Leo 'Canadian Writers of the Past: V Archibald Lampman' in *The Canadian Forum* XIII (May 1933) 301-3

Scott, Duncan Campbell *Lyrics of Earth: Sonnets and Ballads* Toronto: Musson 1925, 276p

– *Selected Poems of Archibald Lampman* Toronto: Ryerson 1947, 176p

Stringer, Arthur 'A Glance at Lampman' in *The Canadian Magazine* II (April 1894) 545-8

– 'Wild Poets I've Known: Archibald Lampman' in *Saturday Night* LVI (24 May 1941) 29

Sutherland, John 'Edgar Allan Poe in Canada' in *The Northern Review* IV (February-March 1951) 22-37

The Poems of Archibald Lampman

(including At the Long Sault)

CONTENTS

CONTENTS

LYRICS OF EARTH

CONTENTS

ALCYONE

CONTENTS vii

SONNETS

viii CONTENTS

CONTENTS

POEMS AND BALLADS

Archibald Lampman.

MEMOIR

More than a century ago in the American colonies of
Great Britain, there were two families of German and
Dutch descent, one surnamed Lampman the other Gesner.
The Lampman family lived in Pennsylvania, and belonged
to the community called Pennsylvania Dutch. At the
outbreak of the American Revolution one of these Lamp-
mans, a Tory with strong feelings in favour of British connec-
tions, turned his face toward the North, and eventually taking
land that the British government had provided for loyalists
like himself, settled near Niagara in the present Province
of Ontario. Colonel John H. Gesner, a contemporary of
this loyal Lampman, was a resident of Long Island, the
family to which he belonged being of Knickerbocker stock.
But he also was a King's man, and when the Revolution was
imminent, he crossed the stretch of sea to Nova Scotia and
settled at Annapolis.

Peter Lampman, the son of the original settler, struck
firm root at Niagara, and the old homestead known as
Mountain Point still remains in possession of the family.
During the war of 1812, both the Lampmans and the Gesners
fought for their land and had their due share in the events of
those times. One of the Gesners was a colonel of militia
and was therefore prominent in the conflict.

While the Lampmans were clearing their land in the
fruitful Niagara peninsula, the Gesners had been making
homes for themselves in the Annapolis valley. David Henry
Gesner, a son of the colonel who had migrated from Long
Island, drifted to Upper Canada, a far journey from the sea
in those days. One may find his name in the record as

Crown Land Agent in the County of Kent, and he is
remembered as a strong man mentally and physically, with
aptitudes for colonization. He settled on the Talbot Road
in the County of Kent, about seven miles from the Village
of Morpeth, where the homestead still stands. His wife was
a Stewart, from the County of Tyrone, Ireland, whose
mother was of Dutch descent, springing from a Knicker-
bocker family called Culver. The fifth child of this union
was Susannah Charlotte, the mother of Archibald Lampman,
the poet.

The sons of Peter Lampman were brought up for differ-
ent employments, and one, Archibald, studied divinity and
took holy orders, and in 1858 was appointed Rector of
Trinity Church, Morpeth. Here he married Susannah Ges-
ner on the 29th of May, 1860, and here was born Archibald
Lampman, the poet, on Sunday morning, the 17th of
November, 1861.

There had been poets and scientists on his mother's side
of the house; the Gesners were an intellectual race and Dr.
Abraham Gesner, Archibald's great-uncle, is, in Nova Scotia
at least, a well-remembered writer and scientist. The Lamp-
mans were men of their hands, fighting King's battles and
winning them too; a valiant, loyal race. So the young
Archibald had men and women for forebears who were
remarkable for their achievements and worthy of remem-
brance and honour.

It was seen as years went by that Archibald resembled
his maternal grandmother Stewart in his disposition, which
was gentle, unselfish and tender, and in the physical charac-
teristics of dark auburn hair and clear brown eyes. His
intellectual endowments came both from the Gesners and
the Lampmans, and if his temperament can be traced to a
maternal source, his father gave him logical power, accuracy
of observation and expression, and his rare gift of language.

In Morpeth Mr. Lampman continued to live until Archi-
bald had entered his sixth year, when a change of residence
was made and for a short time the home was located at
Perrytown, near Port Hope, in the County of Durham.

In October, 1867, he moved to Gore's Landing, a small town on the shore of Rice Lake. Here the family remained for seven years. It is well that these impressionable years of Archibald Lampman's life were passed upon the shores of this beautiful lake. The scenery seemed enchanted the society was congenial, and many forces united to strengthen his love of nature and his powers of observation, and much of his descriptive work is reminiscent of this region.

Unfortunately the only house available for a rectory at Gore's Landing was damp, and in November, 1868, Archibald was stricken with rheumatic fever, and lay suffering acutely for months. It was not until spring that he could walk, and for four years he was lame and during part of the time was compelled to use crutches. His physique was never powerful nor was his health robust, and it may be that the main cause of both lay in this severe illness. But despite his crutches he was active and interested in life, for his spirit was always great and courageous to triumph over any ills of body or estate which he had to bear.

In March, 1870, Mr. Lampman purchased a house in the village and there he sojourned until he left Gore's Landing and the pleasant shores of Rice Lake. Previously to 1870 Archibald's studies had been conducted at home under his father's direction, but in September of that year he entered the school of Mr. F. W. Barron, M.A., of Cambridge, formerly Principal of Upper Canada College. The recollections of the four years he spent there were always vivid and pleasurable. Mr. Barron was a famous schoolmaster. He was thorough in his system, stern in his manner and a strict disciplinarian; but he had the respect of his boys. Many were sent to him who had conquered other masters, but he managed them by rod or by will, and made men of them, some great, and all self-reliant.

Every school day, we are told, the master marched into the room with a cushion upon his outstretched hands, upon that lay the Bible, and upon the Book the rod. He had a liking for Archibald and his clear and ready wit. He laid a deep foundation for his scholarship, taught him how to write beautifully, and grounded him in Latin and Greek. Archibald, during the first year at the school, could not join in the sports; but in January, 1872, his health was so far restored that he was able to run about freely with his companions.

Gradually during the last four years of the residence at Gore's Landing Mr. Lampman's health had begun to fail. The home at Gore's Landing had to be given up, and to Cobourg, a larger town upon the shores of Lake Ontario, the family was next transplanted. Young Archibald, now thirteen, had to leave his beloved flower-beds, and the deep bass pools in which he had fished on Saturday afternoons, and the lovely lake with its sunny water and shimmering rice fields. Cobourg seemed grim and uncertain, merely an arena for struggle and possible failure, compared with this dear spot transfigured by the glamour of childhood.

But when affairs wore their darkest aspect, it became clear that good fortune was with young Archibald in the protection of his mother. She at least would fight conditions, subdue them, would have for her children what she considered their right, cost what it would of her own strength and energy. Through many schemes in which she did not spare herself she succeeded in educating her son and daughters. In the dedication of "Lyrics of Earth" Archibald acknowledged in some part what he owed to the mother who had battled for him in those early days.

In Cobourg, Archibald first attended the Collegiate Institute, and after a year went to Trinity College School at Port Hope. This is an institution of preparation for Trinity College, Toronto, modelled on the English Public Schools. Through the interest taken in him by Bishop Bethune and John Cartwright, Esq., scholarships were given nearly sufficient to cover his expenses at the school. This genuine interest was well repaid, for during his two years' stay at Port Hope he won many prizes and in his last year was Prefect of the school. At the commencement exercises of that year he was chaired by his companions and carried in triumph and with much cheering through the buildings and

school grounds. Although during these years his applica-
tion was intense, he found time to be interested in others,
and while he was Prefect many a disheartened lad at his
gentle bidding and encouragement took up with awakened
trust in himself tasks thrown by in despair.

In September, 1879, he entered Trinity College, Toronto.
There must have been some hard work scattered through the
years at Trinity, for it was in the main by the help of the
scholarships that he won that his course was completed.
But at best he was a desultory student. His love of general
reading was great and many an hour when he ought to have
been labouring at some set task he was poring over the pages
of a history or some narrative of travel, or enjoying a pot of
beer, a pipe and a lively discussion in some friend's quarters.

At Port Hope he was singular for an intense application
which won him nearly all the prizes that were to be gained
in each year, and his memory as a lad shy of the energies of
the cricket crease and foot-ball green might have more
speedily waned had not rumours come from Trinity that
Lampman was not the man he was taken for, that he was a
boon companion, and was to be found foremost in any
innocent wildness that was afoot. And so Dame Rumour kept
his fame aglow at Port Hope, and the boys who were next
year or so to meet him at Trinity had their curiosity roused
and their interest piqued by the discordance between his past
record and his present fame. When they did come within
his circle they found a man who had gained a unique position
in his college by his temperament and character. He was
probably the poorest man in a worldly sense in the school,
and physically the least powerful, yet he had a greater
influence than any of his fellows.

He did not work as hard as many, nor did he play so
successfully, but he was accepted without reserve. He had
done nothing in particular, so far as his companions knew,
he had never written anything that showed genius, but there
was an opinion abroad that Lampman was in some way
different from ordinary men, that he would do something
famous some day.

He was editor of the college paper "Rouge et Noir," so called from the college colours, and "Scribe" of the manuscript journal called "Episkopon." A fair half of his time was spent in writing for these papers both in prose and verse and in the work of editing them.

The poets he had begun to read with care, and he commenced to form poetic ambitions of his own. He laid epic plans, and in the endeavour to realize them he sat long and late with his heroes and demi-gods. These labours were useful, as they taught him the weight and colour of words, gave him exercise in rhythm, and fertility in rhyme. But he left them unfinished and passed on to other work and served his apprenticeship, joyously, full of happy dreams and ambitions. He laid the foundation of a few chapters of what was to be a long novel, which in after years he used to describe with a glow that would lead one to imagine a very paragon of a novel, full of tragic pathos and illuminating laughter, pervaded by deep knowledge of life. But the dissertation would end with his genuine laugh, and the perception by his auditors that the matter was a mere whim.

He graduated in 1882 with second-class honours in classics. This was hardly a matter of surprise to his class-mates or concern to himself. It was beyond question that he could have taken a first had he applied himself, but his final year had been spent in that general reading and social intercourse which he so greatly valued and which was a larger force in his development than many text-books devoured for examination.

There was some doubt as to what he should do in the world, now that he had received his equipment. The first employment that offered was uncongenial. He was appointed assistant master in the High School at Orangeville. He did not dislike the actual labour of tuition, for which he was well prepared, but it was quite impossible for him to enforce discipline and to maintain order in his class. Chaos ruled in his form at the Orangeville High School; the pupils did as they pleased, and the assistant master wished fervently that he might do the same.

But release came shortly from this bondage. One of his friends at college had been Archibald Campbell, son of Sir Alexander Campbell, and through the son's influence with the father, who was then Postmaster-General, he was offered a clerkship in the Civil Service of Canada. He gave up his uncongenial task at Orangeville without regret, and was appointed temporary clerk in the Post Office Department on the 16th of January, 1883. On the 23rd of March following, his position was made permanent, and he was fixed in an employment that was to continue with his life. If an artist be possessed of a private fortune, he is happy indeed; if not, some occupation not subject to the ordinary stress and change of business life is best for him. In the Canadian Civil Service at headquarters there is that element of security, and it is well that Archibald Lampman became a member of the permanent service when he did. He was appointed without reference to any literary achievement, for his name was at that time unknown, and he received the small increments of salary and the single promotion which came to him as the years went by, merely in the ordinary routine, not as a reward for the poetry which was gradually making his name well known. He became an excellent clerk, valuable in his office to those whom he assisted. The work he did not like, and the confinement he found irksome, but he recognized that the life had its compensations, in periods of leisure secure and serene, which he might devote to his one great passion, poetry.

He was fortunate too in his removal to Ottawa. He found in the strenuous climate of the growing city all that is characteristic of Canadian summers and winters. He was on the borders of the wild nature that he loved, and in the midst of a congenial society. To some extent, if not to the limit, he might now follow his inclination. The result was that he began to apply himself steadily to composition.

His first contributions to the public journals were two poems, which may now be found in "Among the Millet"— "The Coming of Winter" and "Three Flower Petals." They appeared in 1884 in "The Week," a literary periodical since discontinued, of which Mr. Chas. G. D. Roberts was at that time the editor.

His first poem presented to a wider public was a quatrain called "Bird Voices" printed in the Century Magazine for May, 1885. The early encouragement of Scribner's Magazine gave him confidence, and the greater part of his contributions to the periodical press appeared in its pages.

During the first year of his sojourn in Ottawa he lived at home, as his father had removed thither from Toronto, and resided in the cottage now No. 144 Nicholas Street. In September, 1887, he married Maud, the youngest daughter of Edward Playter, Esq., M.D., of Toronto. In 1892 a daughter was born to them, and in the early summer of 1894, a son. The loss of this child in the August following was a source of great grief to his father and its poignancy may be traced in the poems "White Pansies" and "We Too Shall Sleep."

In 1895 the death of his father broke the family circle. Archibald was in faithful attendance upon him during his long and trying illness. In his early days his father had taught him the art of verse, as he says in the dedication to "Alcyone," and had sharpened his wits in disputations upon the poets. Pope was the idol of the older man and the model for his own verses, of which he wrote many. Pope was to be upheld before the youngster, and Keats, Tennyson and Coleridge were to be given their proper rank beside the giant. He was a man of strong opinions and scholarly attainments, and to the last he retained his eagerness for discussion on all topics, sacred and profane, and was a worthy antagonist.

In 1895 the poet received the only honour that our country can offer a literary man: he was elected a Fellow of the Royal Society of Canada.

Gradually his poems written between 1884 and 1888 had increased, and in the latter year he decided to collect and publish them. Without taking the useless course of presenting the manuscript of his first book of poems to a publisher, he determined himself to accept the risk. Fortunately

at this time his wife had received a small legacy, which was
faithfully placed at her husband's disposal, and so "Among
the Millet" came into being. It was printed and bound at
a local establishment and everything was done that could be
accomplished with limited skill, experience and equipment
to make the book a success. It brought its author wider
fame and surer standing in the world of letters. Five years
afterwards Messrs. Copeland & Day of Boston, Mass., issued
his second book entitled "Lyrics of Earth," a collection of
poems following the sequence of the seasons.

There is in the years between 1883 and 1899 no incident
or action that the world would call stirring, that would meet
the demands for a relation of adventure or peril. The sixteen
years were full of high endeavour and of fine accomplishment,
but they were outwardly placid and uneventful. They were
varied by change of residence now and then, and every year
by an absence of three or four weeks from the office and its
routine. These weeks were spent in short journeys and
recreation, sometimes in visits to Boston, to Niagara, or to
the lower St. Lawrence; but more frequently, and by prefer-
ence, in camping expeditions. Nowhere was Archibald
Lampman so content as in the great wilderness, which he so
often and so lovingly described. The only existence he
coveted was that of a bushman, to be constantly hidden in
the heart of the woods. There he would neither be solitary
nor lonely, for the clear distance and the tangled undergrowth
were peopled with companionships known to few men nur-
tured as he was.

It was probably upon one of these canoe journeys that
his heart, naturally weak, received the injury from which it
never rallied. In the autumn of 1896 accompanied by two of
his brothers-in-law he went into Lake Temagami by Lake
Nipissing down the Metabechawan River to the Ottawa.
The trip is not an arduous one, but the party was small
and the time limited. After his return from the journey
Mr. Lampman developed a severe and constant pain across
his chest, which increased and would not yield to any

ordinary remedies.   His physicians traced the trouble to
his heart, and then were recalled by his companions the
feats he had performed in the wilds of Temagami, his labours
at the portage and the camping place, and their fruitless
endeavours to restrain him from doing an undue share of the
work. For heavy burdens and tasks requiring great endur-
ance his physique was ill-fitted, yet there was in the man that
robustness of will and tenacity of purpose that prompted him
to lift as if he were a giant and paddle as if he were a trapper.
His weakness, finally called by his physicians enlargement of
the heart, with valvular incompetence, and an aneurism of
the artery at the base, gradually developed, and it became
evident that he could not survive a great while, that he must
leave many of his plans unfinished, many of his dreams
unrealized.

During the winter of 1896-7 he produced several poems,
but he laboured without his wonted spirit, and with perhaps
a foreboding unexpressed that there were many that he
would never write. He was constantly at his desk until
September, 1897, when he enjoyed his last sojourn in the
woods at Lake Achigan, east of Maniwaki. By this beauti-
ful lake, amid dense forest, neighbour of many wild shy
things, he was once more restored at the heart of nature.
After his return he continued his employment until it became
clear that a long rest must be had if he were ever to be even
conditionally well.   Full of hope that many years of life
might be left to him, bearing suffering and fatigue with
absolute patience, he rested quietly during the first months
of 1898. When the spring drew on he was sufficiently well
to walk about slowly in the sunshine, observing the process
of nature, in which he took the old delight, the advent of the
warblers, and the triumph of the fruit blossoms.

It was then that he heard for the first time that when he
was ready he might gain whatever benefit was to be derived
from change of scene and air, that a few of his friends and
admirers had removed the only material obstacle.

In June a son was born to him and when he felt he

could leave home he travelled to Montreal and passed the summer and part of the fall in sojourning at Lake Wayagamac, Digby and Boston. He returned to his work on the 15th of October benefited by the change, and by the prolonged freedom from official labours. But as the winter drew on it became apparent that his strength was gradually declining. He spent these last weeks happily in the correction of the proofs of a new book "Alcyone," which he designed to issue in the spring. It gave him pleasure to look into the future, with this project, around which he had built many hopes. He had again assumed the risk himself, as he had ten years before when "Among the Millet" was published. But on this occasion he had gone to one of the best presses in the world, and the Messrs. Constable & Company of Edinburgh had done the work. It was to be in form such a book as he loved to contemplate, and day by day he was expecting to hear of its completion. But he was never to hold it in his hands.

On the evening of the 8th of February, 1899, he was stricken with a sharp pain in the lungs, and lingered with intermittent suffering until the 10th; then in the first hour of the morning he passed away as if to sleep. He was no more in this world, in which he had worked so steadfastly, and which he understood and loved so well. On Saturday, the 11th, his body was borne to Beechwood Cemetery surrounded by many of the men who had loved and respected him in life.

Archibald Lampman was of middle height, and of a slight form. In the city he walked habitually with a downcast glance, with his eyes fixed upon the ground; in the fields and woods he was alert and observant. His manner was quiet and undemonstrative. His voice was mellow and distinct. The portrait preceding this memoir gives an idea of his features and is the best of several in existence. Before the camera the lines of his face hardened, and the lovely spirit in his eyes departed. It would explain the fascination of his personality if that deep, bright, lucid glance could be preserved, if it could look out upon the old and new readers of his poems with the shadowed sweetness that charmed and attracted in life. Although his face and its expression were in harmony, the index of his character was written in his brow, candid and serene, and in his eyes sincere and affectionate. His brow was finely moulded and over it fell the masses of his brown hair, that glowed with a warm chestnut when the light touched it. His eyes were brown, clear and vivid.

Perfect sincerity was the key-note of his character. He was true to his ideals, in his work and in his life. Born without means and always living on a narrow income, his desire was for the greatest simplicity. A lodge in the forest and the primitive life would have fitted his contemplative mood. And when he built castles his imagination always placed them beside one of our northern lakes where everything was profoundly free and natural. His genial, tranquil temperament lent a quietness to his manner that gave not a hint of his virile spirit. There was no balance between the body of the man and his mind. That was radical and pierced to the sources of things. He was on the side of all good in the wider way. No convention frightened him or obscured his judgment. His writing proves his faith, his courage and the soundness of his morality. In the wider politics he was on the side of socialism and reasonable propaganda to that end, and announced his belief and argued it with courage whenever necessary. Caution might have been prophesied from his want of bodily vigour, but he had an adventurous spirit, and believed in the independence of Canada, and many other things commonly esteemed wild and visionary. Behind all he said and wrote was felt a great reserve of wisdom and integrity.

As a companion he had two manners, one absorbed, thoughtful, reticent; the other happily external, with brilliant conversation, an outpouring of genial criticism on current life or literature, with flashes of whimsical humour, and with a ready and ringing laugh. His talk was always uncommon

in a manner natural to him, expressed in singular words and
uttered in long flowing cadence.

Solitude he loved, and society, and he was always warm
towards any scheme for a union of men, or men and women
of intelligence, where a free discussion of all topics could be
had. His manner with his acquaintances and friends, old
and new, had the charm that Isaac Walton reports of the
behaviour of that admirable poet Dr. John Donne, that
winning behaviour "which when it would entice had a
strange kind of elegant, irresistible art." His deep love of
his own children was but a well-spring of love for all the
children he knew. Again, what he was in his life and in his
work came from sheer sincerity, from a temperament in har-
mony with clear ideals, directed by a mind free from guile.

His poems were principally composed as he walked
either to and from his ordinary employment in the city,
upon excursions into the country, or as he paced about his
writing-room. Lines invented under these conditions would
be transferred to manuscript books, and finally after they
had been perfected, would be written out carefully in his
clear, strong handwriting in volumes of a permanent kind.

Although this was his favorite and natural method of
composing, he frequently wrote his lines as they came to
him, and in many of his note-books can be traced the
development of poems through the constant working of his
fine instinct for form and expression: both were refined until
the artist felt his limit. With Archibald Lampman, as with
all true artists, this was short of his ideal; as he frequently
confessed, there always remained some shade of meaning
that he had not conveyed, some perfection of form that he
had not compassed.

He did not win his knowledge of nature from books,
but from actual observation and from conversations with
men who had studied the science of the special subjects.
Without a thought of literature he would intently observe a
landscape, a flower or a bird, until its true spirit was revealed
to him. Afterwards, it may have been days, weeks or months,

he called upon his knowledge, striving to revive his impression and transcribe it.

To write verses was the one great delight of his life. Everything in his world had reference to poetry. He was restless with a sense of burden when he was not composing, and deep with content when some stanza was taking form gradually in his mind.

Although there were periods during which he added nothing to the volume of his work, the persistence of his effort was remarkable. He did not over-estimate his own powers, and he wrote with no theory and unconscious of any special mission.

It amused him when he was called a didactic poet, not as slighting the term, but all such poems as "Insight," "Truth" and "The Largest Life," having been written from fulness of conviction and experience and prompted only by the joy of production, the idea of didacticism had its humours for him.

He was not a wide reader; books of history and travel were his favorites. During his last illness he read "The Ring and the Book," the novels of Jane Austen, and continued a constant reading of Greek by a reperusal of Pindar, the Odyssey, and the tragedies of Sophocles. Matthew Arnold was his favorite modern poet and he read his works oftener than those of any other; but Keats was the only poet whose method he carefully studied. Of his own sonnets he said: "Here after all is my best work."

His last poem, written on the evenings of the 29th and 30th of January, 1899, was the winter sonnet beginning "The frost that stings like fire upon my cheek." When he had finished its last line his work was done, and his final words are lovingly directed to an aspect of nature, "To silence, frost and beauty everywhere."

He rests in Beechwood Cemetery, part of the wild wood through which he was accustomed to wander speering about the chilly margin of snow-water pools for the first spring flowers. He said it was a good spot in which to lie when all

was over with life.   Even if there be no sense in these houses
of shade, it is a pleasant foreknowledge to be aware that
above one's unrealizing head the snow will sift, the small
ferns rise and the birds come back in nesting-time.   And
though he be forever rapt from such things, careless of them
and unaware, the sternest wind from under the pole star will
blow unconfined over his grave, about it the first hepaticas
will gather in fragile companies, the vesper sparrow will
return to nest in the grass, and from a branch of maple to
sing in the cool dusk.

DUNCAN   CAMPBELL   SCOTT.

AMONG THE MILLET

TO MY WIFE

Though fancy and the might of rhyme,
    That turneth like the tide,
Have borne me many a musing time,
    Belovèd, from thy side,

Ah yet, I pray thee, deem not, Sweet,
    Those hours were given in vain ;
Within these covers to thy feet
    I bring them back again.

AMONG THE MILLET

The dew is gleaming in the grass,
  The morning hours are seven,
And I am fain to watch you pass,
  Ye soft white clouds of heaven.

Ye stray and gather, part and fold;
  The wind alone can tame you;
I think of what in time of old
  The poets loved to name you.

They called you sheep, the sky your sward,
  A field without a reaper;
They called the shining sun your lord,
  The shepherd wind your keeper.

Your sweetest poets I will deem
  The men of old for moulding
In simple beauty such a dream,
  And I could lie beholding,

Where daisies in the meadow toss,
  The wind from morn till even,
For ever shepherd you across
  The shining field of heaven,

APRIL

Pale season, watcher in unvexed suspense,
Still priestess of the patient middle day,
Betwixt wild March's humored petulence
And the warm wooing of green kirtled May,
Maid month of sunny peace and sober gray,
Weaver of flowers in sunward glades that ring
With murmur of libation to the spring;

As memory of pain, all past, is peace,
And joy, dream-tasted, hath the deepest cheer,
So art thou sweetest of all months that lease
The twelve short spaces of the flying year.
The bloomless days are dead, and frozen fear
No more for many moons shall vex the earth,
Dreaming of summer and fruit-laden mirth.

The gray song-sparrows full of spring have sung
Their clear thin silvery tunes in leafless trees;
The robin hops, and whistles, and among
The silver-tasseled poplars the brown bees
Murmur faint dreams of summer harvestries;
The creamy sun at even scatters down
A gold-green mist across the murmuring town.

By the slow streams the frogs all day and night
Dream without thought of pain or heed of ill,
Watching the long warm silent hours take flight,
And ever with soft throats that pulse and thrill,
From the pale-weeded shallows trill and trill,
Tremulous sweet voices, flute-like, answering
One to another glorying in the spring.

All day across the ever-cloven soil,
Strong horses labour, steaming in the sun,
Down the long furrows with slow straining toil,
Turning the brown clean layers; and one by one
The crows gloom over them till daylight done
Finds them asleep somewhere in duskèd lines
Beyond the wheatlands in the northern pines.

The old year's cloaking of brown leaves, that bind
The forest floor-ways, plated close and true—
The last love's labour of the autumn wind—
Is broken with curled flower buds white and blue
In all the matted hollows, and speared through
With thousand serpent-spotted blades up-sprung,
Yet bloomless, of the slender adder-tongue.

In the warm noon the south wind creeps and cools,
Where the red-budded stems of maples throw
Still tangled etchings on the amber pools,
Quite silent now, forgetful of the slow
Drip of the taps, the troughs, and trampled snow,
The keen March mornings, and the silvering rime
And mirthful labour of the sugar prime.

Ah, I have wandered with unwearied feet,
All the long sweetness of an April day,
Lulled with cool murmurs and the drowsy beat
Of partridge wings in secret thickets gray,
The marriage hymns of all the birds at play,
The faces of sweet flowers, and easeful dreams
Beside slow reaches of frog-haunted streams;

Wandered with happy feet, and quite forgot
The shallow toil, the strife against the grain,
Near souls, that hear us call, but answer not,
The loneliness, perplexity and pain,
And high thoughts cankered with an earthly stain;
And then, the long draught emptied to the lees,
I turn me homeward in slow-pacing ease,

Cleaving the cedar shadows and the thin
Mist of gray gnats that cloud the river shore,
Sweet even choruses, that dance and spin
Soft tangles in the sunset; and once more
The city smites me with its dissonant roar.
To its hot heart I pass, untroubled yet,
Fed with calm hope, without desire or fret.

So to the year's first altar step I bring
Gifts of meek song, and make my spirit free
With the blind working of unanxious spring,
Careless with her, whether the days that flee
Pale drouth or golden-fruited plenty see,
So that we toil, brothers, without distress,
In calm-eyed peace and godlike blamelessness.

AN OCTOBER SUNSET

One moment the slim cloudflakes seem to lean
With their sad sunward faces aureoled,
And longing lips set downward brightening
To take the last sweet hand kiss of the king,
Gone down beyond the closing west acold;

Paying no reverence to the slender queen,
That like a curvèd olive leaf of gold
Hangs low in heaven, rounded toward the sun,
Or the small stars that one by one unfold
Down the gray border of the night begun.

THE FROGS

I

Breathers of wisdom won without a quest,
  Quaint uncouth dreamers, voices high and strange;
  Flutists of lands where beauty hath no change,
And wintry grief is a forgotten guest,
Sweet murmurers of everlasting rest,
  For whom glad days have ever yet to run,
  And moments are as aeons, and the sun
But ever sunken half-way toward the west.

Often to me who heard you in your day,
  With close rapt ears, it could not choose but seem
That earth, our mother, searching in what way
  Men's hearts might know her spirit's inmost dream;
    Ever at rest beneath life's change and stir,
    Made you her soul, and bade you pipe for her.

II

In those mute days when spring was in her glee,
  And hope was strong, we knew not why or how,

And earth, the mother, dreamed with brooding
    brow,
Musing on life, and what the hours might be,
When love should ripen to maternity,
    Then like high flutes in silvery interchange
    Ye piped with voices still and sweet and strange,
And ever as ye piped, on every tree

The great buds swelled; among the pensive woods
    The spirits of first flowers awoke and flung
From buried faces the close-fitting hoods,
    And listened to your piping till they fell,
    The frail spring-beauty with her perfumed bell,
The wind-flower, and the spotted adder-tongue.

III

All the day long, wherever pools might be
    Among the golden meadows, where the air
    Stood in a dream, as it were moorèd there
For ever in a noon-tide reverie,
Or where the birds made riot of their glee
    In the still woods, and the hot sun shone down,
    Crossed with warm lucent shadows on the brown
Leaf-paven pools, that bubbled dreamily,

Or far away in whispering river meads
    And watery marshes where the brooding noon,
    Full with the wonder of its own sweet boon,
Nestled and slept among the noiseless reeds,
    Ye sat and murmured, motionless as they,
    With eyes that dreamed beyond the night and day.

IV

And when day passed and over heaven's height,
   Thin with the many stars and cool with dew,
   The fingers of the deep hours slowly drew
The wonder of the ever-healing night,
No grief or loneliness or rapt delight
   Or weight of silence ever brought to you
   Slumber or rest; only your voices grew
More high and solemn; slowly with hushed flight

Ye saw the echoing hours go by, long-drawn,
   Nor ever stirred, watching with fathomless eyes,
   And with your countless clear antiphonies
Filling the earth and heaven, even till dawn,
   Last-risen, found you with its first pale gleam,
   Still with soft throats unaltered in your dream.

V

And slowly as we heard you, day by day,
   The stillness of enchanted reveries
   Bound brain and spirit and half-closèd eyes,
In some divine sweet wonder-dream astray;
To us no sorrow or upreared dismay
   Nor any discord came, but evermore
   The voices of mankind, the outer roar,
Grew strange and murmurous, faint and far away.

Morning and noon and midnight exquisitely,
   Rapt with your voices, this alone we knew,

Cities might change and fall, and men might die,
  Secure were we, content to dream with you
    That change and pain are shadows faint and fleet,
    And dreams are real, and life is only sweet.

AN IMPRESSION

I heard the city time-bells call
  Far off in hollow towers,
And one by one with measured fall
  Count out the old dead hours;

I felt the march, the silent press
  Of time, and held my breath;
I saw the haggard dreadfulness
  Of dim old age and death.

SPRING ON THE RIVER

O Sun, shine hot on the river;
  For the ice is turning an ashen hue,
· And the still bright water is looking through,
  And the myriad streams are greeting you
With a ballad of life to the giver,
  From forest and field and sunny town,
  Meeting and running and tripping down,
With laughter and song to the river.

Oh! the din on the boats by the river;
  The barges are ringing while day avails,

With sound of hewing and hammering nails,
Planing and painting and swinging pails,
All day in their shrill endeavour;
For the waters brim over their wintry cup,
And the grinding ice is breaking up,
And we must away down the river.

Oh! the hum and the toil of the river;
The ridge of the rapid sprays and skips;
Loud and low by the water's lips,
Tearing the wet pines into strips,
The saw-mill is moaning ever.
The little gray sparrow skips and calls
On the rocks in the rain of the waterfalls,
And the logs are adrift in the river.

Oh! restlessly whirls the river;
The rivulets run and the cataract drones;
The spiders are flitting over the stones;
Summer winds float and the cedar moans;
And the eddies gleam and quiver.
O Sun, shine hot, shine long and abide
In the glory and power of thy summer tide
On the swift longing face of the river.

WHY DO YE CALL THE POET LONELY

Why do ye call the poet lonely,
Because he dreams in lonely places?
He is not desolate, but only
Sees, where ye cannot, hidden faces.

HEAT

From plains that reel to southward, dim,
   The road runs by me white and bare;
Up the steep hill it seems to swim
   Beyond, and melt into the glare.
Upward half-way, or it may be
   Nearer the summit, slowly steals
A hay-cart, moving dustily
   With idly clacking wheels.

By his cart's side the wagoner
   Is slouching slowly at his ease,
Half-hidden in the windless blur
   Of white dust puffing to his knees.
This wagon on the height above,
   From sky to sky on either hand,
Is the sole thing that seems to move
   In all the heat-held land.

Beyond me in the fields the sun
   Soaks in the grass and hath his will;
I count the marguerites one by one;
   Even the buttercups are still.
On the brook yonder not a breath
   Disturbs the spider or the midge.
The water-bugs draw close beneath
   The cool gloom of the bridge.

Where the far elm-tree shadows flood
   Dark patches in the burning grass,
The cows, each with her peaceful cud,

Lie waiting for the heat to pass.
From somewhere on the slope near by
   Into the pale depth of the noon
A wandering thrush slides leisurely
   His thin revolving tune.

In intervals of dreams I hear
   The cricket from the droughty ground;
The grasshoppers spin into mine ear
   A small innumerable sound.
I lift mine eyes sometimes to gaze:
   The burning sky-line blinds my sight:
The woods far off are blue with haze:
   The hills are drenched in light.

And yet to me not this or that
   Is always sharp or always sweet;
In the sloped shadow of my hat
   I lean at rest, and drain the heat;
Nay more, I think some blessèd power
   Hath brought me wandering idly here:
In the full furnace of this hour
   My thoughts grow keen and clear.

AMONG THE TIMOTHY

Long hours ago, while yet the morn was blithe,
   Nor sharp athirst had drunk the beaded dew,
A mower came, and swung his gleaming scythe
   Around this stump, and, shearing slowly, drew
Far round among the clover, ripe for hay,
   A circle clean and gray;

And here among the scented swathes that gleam,
　Mixed with dead daisies, it is sweet to lie
　And watch the grass and the few-clouded sky,
　　Nor think but only dream.

For when the noon was turning, and the heat
　Fell down most heavily on field and wood,
I too came hither, borne on restless feet,
　Seeking some comfort for an aching mood.
　Ah! I was weary of the drifting hours,
　　The echoing city towers,
The blind gray streets, the jingle of the throng,
　Weary of hope that like a shape of stone
　Sat near at hand without a smile or moan,
　　And weary most of song.

And those high moods of mine that sometime made
　My heart a heaven, opening like a flower
A sweeter world where I in wonder strayed,
　Begirt with shapes of beauty and the power
　Of dreams that moved through that enchanted
　　clime
　　With changing breaths of rhyme,
Were all gone lifeless now, like those white leaves
　That hang all winter, shivering dead and blind
　Among the sinewy beeches in the wind,
　　That vainly calls and grieves.

Ah! I will set no more mine overtaskèd brain
　To barren search and toil that beareth nought,
For ever following with sore-footed pain
　The crossing pathways of unbournèd thought;

But let it go, as one that hath no skill,
    To take what shape it will,
An ant slow-burrowing in the earthy gloom,
    A spider bathing in the dew at morn,
    Or a brown bee in wayward fancy borne
        From hidden bloom to bloom.

Hither and thither o'er the rocking grass
    The little breezes, blithe as they are blind,
Teasing the slender blossoms pass and pass,
    Soft-footed children of the gipsy wind,
    To taste of every purple-fringèd head
        Before the bloom is dead;
And scarcely heed the daisies that, endowed
    With stems so short they cannot see, up-bear
    Their innocent sweet eyes distressed, and stare
        Like children in a crowd.

Not far to fieldward in the central heat,
    Shadowing the clover, a pale poplar stands
With glimmering leaves that, when the wind comes,
        beat
    Together like innumerable small hands,
    And with the calm, as in vague dreams astray,
        Hang wan and silver-gray;
Like sleepy maenads, who in pale surprise,
    Half-wakened by a prowling beast, have crept
    Out of the hidden covert, where they slept,
        At noon with languid eyes.

The crickets creak, and through the noonday glow,
    That crazy fiddler of the hot mid-year,

The dry cicada plies his wiry bow
  In long-spun cadence, thin and dusty sere;
  From the green grass the small grasshoppers' din
    Spreads soft and silvery thin;
And ever and anon a murmur steals
  Into mine ears of toil that moves alway,
  The crackling rustle of the pitch-forked hay
    And lazy jerk of wheels.

As so I lie and feel the soft hours wane,
  To wind and sun and peaceful sound laid bare,
That aching dim discomfort of the brain
  Fades off unseen, and shadowy-footed care
  Into some hidden corner creeps at last
    To slumber deep and fast;
And gliding on, quite fashioned to forget,
  From dream to dream I bid my spirit pass
  Out into the pale green ever-swaying grass
    To brood, but no more fret.

.And hour by hour among all shapes that grow
  Of purple mints and daisies gemmed with gold
In sweet unrest my visions come and go;
  I feel and hear and with quiet eyes behold;
  And hour by hour, the ever-journeying sun,
    In gold and shadow spun,
Into mine eyes and blood, and through the dim
  Green glimmering forest of the grass shines down,
  Till flower and blade, and every cranny brown,
    And I are soaked with him.

FREEDOM

Out of the heart of the city begotten
  Of the labour of men and their manifold hands,
Whose souls, that were sprung from the earth in
      her morning,
No longer regard or remember her warning,
  Whose hearts in the furnace of care have forgotten
  For ever the scent and the hue of her lands;

Out of the heat of the usurer's hold,
  From the horrible crash of the strong man's feet;
Out of the shadow where pity is dying;
Out of the clamour where beauty is lying,
  Dead in the depth of the struggle for gold;
  Out of the din and the glare of the street;

Into the arms of our mother we come,
  Our broad strong mother, the innocent earth,
Mother of all things beautiful, blameless,
Mother of hopes that her strength makes tameless,
  Where the voices of grief and of battle are dumb,
  And the whole world laughs with the light of
      her mirth.

Over the fields, where the cool winds sweep,
  Black with the mould and brown with the loam,
Where the thin green spears of the wheat are
      appearing,
And the high-ho shouts from the smoky clearing;
  Over the widths where the cloud shadows creep;
  Over the fields and the fallows we come;
  2

Over the swamps with their pensive noises,
  Where the burnished cup of the marigold
    gleams;
Skirting the reeds, where the quick winds shiver
  On the swelling breast of the dimpled river,
  And the blue of the kingfisher hangs and poises,
    Watching a spot by the edge of the streams;

  By the miles of the fences warped and dyed
    With the white-hot noons and their withering
      fires.
Where the rough bees trample the creamy bosoms
Of the hanging tufts of the elder blossoms,
    And the spiders weave, and the gray snakes hide,
      In the crannied gloom of the stones and the
        briers;

  Over the meadow lands sprouting with thistle,
    Where the humming wings of the blackbirds
      pass,
Where the hollows are banked with the violets
      flowering,
And the long-limbed pendulous elms are towering,
  Where the robins are loud with their voluble
      whistle,
      And the ground-sparrow scurries away through
        the grass,

  Where the restless bobolink loiters and woos
    Down in the hollows and over the swells,
Dropping in and out of the shadows,
Sprinkling his music about the meadows,

Whistles and little checks and coos,
  And the tinkle of glassy bells;

Into the dim woods full of the tombs
  Of the dead trees soft in their sepulchres,
Where the pensive throats of the shy birds hidden,
Pipe to us strangely entering unbidden,
  And tenderly still in the tremulous glooms
    The trilliums scatter their white-winged stars;

Up to the hills where our tired hearts rest,
  Loosen, and halt, and regather their dreams;
Up to the hills, where the winds restore us,
Clearing our eyes to the beauty before us,
  Earth with the glory of life on her breast,
    Earth with the gleam of her cities and streams.

Here we shall commune with her and no other;
  Care and the battle of life shall cease;
Men, her degenerate children, behind us,
Only the might of her beauty shall bind us,
  Full of rest, as we gaze on the face of our mother,
    Earth in the health and the strength of her
      peace.

MORNING ON THE LIEVRE

Far above us where a jay
Screams his matins to the day,
Capped with gold and amethyst,
Like a vapour from the forge

Of a giant somewhere hid,
Out of hearing of the clang
Of his hammer, skirts of mist
Slowly up the woody gorge
Lift and hang.

Softly as a cloud we go,
Sky above and sky below,
Down the river; and the dip
Of the paddles·scarcely breaks,
With the little silvery drip
Of the water as it shakes
From the blades, the crystal deep
Of the silence of the morn,
Of the forest yet asleep;
And the river reaches borne
In a mirror, purple gray,
Sheer away
To the misty line of light,
Where the forest and the stream
In the shadow meet and plight,
Like a dream.

From amid a stretch of reeds,
Where the lazy river sucks
All the water as it bleeds
From a little curling creek,
And the muskrats peer and sneak
In around the sunken wrecks
Of a tree that swept the skies
Long ago,
On a sudden seven ducks

With a splashy rustle rise,
Stretching out their seven necks,
One before, and two behind,
And the others all arow,
And as steady as the wind
With a swivelling whistle go,
Through the purple shadow led,
Till we only hear their whir
In behind a rocky spur,
Just ahead.

IN OCTOBER

Along the waste, a great way off, the pines
    Like tall slim priests of storm, stand up and bar
The low long strip of dolorous red that lines
    The under west, where wet winds moan afar.
The cornfields all are brown, and brown the meadows
    With the blown leaves' wind-heapèd traceries,
And the brown thistle stems that cast no shadows,
    And bear no bloom for bees.

As slowly earthward leaf by red leaf slips,
    The sad trees rustle in chill misery,
A soft strange inner sound of pain-crazed lips,
    That move and murmur incoherently;
As if all leaves, that yet have breath, were sighing,
    With pale hushed throats, for death is at the door,
So many low soft masses for the dying
    Sweet leaves that live no more.

Here I will sit upon this naked stone,
   Draw my coat closer with my numbèd hands,
And hear the ferns sigh, and the wet woods moan,
   And send my heart out to the ashen lands;
And I will ask myself what golden madness,
   What balmèd breaths of dreamland spicery,
What visions of soft laughter and light sadness
   Were sweet last month to me.

The dry dead leaves flit by with thin weird tunes,
   Like failing murmurs of some conquered creed,
Graven in mystic markings with strange runes,
   That none but stars and biting winds may read;
Here I will wait a little; I am weary,
   Not torn with pain of any lurid hue,
But only still and very gray and dreary,
   Sweet sombre lands, like you.

LAMENT OF THE WINDS

We in sorrow coldly witting,
In the bleak world sitting, sitting,
   By the forest, near the mould,
Heard the summer calling, calling,
Through the dead leaves falling, falling,
   That her life grew faint and old.

And we took her up, and bore her,
With the leaves that moaned before her,
   To the holy forest bowers,
Where the trees were dense and serried,

And her corpse we buried, buried,
  In the graveyard of the flowers.

Now the leaves, as death grows vaster,
Yellowing deeper, dropping faster,
  All the grave wherein she lies
With their bodies cover, cover,
With their hearts that love her, love her,
  For they live not when she dies.

BALLADE OF SUMMER'S SLEEP

Sweet summer is gone; they have laid her away—
  The last sad hours that were touched with her
            grace—
In the hush where the ghosts of the dead flowers
            play;
  The sleep that is sweet of her slumbering space
Let not a sight nor a sound erase
  Of the woe that hath fallen on all the lands:
Gather ye, Dreams, to her sunny face,
  Shadow her head with your golden hands.

The woods that are golden and red for a day
  Girdle the hills in a jewelled case,
Like a girl's strange mirth, ere the quick death slay
  The beautiful life that he hath in chase.
  Darker and darker the shadows pace
    Out of the north to the southern sands,
  Ushers bearing the winter's mace:
    Keep them away with your woven hands.

The yellow light lies on the wide wastes gray,
  More bitter and cold than the winds that race
From the skirts of the autumn, tearing away,
  This way and that way, the woodland lace,
  In the autumn's cheek is a hectic trace;
    Behind her the ghost of the winter stands;
  Sweet summer will moan in her soft gray place;
  Mantle her head with your glowing hands.

Envoi.

Till the slayer be slain and the spring displace
  The might of his arms with her rose-crowned bands,
Let her heart not gather a dream that is base:
  Shadow her head with your golden hands.

WINTER

The long days came and went; the riotous bees
  Tore the warm grapes in many a dusty vine,
And men grew faint and thin with too much ease,
      And Winter gave no sign;
But all the while beyond the northmost woods
  He sat and smiled and watched his spirits play
  In elfish dance and eerie roundelay,
      Tripping in many moods
With snowy curve and fairy crystal shine.

But now the time is come: with southward speed
  The elfin spirits pass: a secret sting
Hath fallen and smitten flower and fruit and weed,
      And every leafy thing.

The wet woods moan : the dead leaves break and fall ;
 In still night-watches wakeful men have heard
 The muffled pipe of many a passing bird,
         High over hut and hall,
Straining to southward with unresting wing.

And then they come with colder feet, and fret
 The winds with snow, and tuck the streams to sleep
With icy sheet and gleaming coverlet,
         And fill the valleys deep
With curvèd drifts, and a strange music raves
 Among the pines, sometimes in wails, and then
 In whistled laughter, till affrighted men
         Draw close, and into caves
And earthy holes the blind beasts curl and creep.

And so all day above the toiling heads
 Of men's poor chimneys, full of impish freaks,
Tearing and twisting in tight-curlèd shreds
         The vain unnumbered reeks,
The Winter speeds his fairies forth and mocks
 Poor bitten men with laughter icy cold,
 Turning the brown of youth to white and old
         With hoary-woven locks,
And gray men young with roses in their cheeks.

And after thaws, when liberal water swells
 The bursting eaves, he biddeth drip and grow
The curly horns of ribbèd icicles
         In many a beard-like row.

In secret moods of mercy and soft dole,
  Old warpèd wrecks and things of mouldering death
  That summer scorns and man abandoneth
    His careful hands console
With lawny robes and draperies of snow.

And when night comes, his spirits with chill feet,
  Winged with white mirth and noiseless mockery,
Across men's pallid windows peer and fleet,
    And smiling silverly
Draw with mute fingers on the frosted glass
  Quaint fairy shapes of icèd witcheries,
  Pale flowers and glinting ferns and frigid trees
    And meads of mystic grass,
Graven in many an austere phantasy.

But far away the Winter dreams alone,
  Rustling among his snow-drifts, and resigns
Cold fondling ears to hear the cedars moan
    In dusky-skirted lines
Strange answers of an ancient runic call;
  Or somewhere watches with his antique eyes,
  Gray-chill with frosty-lidded reveries,
    The silvery moonshine fall
In misty wedges through his girth of pines.

Poor mortals haste and hide away: creep soon
  Into your icy beds: the embers die;
And on your frosted panes the pallid moon
    Is glimmering brokenly.

Mutter faint prayers that spring will come e'erwhile,
  Scarring with thaws and dripping days and nights
  The shining majesty of him that smites
        And slays you with a smile
Upon his silvery lips, of glinting mockery.

WINTER HUES RECALLED

Life is not all for effort; there are hours
When fancy breaks from the exacting will,
And rebel thought takes schoolboy's holiday,
Rejoicing in its idle strength.   'Tis then,
And only at such moments, that we know
The treasure of hours gone—scenes once beheld,
Sweet voices and words bright and beautiful,
Impetuous deeds that woke the God within us,
The loveliness of forms and thoughts and colours,
A moment marked and then as soon forgotten.
These things are ever near us, laid away,
Hidden and waiting the appropriate times,
In the quiet garner-house of memory.
There in the silent unaccounted depth,
  Beneath the heated strainage and the rush,
That teem the noisy surface of the hours,
All things that ever touched us are stored up,
Growing more mellow like sealed wine with age;
We thought them dead, and they are but asleep.
In moments when the heart is most at rest
And least expectant, from the luminous doors,

And sacred dwelling-place of things unfeared,
They issue forth, and we who never knew
Till then how potent and how real they were,
Take them, and wonder, and so bless the hour.

Such gifts are sweetest when unsought.   To me,
As I was loitering lately in my dreams,
Passing from one remembrance to another,
Like him who reads upon an outstretched map,
Content and idly happy, there rose up,
Out of that magic well-stored picture house,
No dream, rather a thing most keenly real,
The memory of a moment, when with feet
Arrested and spell-bound, and captured eyes,
Made wide with joy and wonder, I beheld
The spaces of a white and wintry land
Swept with the fire of sunset, all its width,
Vale, forest, town and misty eminence,
A miracle of colour and of beauty.

I had walked out, as I remember now,
With covered ears, for the bright air was keen,
To southward up the gleaming snow-packed fields,
With the snowshoer's long rejoicing stride,
Marching at ease.   It was a radiant day
In February, the month of the great struggle
'Twixt sun and frost, when with advancing spears,
The glittering golden vanguard of the spring
Holds the broad winter's yet unbroken rear
In long-closed wavering contest.   Thin pale threads
Like streaks of ash across the far-off blue
Were drawn, nor seemed to move.   A brooding
        silence

Kept all the land, a stillness as of sleep;
But in the east the gray and motionless woods,
Watching the great sun's fiery slow decline,
Grew deep with gold.   To westward all was silver.
An hour had passed above me; I had reached
The loftiest level of the snow-piled fields,
Clear-eyed, but unobservant, noting not
That all the plain beneath me and the hills
Took on a change of colour splendid, gradual,
Leaving no spot the same; nor that the sun
Now like a fiery torrent overflamed
The great line of the west.   Ere yet I turned
With long stride homeward, being heated
With the loose swinging motion, weary too,
Nor uninclined to rest, a buried fence,
Whose topmost log just shouldered from the snow.
Made me a seat, and thence with heated cheeks,
Grazed by the northwind's edge of stinging ice,
I looked far out upon the snow-bound waste,
The lifting hills and intersecting forests,
The scarce marked courses of the buried streams,
And as I looked lost memory of the frost,
Transfixed with wonder, overborne with joy.
I saw them in their silence and their beauty,
Swept by the sunset's rapid hand of fire,
Sudden, mysterious, every moment deepening
To some new majesty of rose or flame.
The whole broad west was like a molten sea
Of crimson.   In the north the light-lined hills
Were veiled far off as with a mist of rose
Wondrous and soft.   Along the darkening east

The gold of all the forests slowly changed
To purple.   In the valley far before me,
Low sunk in sapphire shadows, from its hills,
Softer and lovelier than an opening flower,
Uprose a city with its sun-touched towers,
A bunch of amethysts.

                    Like one spell-bound
Caught in the presence of some god, I stood,
Nor felt the keen wind and the deadly air,
But watched the sun go down, and watched the gold
Fade from the town and the withdrawing hills,
Their westward shapes athwart the dusky red
Freeze into sapphire, saw the arc of rose
Rise ever higher in the violet east,
Above the frore front of the uprearing night
Remorsefully soft and sweet.   Then I awoke
As from a dream, and from my shoulders shook
The warning chill, till then unfelt, unfeared.

STORM

Out of the gray northwest, where many a day gone by
    Ye tugged and howled in your tempestuous grot,
And evermore the huge frost giants lie,
    Your wizard guards in vigilance unforgot,
Out of the gray northwest, for now the bonds are
        riven,
On wide white wings your thongless flight is driven,
    That lulls but resteth not.

And all the gray day long, and all the dense wild
    night,
Ye wheel and hurry with the sheeted snow,
By cedared waste and many a pine-dark height,
    Across white rivers frozen fast below;
Over the lonely forests, where the flowers yet sleeping
Turn in their narrow beds with dreams of weeping
    In some remembered woe;

Across the unfenced wide marsh levels, where the dry
    Brown ferns sigh out, and last year's sedges scold
In some drear language, rustling haggardly
    Their thin dead leaves and dusky hoods of gold;
Across gray beechwoods where the pallid leaves
        unfalling
In the blind gusts like homeless ghosts are calling
    With voices cracked and old;

Across the solitary clearings, where the low
    Fierce gusts howl through the blinded woods, and
        round
The buried shanties all day long the snow
    Sifts and piles up in many a spectral mound;
Across lone villages in eerie wildernesses
Whose hidden life no living shape confesses
    Nor any human sound;

Across the serried masses of dim cities, blown
    Full of the snow that ever shifts and swells,
While far above them all their towers of stone
    Stand and beat back your fierce and tyrannous
        spells,

And hour by hour send out, like voices torn and
      broken
Of battling giants that have grandly spoken,
   The veering sound of bells;

So day and night, O Wind, with hiss and moan you
      fleet,
   Where once long gone on many a green-leafed day
Your gentler brethren wandered with light feet
   And sang, with voices soft and sweet as they,
The same blind thought that you with wilder might
      are speaking,
Seeking the same strange thing that you are seeking
   In this your stormier way.

O Wind, wild-voicèd brother, in your northern cave,
   My spirit also being so beset
With pride and pain, I heard you beat and rave,
   Grinding your chains with furious howl and fret,
Knowing full well that all earth's moving things
      inherit
The same chained might and madness of the spirit,
   That none may quite forget.

You in your cave of snows, we in our narrow girth
   Of need and sense, for ever chafe and pine;
Only in moods of some demonic birth
   Our souls take fire, our flashing wings untwine;
Even like you, mad Wind, above our broken prison,
With streaming hair and maddened eyes uprisen,
   We dream ourselves divine;

Mad moods that come and go in some mysterious
      way,
  That flash and fall, none knoweth how or why,
O Wind, our brother, they are yours to-day,
  The stormy joy, the sweeping mastery;
Deep in our narrow cells, we hear you, we awaken,
With hands afret and bosoms strangely shaken,
  We answer to your cry.

I most that love you, Wind, when you are fierce and
      free,
  In these dull fetters cannot long remain;
Lo, I will rise and break my thongs and flee
  Forth to your drift and beating, till my brain
Even for an hour grow wild in your divine embraces,
And then creep back into mine earthly traces,
  And bind me with my chain.

Nay, Wind, I hear you, desperate brother, in your
      might
  Whistle and howl; I shall not tarry long,
And though the day be blind and fierce, the night
  Be dense and wild, I still am glad and strong
To meet you face to face; through all your gust and
      drifting
With brow held high, my joyous hands uplifting,
  I cry you song for song.

3

MIDNIGHT

From where I sit, I see the stars,
  And down the chilly floor
The moon between the frozen bars
  Is glimmering dim and hoar.

Without in many a peakèd mound
  The glinting snowdrifts lie;
There is no voice or living sound;
  The embers slowly die.

Yet some wild thing is in mine ear;
  I hold my breath and hark;
Out of the depth I seem to hear
  A crying in the dark;

No sound of man or wife or child,
  No sound of beast that groans,
Or of the wind that whistles wild,
  Or of the tree that moans:

I know not what it is I hear;
  I bend my head and hark:
I cannot drive it from mine ear,
  That crying in the dark.

SONG OF THE STREAM-DROPS

By silent forest and field and mossy stone,
  We come from the wooded hill, and we go to the
    sea.
We labour, and sing sweet songs, but we never
    moan,
  For our mother, the sea, is calling us cheerily.
We have heard her calling us many and many a day
From the cool gray stones and the white sands far
    away.

  The way is long, and winding and slow is the track,
    The sharp rocks fret us, the eddies bring us
      delay,
  But we sing sweet songs to our mother, and
      answer her back;
    Gladly we answer our mother, sweetly repay.
Oh, we hear, we hear her singing wherever we roam,
Far, far away in the silence, calling us home.

  Poor mortal, your ears are dull, and you cannot
      hear;
    But we, we hear it, the breast of our mother
      abeat;
  Low, far away, sweet and solemn and clear,
    Under the hush of the night, under the noontide
      heat;
And we sing sweet songs to our mother, for so we
    shall please her best,
Songs of beauty and peace, freedom and infinite rest.

We sing, and sing, through the grass and the
    stones and the reeds,
  And we never grow tired, though we journey
    ever and aye,
Dreaming, and dreaming, wherever the long way
    leads,
  Of the far cool rocks and the rush of the wind
    and the spray.
Under the sun and the stars we murmur and dance
    and are free,
And we dream and dream of our mother, the width
    of the sheltering sea.

BETWEEN THE RAPIDS

The point is turned; the twilight shadow fills
  The wheeling stream, the soft receding shore,
And on our ears from deep among the hills
  Breaks now the rapid's sudden quickening roar.
Ah, yet the same, or have they changed their face,
  The fair green fields, and can it still be seen,
The white log cottage near the mountain's base,
  So bright and quiet, so home-like and serene?
Ah, well I question, for as five years go,
How many blessings fall, and how much woe.

Aye there they are, nor have they changed their
    cheer,
  The fields, the hut, the leafy mountain brows;
Across the lonely dusk again I hear
  The loitering bells, the lowing of the cows,

The bleat of many sheep, the stilly rush
  Of the low whispering river, and through all,
Soft human tongues that break the deepening hush
  With faint-heard song or desultory call:
O comrades hold, the longest reach is past;
The stream runs swift, and we are flying fast.

The shore, the fields, the cottage just the same,
  But how with those whose memory makes them
    sweet?
Oh if I called them, hailing name by name,
  Would the same lips the same old shouts repeat?
Have the rough years, so big with death and ill,
  Gone lightly by and left them smiling yet?
Wild black-eyed Jeanne whose tongue was never
    still,
  Old wrinkled Picaud, Pierre and pale Lisette,
The homely hearts that never cared to range,
While life's wide fields were filled with rush and
    change.

And where is Jacques, and where is Virginie?
  I cannot tell; the fields are all a blur.
The lowing cows whose shapes I scarcely see,
  Oh do they wait and do they call for her?
And is she changed, or is her heart still clear
  As wind or morning, light as river foam?
Or have life's changes borne her far from here,
  And far from rest, and far from help and home?
Ah comrades, soft, and let us rest awhile,
For arms grow tired with paddling many a mile.

The woods grow wild, and from the rising shore
   The cool wind creeps, the faint wood odours steal;
Like ghosts adown the river's blackening floor
   The misty fumes begin to creep and reel.
Once more I leave you, wandering toward the night,
   Sweet home, sweet heart, that would have held me
      in;
Whither I go I know not, and the light
   Is faint before, and rest is hard to win.
Ah sweet ye were and near to heaven's gate;
But youth is blind and wisdom comes too late.

Blacker and loftier grow the woods, and hark!
   The freshening roar!   The chute is near us now,
And dim the canyon grows, and inky dark
   The water whispering from the birchen prow.
One long last look, and many a sad adieu,
   While eyes can see and heart can feel you yet,
I leave sweet home and sweeter hearts to you,
   A prayer for Picaud, one for pale Lisette,
A kiss for Pierre and little Jacques for thee,
A sigh for Jeanne, a sob for Virginie.

Oh, does she still remember?   Is the dream
   Now dead, or has she found another mate?
So near, so dear; and ah, so swift the stream;
   Even now perhaps it were not yet too late.
But oh, what matter; for before the night
   Has reached its middle, we have far to go:
Bend to your paddles, comrades: see, the light
   Ebbs off apace; we must not linger so.
Aye thus it is! Heaven gleams and then is gone:
Once, twice, it smiles, and still we wander on.

NEW YEAR'S EVE

Once on the year's last eve in my mind's might
  Sitting in dreams, not sad, nor quite elysian,
  Balancing all 'twixt wonder and derision,
Methought my body and all this world took flight,
And vanished from me, as a dream, outright;
  Leaning out thus in sudden strange decision,
  I saw as in the flashing of a vision,
Far down between the tall towers of the night,
  Borne by great winds in awful unison,
    The teeming masses of mankind sweep by,
    Even as a glittering river with deep sound
  And innumerable banners, rolling on,
    Over the starry border-glooms that bound
    The last gray space in dim eternity.

And all that strange unearthly multitude
  Seemed twisted in vast seething companies,
  That evermore, with hoarse and terrible cries
And desperate encounter at mad feud,
Plunged onward, each in its implacable mood
  Borne down over the trampled blazonries
  Of other faiths and other phantasies,
Each following furiously, and each pursued;
  So sped they on with tumult vast and grim,
    But ever meseemed beyond them I could see
    White-haloed groups that sought perpetually
    The figure of one crowned and sacrificed;
  And faint, far forward, floating tall and dim,
    The banner of our Lord and Master, Christ.

UNREST

All day upon the garden bright
  The sun shines strong,
But in my heart there is no light,
  Nor any song.

Voices of merry life go by,
  Adown the street;
But I am weary of the cry
  And drift of feet.

With all dear things that ought to please
  The hours are blessed,
And yet my soul is ill at ease,
  And cannot rest.

Strange Spirit, leave me not too long,
  Nor stint to give,
For if my soul have no sweet song,
  It cannot live.

SONG

Songs that could span the earth,
  When leaping thought had stirred them,
In many an hour since birth,
  We heard or dreamed we heard them.

Sometimes to all their sway
  We yield ourselves half fearing,
Sometimes with hearts grown gray
  We curse ourselves for hearing.

We toil and but begin;
In vain our spirits fret them,
We strive, and cannot win,
Nor evermore forget them.

A light that will not stand,
That comes and goes in flashes,
Fair fruits that in the hand
Are turned to dust and ashes.

Yet still the deep thoughts ring
Around and through and through us,
Sweet mights that make us sing,
But bring no resting to us.

ONE DAY

The trees rustle; the wind blows
Merrily out of the town;
The shadows creep, the sun goes
Steadily over and down.

In a brown gloom the moats gleam;
Slender the sweet wife stands;
Her lips are red; her eyes dream;
Kisses are warm on her hands.

The child moans; the hours slip
Bitterly over her head;
In a gray dusk, the tears drip;
Mother is up there—dead.

The hermit hears the strange bright
   Murmur of life at play;
In the waste day and the waste night
   Times to rebel and to pray.

The labourer toils in gray wise,
   Godlike and patient and calm;
The beggar moans; his bleared eyes
   Measure the dust in his palm.

The wise man marks the flow and ebb
   Hidden and held aloof:
In his deep mind is laid the web,
   Shuttles are driving the woof.

SLEEP

If any man, with sleepless care oppressed,
On many a night had risen, and addressed
His hand to make him out of joy and moan
An image of sweet sleep in carven stone,
Light touch by touch, in weary moments planned,
He would have wrought her with a patient hand,
Not like her brother death, with massive limb
And dreamless brow, unstartled, changeless, dim,
But very fair, though fitful and afraid,
More sweet and slight than any mortal maid.
Her hair he would have carved a mantle smooth
Down to her tender feet to wrap and soothe
All fevers in, yet barbèd here and there
With many a hidden sting of restless care;
Her brow most quiet, thick with opiate rest,

Yet watchfully lined, as if some hovering guest
Of noiseless doubt were there; so too her eyes
His light hand would have carved in cunning wise
Broad with all languor of the drowsy South,

Most beautiful, but held askance; her mouth
More soft and round than any rose half-spread,
Yet ever twisted with some nervous dread.
He would have made her with one marble foot,
Frail as a snow-white feather, forward put,
Bearing sweet medicine for all distress,
Smooth languor and unstrung forgetfulness;
The other held a little back for dread;
One slender moon-pale hand held forth to shed
Soft slumber dripping from its pearly tip
Into wide eyes; the other on her lip.
So in the watches of his sleepless care
The cunnning artist would have wrought her fair;
Shy goddess, at keen seeking most afraid,
Yet often coming when we least have prayed.

THREE FLOWER PETALS

What saw I yesterday walking apart
    In a leafy place where the cattle wait?
Something to keep for a charm in my heart—
    A little sweet girl in a garden gate.
Laughing she lay in the gold sun's might,
    And held for a target to shelter her,
In her little soft fingers, round and white,
    The gold-rimmed face of a sunflower.

Laughing she lay on the stone that stands
   For a rough-hewn step in that sunny place,
And her yellow hair hung down to her hands,
   Shadowing over her dimpled face.
Her eyes like the blue of the sky, made dim
   With the might of the sun that looked at her,
Shone laughing over the serried rim,
   Golden set, of the sunflower.

Laughing, for token she gave to me
   Three petals out of the sunflower.
When the petals are withered and gone, shall be
   Three verses of mine for praise of her,
That a tender dream of her face may rise,
   And lighten me yet in another hour,
Of her sunny hair and her beautiful eyes,
   Laughing over the gold sunflower.

PASSION

As a weed beneath the ocean,
   As a pool beneath a tree
Answers with each breath or motion
   An imperious mastery;

So my spirit swift with passion
   Finds in every look a sign,
Catching in some wondrous fashion
   Every mood that governs thine.

In a moment it will borrow,
　　Flashing in a gusty train,
Laughter and desire and sorrow
　　Anger and delight and pain.

A BALLADE OF WAITING

No girdle hath weaver or goldsmith wrought
　　So rich as the arms of my love can be;
No gems with a lovelier lustre fraught
　　Than her eyes, when they answer me liquidly.
　Dear Lady of Love, be kind to me
　　In days when the waters of hope abate,
　And doubt like a shimmer on sand shall be,
　　In the year yet, Lady, to dream and wait.

Sweet mouth, that the wear of the world hath taught
　　No glitter of wile or traitorie,
More soft than a cloud in the sunset caught,
　　Or the heart of a crimson peony;
　O turn not its beauty away from me;
　　To kiss it and cling to it early and late
　Shall make sweet minutes of days that flee,
　　In the year yet, Lady, to dream and wait.

Rich hair, that a painter of old had sought
　　For the weaving of some soft phantasy,
Most fair when the streams of it run distraught
　　On the firm sweet shoulders yellowly;

Dear Lady, gather it close to me,
  Weaving a nest for the double freight
Of cheeks and lips that are one and free,
  For the year yet, Lady, to dream and wait.

Envoi

So time shall be swift till thou mate with me,
  For love is mightiest next to fate,
And none shall be happier, Love, than we,
  In the year yet, Lady, to dream and wait.

BEFORE SLEEP

Now the creeping nets of sleep
  Stretch about and gather nigh,
And the midnight dim and deep
  Like a spirit passes by,
Trailing from her crystal dress
  Dreams and silent frostiness.

Yet a moment, ere I be
  Tangled in the snares of night,
All the dreamy heart of me
  To my Lady takes its flight,
To her chamber where she lies,
  Wrapt in midnight phantasies.

Over many a glinting street
  And the snow-capped roofs of men,
Towers that tremble with the beat
  Of the midnight bells, and then,

Where my body may not be,
  Stands my spirit holily.

Wake not, Lady, wake not soon:
  Through the frosty windows fall
Broken glimmers of the moon
  Dimly on the floor and wall;
Wake not, Lady, never care,
  'Tis my spirit kneeling there.

Let him kneel a moment now,
  For the minutes fly apace;
Let him see the sleeping brow,
  And the sweetly rounded face:
He shall tell me soon aright
  How my Lady looks to-night.

How her tresses out and in
  Fold in many a curly freak,
Round about the snowy chin
  And the softly tinted cheek,
Where no sorrows now can weep,
  And the dimples lie asleep.

How her eyelids meet and match,
  Gathered in two dusky seams,
Each the little creamy thatch
  Of an azure house of dreams,
Or two flowers that love the light
  Folded softly up at night.

How her bosom, breathing low,
  Stirs the wavy coverlet

With a motion soft and slow:
  O, my Lady, wake not yet;
There without a thought of guile
  Let my spirit dream a while.

Yet my spirit back to me,
  Hurry soon and have a care;
Love will turn to agony,
  If you rashly linger there;
Bending low as spirits may,
  Touch her lips and come away.

So, fond spirit, beauty-fed,
  Turning when your watch is o'er,
Weave a cross above the bed
  And a sleep-rune on the floor,
That no evil enter there,
  Ugly shapes and dreams beware.

Then, ye looming nets of sleep,
  Ye may have me all your own,
For the night is wearing deep
  And the ice-winds whisk and moan;
Come with all your drowsy stress,
  Dreams and silent frostiness.

A SONG

  O night and sleep,
  Ye are so soft and deep,
I am so weary, come ye soon to me.
  O hours that creep,

With so much time to weep,
I am so tired, can ye no swifter be?

Come, night, anear;
I'll whisper in thine ear
What makes me so unhappy, full of care;
Dear night, I die
For love, that all men buy
With tears, and know not it is dark despair.

Dear night, I pray,
How is it that men say
That love is sweet?   It is not sweet to me.
For one boy's sake
A poor girl's heart must break;
So sweet, so true, and yet it could not be!

Oh, I loved well,
Such love as none can tell:
It was so true, it could not make him know:
For he was blind,
All light and all unkind:
Oh, had he known, would he have hurt me so?

O night and sleep,
Ye are so soft and deep,
I am so weary, come ye soon to me.
O hours that creep,
With so much time to weep,
I am so tired, can ye no swifter be?

4

WHAT DO POETS WANT WITH GOLD?

What do poets want with gold,
   Cringing slaves and cushioned ease;
Are not crusts and garments old
   Better for their souls than these?

Gold is but the juggling rod
Of a false usurping god,
Graven long ago in hell
With a sombre stony spell,
Working in the world for ever.
Hate is not so strong to sever
Beating human heart from heart.
Soul from soul we shrink and part,
And no longer hail each other
With the ancient name of brother.
Give the simple poet gold,
 And his song will die of cold.
He must walk with men that reel
On the rugged path, and feel
Every sacred soul that is
Beating very near to his.
Simple, human, careless, free,
As God made him, he must be:
For the sweetest song of bird
Is the hidden tenor heard
In the dusk, at even-flush,
From the forest's inner hush,
Of the simple hermit thrush.

What do poets want with love?
  Flowers that shiver out of hand,
And the fervid fruits that prove
  Only bitter broken sand?

Poets speak of passion best,
When their dreams are undistressed,
And the sweetest songs are sung,
E'er the inner heart is stung.
Let them dream; 'tis better so;
Ever dream, but never know.
If their spirits once have drained
All that goblet crimson-stained,
Finding what they dreamed divine,
Only earthly sluggish wine,
Sooner will the warm lips pale,
And the flawless voices fail,
Sooner come the drooping wing,
And the afterdays that bring
No such songs as did the spring.

THE KING'S SABBATH

Once idly in his hall King Olave sat
  Pondering, and with his dagger whittled chips;
  And one drew near to him with austere lips,
Saying, "To-morrow is Monday," and at that
The king said nothing, but held forth his flat
  Broad palm, and bending on his mighty hips,
  Took up and mutely laid thereon the slips
Of scattered wood, as on a hearth, and gat

From off the embers near, a burning brand.
   Kindling the,pile with this, the dreaming Dane
Sat silent with his eyes set and his bland
     Proud mouth, tight-woven, smiling, drawn with
       pain,
     Watching the fierce fire flare, and wax, and wane,
Hiss and burn down upon his shrivelled hand.

THE LITTLE HANDMAIDEN

The King's son walks in the garden fair—
    Oh, the maiden's heart is merry!
He little knows for his toil and care,
That the bride is gone and the bower is bare.
    Put on garments of white, my maidens!

The sun shines bright through the casement high—
    Oh, the maiden's heart is merry!
The little handmaid, with a laughing eye,
Looks down on the King's son strolling by.
    Put on garments of white, my maidens!

" He little knows that the bride is gone,
    And the Earl knows little as he;
She is fled with her lover afar last night,
    And the King's son is left to me."

And back to her chamber with velvety step
    The little handmaid did glide,
And a gold key took from her bosom sweet,
    And opened the great chests wide.

She bound her hair with a band of blue,
    And a garland of lilies sweet;
And put on her delicate silken shoes,
    With roses on both her feet.

She clad her body in spotless white,
    With a girdle as red as blood.
The glad white raiment her beauty bound,
    As the sepals bind the bud.

And round and round her white neck she flung
    A necklace of sapphires blue;
On one white finger of either hand
    A shining ring she drew.

Then down the stairway and out the door
    She glided, as soft and light,
As an airy tuft of a thistle seed
    Might glide through the grasses bright.

And into the garden sweet she stole—
    The little birds carolled loud—
Her beauty shone as a star might shine
    In the rift of a morning cloud.

The King's son walked in the garden fair,
    And the little handmaiden came,
Through the midst of a shimmer of roses red,
    Like a sunbeam through a flame.

The King's son marvelled, his heart leaped up,
    " And art thou my bride?" said he,
" For, North or South, I have never beheld
    A lovelier maid than thee."

" And dost thou love me?" the little maid cried,
    " A fine King's son, I wis!"
The King's son took her with both his hands,
    And her ruddy lips did kiss.

The little maid laughed till the beaded tears
        Ran down in a silver rain.
" O foolish King's son!" and she clapped her hands,
    Till the gold rings rang again.

"O King's son foolish and fooled art thou,
    For a goodly game is played;
Thy bride is away with her lover last night,
    And I am her little handmaid."

And the King's son sware a great oath: said he,–
    Oh, the maiden's heart is merry!
" If the Earl's fair daughter a traitress be,
The little handmaid is enough for me."
    Put on garments of white, my maidens!

The King's son walks in the garden fair—
    Oh, the maiden's heart is merry!
And the little handmaiden walketh there,
But the old Earl pulleth his beard for care.
    Put on garments of white, my maidens!

ABU MIDJAN

Underneath a tree at noontide
    Abu Midjan sits distressed,
Fetters on his wrists and ankles,
    And his chin upon his breast;

For the Emir's guard had taken,
  As they passed from line to line,
Reeling in the camp at midnight,
  Abu Midjan drunk with wine.

Now he sits and rolls uneasy,
  Very fretful, for he hears,
Near at hand, the shout of battle,
  And the din of driving spears.

Both his heels in wrath are digging
  Trenches in the grassy soil,
And his fingers clutch and loosen,
  Dreaming of the Persian spoil.

To the garden, over-weary
  Of the sound of hoof and sword,
Came the Emir's gentle lady,
  Anxious for her fighting lord.

Very sadly, Abu Midjan,
  Hanging down his head for shame,
Spake in words of soft appealing
  To the tender-hearted dame.

" Lady, while the doubtful battle
  Ebbs and flows upon the plains,
Here in sorrow, meek and idle,
  Abu Midjan sits in chains.

" Surely Saad would be safer
  For the strength of even me;
Give me then his armour, Lady,
  And his horse, and set me free.

" When the day of fight is over,
　With the spoil that he may earn,
To his chains, if he is living,
　Abu Midjan will return."

She, in wonder and compassion,
　Had not heart to say him nay;
So, with Saad's horse and armour,
　Abu Midjan rode away.

Happy from the fight at even,
　Saad told his wife at meat,
How the army had been succoured
　In the fiercest battle-heat,

By a stranger horseman, coming
　When their hands were most in need,
And he bore the arms of Saad,
　And was mounted on his steed;

How the faithful battled forward,
　Mighty where the stranger trod,
Till they deemed him more than mortal,
　And an angel sent from God.

Then the lady told her master
　How she gave the horse and mail
To the drunkard, and had taken
　Abu Midjan's word for bail.

To the garden went the Emir,
　Running to the tree, and found
Torn with many wounds and bleeding,
　Abu Midjan meek and bound.

And the Emir loosed him, saying,
    As he gave his hand for sign,
" Never more shall Saad's fetters
    Chafe thee for a draught of wine."

Three times to the ground in silence
    Abu Midjan bent his head;
Then with glowing eyes uplifted,
    To the Emir spake and said:

" While an earthly lord controlled me,
    All things for the wine I bore;
Now since God alone doth judge me,
    Abu Midjan drinks no more."

THE WEAVER

All day, all day, round the clacking net
    The weaver's fingers fly;
Gray dreams like frozen mists are set
    In the hush of the weaver's eye;
A voice from the dusk is calling yet,
    "O, come away, or we die!"

Without is a horror of hosts that fight,
    That rest not, and cease not to kill,
The thunder of feet and the cry of flight,
    A slaughter weird and shrill;
Gray dreams are set in the weaver's sight,
    The weaver is weaving still.

" Come away, dear soul, come away, or we die;
    Hear'st thou the rush!   Come away;
The people are slain at the gates, and they fly;
    The kind God hath left them this day;
The battle-axe cleaves, and the foemen cry,
    And the red swords swing and slay."

" Nay, wife, what boots it to fly from pain,
    When pain is wherever we fly?
And death is a sweeter thing than a chain:
    'Tis sweeter to sleep than to cry.
The kind God giveth the days that wane;
    If the kind God hath said it, I die."

And the weaver wove, and the good wife fled,
    And the city was made a tomb,
And a flame that shook from the rocks overhead
    Shone into that silent room,
And touched like a wide red kiss on the dead
    Brown weaver slain at his loom.

Yet I think that in some dim shadowy land,
    Where no suns rise or set,
Where the ghost of a whilom loom doth stand
    Round the dusk of its silken net,
For ever flieth his shadowy hand,
    And the weaver is weaving yet.

THE THREE PILGRIMS

In days, when the fruit of men's labour was sparing,
  And hearts were weary and nigh to break,
A sweet grave man with a beautiful bearing
  Came to us once in the fields and spake.

He told us of Roma, the marvellous city,
  And of One that came from the living God,
The Virgin's Son who, in heavenly pity,
  Bore for His people the rood and rod,

And how at Roma the gods were broken,
  The new was strong, and the old nigh dead,
And love was more than a bare word spoken,
  For the sick were healed and the poor were fed;

And we sat mute at his feet, and hearkened:
  The grave man came in an hour, and went,
But a new light shone on a land long darkened,
  Where toil was weary, and hope was spent.

So we came south, till we saw the city,
  Speeding three of us, hand in hand,·
Seeking peace and the bread of pity,
  Journeying out of the Umbrian land;

And we stood long in a dream and waited,
  Watching and praying and purified,
And came at last to the walls belated,
  Entering in at the eventide;

And many met us with song and dancing,
  Mantled in skins and crowned with flowers,
Waving goblets and torches glancing,
  Faces drunken, that grinned in ours;

And one, that ran in the midst, came near us—
  " Crown yourselves for the feast," he said;
But we cried out, that the God might hear us,
  " Where is Jesus, the living bread?"

And they took us each by the hand with laughter;
  Their eyes were haggard and red with wine:
They haled us on, and we followed after,
  " We will show you the new god's shrine."

Ah, woe to our tongues, that, for ever unsleeping,
  Must still uncover the old hot care,
The soothing ash from the embers sweeping,
  Wherever the soles of our sad feet fare.

Ah, we were simple of mind, not knowing
  How dreadful the heart of a man might be;
But the knowledge of evil is mighty of growing:
  Only the deaf and the blind are free.

We came to a garden of beauty and pleasure—
  It was not the way that our own feet chose—
Where a revel was whirling in many a measure,
  And the myriad roar of a great crowd rose;

And the midmost round of the garden was reddened
  With pillars of fire in a great high ring—

One look—and our souls for ever were deadened,
    Though our feet yet move, and our dreams yet
        sting;

For we saw that each was a live man flaming,
    Limbs that a human mother bore,
And a thing of horror was done, past naming,
    And the crowd spun round, and we saw no more.

And he that ran in the midst, descrying,
    Lifted his hand with a foul red sneer,
And smote us each and the other, crying,
    " Thus we worship the new god here.

" The Cæsar comes, and the people's pæans
    Hail his name for the new-made light,
Pitch and the flesh of the Galileans,
    Torches fit for a Roman night."

And we fell down to the earth, and sickened,
    Moaning, three of us, head by head,
"Where is He whom the good God quickened?
    Where is Jesus, the living bread?"

Yet ever we heard, in the foul mirth turning,
    Man and woman and child go by,
And ever the yells of the charred men burning,
    Piercing heavenward, cry on cry;

And we lay there, till the frightful revel
    Died in the dawn with a few short moans
Of some that knelt in the wan and level
    Shadows that fell from the blackened bones.

Numb with horror and sick with pity,
　The heart of each as an iron weight,
We crept in the dawn from the awful city,
　Journeying out of the seaward gate.

The great sun flamed on the sea before us;
　A soft wind blew from the scented south;
But our eyes knew not of the steps that bore us
　Down to the ships at the Tiber's mouth;

Then we prayed, as we turned our faces
　Over the sea, to the living God,
That our ways might be in the fierce bare places,
　Where never the foot of a live man trod.

So we set sail in the noon, not caring
　Whither the prow of the dark ship came,
No more over the old ways faring;
　For the sea was cold, but the land was flame:

And the keen ship sped, and a deadly coma
　Blotted away from our eyes for ever,
Tower on tower, the great city Roma,
　Palace and temple and winding river.

THE COMING OF WINTER

Out of the Northland sombre weirds are calling;
A shadow falleth southward day by day;
Sad summer's arms grow cold; his fire is falling;
　His feet draw back to give the stern one way.

It is the voice and shadow of the slayer,
  Slayer of loves, sweet world, slayer of dreams;
Make sad thy voice with sober plaint and prayer;
  Make gray thy woods, and darken all thy streams.

Black grows the river, blacker drifts the eddy;
  The sky is gray; the woods are cold below:
O make thy bosom and thy sad lips ready
  For the cold kisses of the folding snow.

EASTER EVE

Hear me, brother, gently met,
Just a little, turn not yet,
Thou shalt laugh, and soon forget:
    Now the midnight draweth near.
I have little more to tell;
Soon with hollow stroke and knell,
Thou shalt count the palace bell,
    Calling that the hour is here.

Burdens black and strange to bear,
I must tell, and thou must share,
Listening with that stony stare,
    Even as many a man before.
Years have lightly come and gone
In their jocund unison,
But the tides of life roll on——
    They remember now no more

Once upon a night of glee,
In an hour of revelry,

As I wandered restlessly,
    I beheld with burning eye
How a pale procession rolled
Through a quarter quaint and old,
With its banners and its gold,
    And the crucifix went by.

Well I knew that body brave
That was pierced and hung to save,
But my flesh was now a grave
    For the soul that gnashed within
He that they were bearing by,
With their banners white and high,
He was pure, and foul was I,
    And his whiteness mocked my sin.

Ah, meseemed that even he,
Would not wait to look on me,
In my years and misery,
    Things that he alone could heal.
In mine eyes I felt the flame
Of a rage that nought could tame,
And I cried and cursed his name,
    Till my brain began to reel.

In a moment I was 'ware
How that many watching there,
Fearfully with blanch and stare,
    Crossed themselves, and shrank away;
Then upon my reeling mind,
Like a sharp blow from behind,
Fell the truth, and left me blind,
    Hopeless now, and all astray.

O'er the city wandering wide,
Seeking but some place to hide,
Where the sounds of mirth had died,
    Through the shaken night I stole;
From the ever-eddying stream
Of the crowds that did but seem
Like processions in a dream
    To my empty echoing soul.

Till I came at last alone
To a hidden street of stone,
Where the city's monotone
    On the silence fell no more.
Then I saw how one in white,
With a footstep mute and light,
Through the shadow of the night
    Like a spirit paced before.

And a sudden stillness came
Through my spirit and my frame,
And a spell without a name
    Held me in his mystic track.
Though his presence seemed so mild
Yet he led me like a child,
With a yearning strange and wild,
    That I dared not turn me back.

Oh, I could not see his face,
Nor behold his utmost grace,
Yet I might not change my pace,
    Fastened by a strange belief;
5

For his steps were sad and slow,
And his hands hung straight below,
And his head was bowed, as though
        Pressed by some immortal grief.

So I followed, yet not I
Held alone that company:
Every silent passer-by
        Paled and turned and joined with me;
So we followed still and fleet,
While the city, street by street,
Fell behind our rustling feet
        Like a deadened memory.

Where the sound of sin and riot
Broke upon the night's dim quiet,
And the solemn bells hung nigh it
        Echoed from their looming towers;
Where the mourners wept alway,
Watching for the morning gray;
Where the weary toiler lay,
        Husbanding the niggard hours;

By the gates where all night long
Guests in many a joyous throng,
With the sound of dance and song,
        Dreamed in golden palaces;
Still he passed, and door by door
Opened with a pale outpour,
And the revel rose no more
        Hushed in deeper phantasies.

As we passed, the talk and stir
Of the quiet wayfarer
And the noisy banqueter
    Died upon the midnight dim.
They that reeled in drunken glee
Shrank upon the trembling knee,
And their jests died suddenly,
    As they rose and followed him.

From the street and from the hall,
From the flare of festival
None that saw him stayed, but all
    Followed where his wonder would;
And our feet at first so few
Gathered as those white feet drew,
Till at last our number grew
    To a thronging multitude;

And the hushed and awful beat
Of our pale unnumbered feet
Made a murmur strange and sweet,
    As we followed evermore.
Now the night was almost passed,
And the dawn was overcast,
When the stranger stayed at last
    At a great cathedral door.

Never word the stranger said,
 But he slowly raised his head,
And the vast doors openèd
    By an unseen hand withdrawn;

And in silence wave on wave,
Like an army from the grave,
Up the aisles and up the nave,
    All that spectral crowd rolled **on.**

As I followed close behind,
Knowledge like an awful wind
Seemed to blow my naked mind
    Into darkness black and bare;
Yet with longing wild and dim,
And a terror vast and grim,
Nearer still I pressed to him,
    Till I almost touched his hair.

From the gloom so strange and eerie,
From the organ low and dreary,
Rose the wailing miserere,
    By mysterious voices sung;
And a dim light shone, none knew
How it came, or whence it grew—
From the dusky roof and through
    All the solemn spaces flung.

But the stranger still passed on,
Till he reached the altar stone,
And with body white and prone
    Sunk his forehead to the floor;
And I saw in my despair,
Standing like a spirit there,
How his head was bruised and bare,
    And his hands were clenched before,

How his hair was fouled and knit
With the blood that clotted it,
Where the prickled thorns had bit
    In his crownèd agony;
In his hands so wan and blue,
Leaning out, I saw the two
Marks of where the nails pierced through,
    Once on gloomy Calvary.

Then with trembling throat I owned
All my dark sin unatoned,
Telling it with lips that moaned;
    And methought an echo came
From the bended crowd below,
Each one breathing faint and low,
Sins that none but he might know:
    " Master I did curse thy name."

And I saw him slowly rise
With his sad unearthly eyes,
Meeting mine with meek surprise,
    And a voice came solemnly:
" Never more on mortal ground
For thy soul shall rest be found,
But when bells at midnight sound
    Thou must rise and come with me."

Then my forehead smote the floor,
Swooning, and I knew no more,
Till I heard the chancel door
    Open for the choristers;

But the stranger's form was gone,
And the church was dim and lone;
Through the silence, one by one
    Stole the early worshippers.

I am aging now I know;
That was many years ago,
Yet or I shall rest below
    In the grave where none intrude,
Night by night I roam the street,
And that awful form I meet,
And I follow pale and fleet,
    With a ghostly multitude.

Every night I see his face,
With its sad and burdened grace,
And the torn and bloody trace
    That in hands and feet he has.
Once my life was dark and bad;
Now its days are strange and sad,
And the people call me mad:
    See, they whisper as they pass!

Even now the echoes roll
From the swinging bells that toll;
It is midnight, now my soul
    Hasten, for he glideth by.
Stranger, 'tis no phantasy:
Look! my master waits for me
Mutely, but thou canst not see
    With thy mortal blinded eye.

THE ORGANIST

In his dim chapel day by day
The organist was wont to play,
And please himself with fluted reveries;
And all the spirit's joy and strife,
The longing of a tender life,
Took sound and form upon the ivory keys;
And though he seldom spoke a word,
The simple hearts that loved him heard
His glowing soul in these.

One day as he was rapt, a sound
Of feet stole near; he turned and found
A little maid that stood beside him there.
She started, and in shrinking wise
Besought him with her liquid eyes
And little features, very sweet and spare.
"You love the music, child," he said,
And laid his hand upon her head,
And smoothed her matted hair.

She answered, " At the door one day
I sat and heard the organ play;
I did not dare to come inside for fear;
But yesterday, a little while,
I crept half up the empty aisle
And heard the music sounding sweet and clear;
To-day I thought you would not mind,
For, master dear, your face was kind,
And so I came up here."

" You love the music, then," he said,
And still he stroked her golden head,
And followed out some winding reverie;
  " And you are poor?" said he at last;
  The maiden nodded, and he passed
His hand across his forehead dreamingly;
  "And will you be my friend?" he spake,
  And on the organ learn to make
    Grand music here with me?"

And all the little maiden's face
Was kindled with a grateful grace;
" O, master, teach me; I will slave for thee!"
  She cried; and so the child grew dear
  To him, and slowly year by year
He taught her all the organ's majesty;
  And gave her from his slender store
  Bread and warm clothing, that no more
    Her cheeks were pinched to see.

And year by year the maiden grew
Taller and lovelier, and the hue
Deepened upon her tender cheeks untried.
  Rounder, and queenlier, and more fair
  Her form grew, and her golden hair
Fell yearly richer at the master's side.
  In speech and bearing, form and face,
  Sweeter and graver, grace by grace,
    Her beauties multiplied.

And sometimes at his work a glow
Would touch him, and he murmured low,

" How beautiful she is?" and bent his head;
  And sometimes when the day went by
  And brought no maiden he would sigh,
And lean and listen for her velvet tread;
  And he would drop his hands and say,
  " My music cometh not to-day;
    Pray God she be not dead!"

So the sweet maiden filled his heart,
  And with her growing grew his art,
For day by day more wondrously he played.
  Such heavenly things the master wrought,
  That in his happy dreams he thought
The organ's self did love the gold-haired maid;
  But she, the maiden, never guessed
  What prayers for her in hours of rest
    The sombre organ prayed.

At last, one summer morning fair,
  The maiden came with braided hair
And took his hands, and held them eagerly.
  " To-morrow is my wedding day;
  Dear master, bless me that the way
Of life be smooth, not bitter unto me."
  He stirred not; but the light did go
  Out of his shrunken cheeks, and oh!
    His head hung heavily.

" You love him, then?"   " I love him well,"
  She answered, and a numbness fell
Upon his eyes and all his heart that bled.
  A glory, half a smile, abode
  Within the maiden's eyes and glowed

Upon her parted lips.   The master said,
  " God bless and bless thee, little maid,
  With peace and long delight," and laid
    His hands upon her head.

  And she was gone; and all that day
  The hours crept up and slipped away,
And he sat still, as moveless as a stone.
  The night came down, with quiet stars,
  And darkened him : in coloured bars
Along the shadowy aisle the moonlight shone.
  And then the master woke and passed
  His hands across the keys at last,
    And made the organ moan.

  The organ shook, the music wept;
  For sometimes like a wail it crept
In broken moanings down the shadows **drear**;
  And otherwhiles the sound did swell,
  And like a sudden tempest fell
Through all the windows wonderful and **clear**.
  The people gathered from the street,
  And filled the chapel seat by seat—
    They could not choose but hear.

  And there they sat till dawning light,
  Nor ever stirred for awe.   " To-night,
The master hath a noble mood," they said.
  But on a sudden ceased the sound :
  Like ghosts the people gathered round,

And on the keys they found his fallen head.
   The silent organ had received
   The master's broken heart relieved,
    And he was white and dead.

THE MONK

In Nino's chamber not a sound intrudes
   Upon the midnight's tingling silentness,
Where Nino sits before his book and broods,
   Thin and brow-burdened with some fine distress,
Some gloom that hangs about his mournful moods
   His weary bearing and neglected dress:
So sad he sits, nor ever turns a leaf—
Sorrow's pale miser o'er his hoard of grief.

Young Nino and Leonora, they had met
   Once at a revel by some lover's chance,
And they were young with hearts already set
   To tender thoughts, attunèd to romance;
Wherefore it seemed they never could forget
   That winning touch, that one bewildering glance:
But found at last a shelter safe and sweet,
Where trembling hearts and longing hands might
     meet.

Ah, sweet their dreams, and sweet the life they led
   With that great love that was their bosoms' all,
Yet ever shadowed by some circling dread
   It gloomed at moments deep and tragical,

And so for many a month they seemed to tread
   With fluttering hearts, whatever might befall,
Half glad, half sad, their sweet and secret way
To the soft tune of some old lover's lay.

But she is gone, alas he knows not where,
   Or how his life that tender gift should lose:
Indeed his love was ever full of care,
   The hasty joys and griefs of him who woos,
Where sweet success is neighbour to despair,
   With stolen looks and dangerous interviews:
But one long week she came not, nor the next,
And so he wandered here and there perplext;

Nor evermore she came.   Full many days
   He sought her at their trysts, devised deep schemes
To lure her back, and fell on subtle ways
   To win some word of her; but all his dreams
Vanished like smoke, and then in sore amaze
   From town to town, as one that crazèd seems,
He wandered, following in unhappy quest
Uncertain clues that ended like the rest.

And now this midnight, as he sits forlorn,
   The printed page for him no meaning bears;
With every word some torturing dream is born;
   And every thought is like a step that scares
Old memories up to make him weep and mourn.
   He cannot turn but from their latchless lairs,
The weary shadows of his lost delight
Rise up like dusk birds through the lonely night.

And still with questions vain he probes his grief,
  Till thought is wearied out, and dreams grow dim.
What bitter chance, what woe beyond belief
  Could keep his lady's heart so hid from him?
Or was her love indeed but light and brief,
  A passing thought, a moment's dreamy whim?
Aye there it stings, the woe that never sleeps:
Poor Nino leans upon his book, and weeps.

Until at length the sudden grief that shook
  His piercèd bosom like a gust is past,
And laid full weary on the wide-spread book,
  His eyes grow dim with slumber light and fast;
But scarcely have his dreams had time to look
  On lands of kindlier promise, when aghast
He starts up softly, and in wondering wise
Listens atremble with wide open eyes.

What sound was that? Who knocks like one in dread
  With such swift hands upon his outer door?
Perhaps some beggar driven from his bed
  By gnawing hunger he can bear no more,
Or questing traveller with confusèd tread,
  Straying, bewildered in the midnight hoar.
Nino uprises, scared, he knows not how,
The dreams still pale about his burdened brow.

The heavy bolt he draws, and unawares
  A stranger enters with slow steps, unsought,
A long-robed monk, and in his hand he bears
  A jewelled goblet curiously wrought;

But of his face beneath the cowl he wears
   For all his searching Nino seeth nought;
And slowly past him with long stride he hies,
While Nino follows with bewildered eyes.

Straight on he goes with dusky rustling gown.
   His steps are soft, his hands are white and fine;
And still he bears the goblet on whose crown
   A hundred jewels in the lamplight shine;
And ever from its edges dripping down
   Falls with dark stain the rich and lustrous wine,
Wherefrom through all the chamber's shadowy deeps
A deadly perfume like a vapour creeps.

And now he sets it down with careful hands
   On the slim table's polished ebony;
And for a space as if in dreams he stands,
   Close hidden in his sombre drapery.
" O lover, by thy lady's last commands,
   I bid thee hearken, for I bear with me
A gift to give thee and a tale to tell
From her who loved thee, while she lived, too well."

The stranger's voice falls slow and solemnly.
   'Tis soft, and rich, and wondrous deep of tone;
And Nino's face grows white as ivory,
   Listening fast-rooted like a shape of stone.
Ah, blessèd saints, can such a dark thing be?
   And was it death, and is Leonora gone?
Oh, love is harsh, and life is frail indeed,
That gives men joy, and then so makes them bleed

" There is the gift I bring "; the stranger's head
   Turns to the cup that glitters at his side:
" And now my tongue draws back for very dread,
   Unhappy youth, from what it must not hide.
The saddest tale that ever lips have said;
   Yet thou must know how sweet Leonora died,
A broken martyr for love's weary sake,
And left this gift for thee to leave or take."

Poor Nino listens with that marble face,
   And eyes that move not, strangely wide and set.
The monk continues with his mournful grace:
   " She told me, Nino, how you often met
In secret, and your plighted loves kept pace
   Together, tangled in the self-same net;
Your dream's dark danger and its dread you knew,
And still you met, and still your passion grew.

"And aye with that luxurious fire you fed
   Your dangerous longing daily, crumb by crumb;
Nor ever cared that still above your head
   The shadow grew; for that your lips were dumb.
You knew full keenly you could never wed:
   'Twas all a dream: the end must surely come;
For not on thee her father's eyes were turned
To find a son, when mighty lords were spurned.

" Thou knowest that new-sprung prince, that proud
      upstart,
   Pisa's new tyrant with his armèd thralls,
Who bends of late to take the people's part,
   Yet plays the king among his marble halls,

Whose gloomy palace in our city's heart
   Frowns like a fortress with its loop-holed walls.
'Twas him he sought for fair Leonora's hand,
That so his own declining house might stand.

" The end came soon; 'twas never known to thee;
   But, when your love was scarce a six months old,
She sat one day beside her father's knee,
   And in her ears the dreadful thing was told.
Within one month her bridal hour should be
   With Messer Gianni for his power and gold;
And as she sat with whitened lips the while,
The old man kissed her, with his crafty smile.

"Poor pallid lady, all the woe she felt
   Thou, wretched Nino, thou alone canst know.
Down at his feet with many a moan she knelt,
   And prayed that he would never wound her so.
Ah, tender saints! it was a sight to melt
   The flintiest heart; but his could never glow.
He sat with clenchèd hands and straightened head,
And frowned, and glared, and turned from white to
      red.

"And still with cries about his knees she clung,
   Her tender bosom broken with her care.
His words were brief, with bitter fury flung:
   'The father's will the child must meekly bear;
I am thy father, thou a girl and young.'
   Then to her feet she rose in her despair,
And cried with tightened lips and eyes aglow,
One daring word, a straight and simple, 'No!'

"Her father left her with wild words, and sent
  Rough men who dragged her to a dungeon deep,
Where many a weary soul in darkness pent
  For many a year had watched the slow days creep,
And there he left her for his dark intent,
  Where madness breeds and sorrows never sleep.
Coarse robes he gave her, and her lips he fed
With bitter water and a crust of bread.

"And day by day still following out his plan,
  He came to her and with determined spite
Strove with soft words and then with curse and ban
  To bend her heart so wearied to his might,
And aye she bode his bitter pleasure's span,
  As one that hears, but hath not sense or sight.
Ah, Nino, still her breaking heart held true:
Poor lady sad, she had no thought but you.

" The father tired at last and came no more,
  But in his settled anger bade prepare
The marriage feast with all luxurious store,
  With pomps and shows and splendours rich and
      rare;
And so in toil another fortnight wore,
  Nor knew she aught what things were in the air,
Till came the old lord's message brief and coarse:
Within three days she should be wed by force.

"And all that noon and weary night she lay,
  Poor child, like death upon her prison stone,
And none that came to her but crept away,
  Sickened at heart to see her lips so moan,
6

Her eyes so dim within their sockets gray,
　　Her tender cheeks so thin and ghastly grown;
But when the next morn's light began to stir,
She sent and prayed that I might be with her.

" This boon he gave: perchance he deemed that I,
　　The chaplain of his house, her childhood's friend,
With patient tones and holy words, might try
　　To soothe her purpose to his gainful end.
I bowed full low before his crafty eye,
　　But knew my heart had no base help to lend.
That night with many a silent prayer I came
To poor Leonora in her grief and shame.

" But she was strange to me: I could not speak
　　For glad amazement, mixed with some dark fear;
I saw her stand no longer pale and weak,
　　But a proud maiden, queenly and most clear,
With flashing eyes and vermeil in her cheek:
　　And on the little table, set anear,
I marked two goblets of rare workmanship
With some strange liquor crownèd to the lip.

"And then she ran to me and caught my hand,
　　Tightly imprisoned in her meagre twain,
And like the ghost of sorrow she did stand,
　　And eyed me softly with a liquid pain:
'O father, grant, I pray thee, I command,
　　One boon to me, I'll never ask again,
One boon to me and to my love, to both;
Dear father, grant, and bind it with an oath.'

" This granted I, and then with many a wail
  She told me all the story of your woe,
And when she finished, lightly but most pale,
  To those two brimming goblets she did go,
And one she took within her fingers frail,
  And looked down smiling in its crimson glow:
'And now thine oath I'll tell; God grant to thee
No rest in grave, if thou be false to me.

" 'Alas poor me! whom cruel hearts would wed
  On the sad morrow to that wicked lord;
But I'll not go; nay, rather I'll be dead,
  Safe from their frown and from their bitter word.
Without my Nino life indeed were sped;
  And sith we two can never more accord
In this drear world, so weary and perplext,
We'll die, and win sweet pleasure in the next.

" ' O father, God will never give thee rest,
  If thou be false to what thy lips have sworn,
And false to love, and false to me distressed,
  A helpless maid, so broken and outworn.
This cup—she put it softly to her breast—
  I pray thee carry, ere the morrow morn,
To Nino's hand, and tell him all my pain;
This other with mine own lips I will drain.'

" Slowly she raised it to her lips, the while
  I darted forward, madly fain to seize
Her dreadful hands, but with a sudden wile
  She twisted and sprang from me with bent knees,

And rising turned upon me with a smile,
  And drained her goblet to the very lees.
' O priest, remember, keep thine oath,' she cried,
And the spent goblet fell against her side.

"And then she moaned and murmured like a bell:
  ' My Nino, my sweet Nino!' and no more
She said, but fluttered like a bird and fell
  Lifeless as marble to the footworn floor;
And there she lies even now in lonely cell,
  Poor lady, pale with all the grief she bore,
She could not live and still be true to thee,
And so she's gone where no rude hands can be."

The monk's voice pauses like some mournful flute,
  Whose pondered closes for sheer sorrow fail,
And then with hand that seems as it would suit
  A soft girl best, it is so light and frail,
He turns half round, and for a moment mute
  Points to the goblet, and so ends his tale:
" Mine oath is kept, thy lady's last command;
'Tis but a short hour since it left her hand."

So ends the stranger: surely no man's tongue
  Was e'er so soft, or half so sweet as his.
Oft as he listened, Nino's heart had sprung
  With sudden start as from a spectre's kiss;
For deep in many a word he deemed had rung
  The liquid fall of some loved emphasis;
And so it pierced his sorrow to the core,
The ghost of tones that he should hear no more.

But now the tale is ended, and still keeps
  The stranger hidden in his dusky weed;
And Nino stands, wide-eyed, as one that sleeps,
  And dimly wonders how his heart doth bleed.
Anon he bends, yet neither moans nor weeps,
  But hangs atremble, like a broken reed;
"Ah! bitter fate, that lured and sold us so,
Poor lady mine; alas for all our woe!"

But even as he moans in such dark mood,
  His wandering eyes upon the goblet fall.
O, dreaming heart! O, strange ingratitude.
  So to forget his lady's lingering call,
Her parting gift, so rich, so crimson-hued,
  The lover's draught, that shall be cure for all.
He lifts the goblet lightly from its place,
And smiles and rears it with his courtly grace.

" O lady sweet, I shall not long delay:
  This gift of thine shall bring me to thine eyes.
Sure God will send on no unpardoned way
  The faithful soul, that at such bidding dies.
When thou art gone, I cannot longer stay
  To brave this world with all its wrath and lies,
Where hands of stone and tongues of dragon's breath
Have bruised mine angel to her piteous death."

And now the gleaming goblet hath scarce dyed
  His lips' thin pallor with its deathly red,
When Nino starts in wonder, fearful-eyed,
  For, lo! the stranger with outstretchèd head

Springs at his face one soft and sudden stride,
   And from his hand the deadly cup hath sped,
Dashed to the ground, and all its seeded store
Runs out like blood upon the marble floor.

" O Nino, my sweet Nino! speak to me,
   Nor stand so strange, nor look so deathly pale.
'Twas all to prove thy heart's dear constancy
   I brought that cup and told that piteous tale.
Ah! chains and cells and cruel treachery
   Are weak indeed when women's hearts assail.
Art angry, Nino?"   'Tis no monk that cries,
But sweet Leonora with her love-lit eyes.

She dashes from her brow the pented hood;
   The dusky robe falls rustling to her feet;
And there she stands, as aye in dreams she stood.
   Ah, Nino, see! Sure man did never meet
So warm a flower from such a sombre bud,
   So trembling fair, so wan, so pallid sweet.
Aye, Nino, down like saint upon thy knee,
And soothe her hands with kisses warm and free.

And now with broken laughter on her lips,
   And now with moans remembering of her care,
She weeps and smiles, and like a child she slips
   Her lily fingers through his curly hair,
The while her head with all it's sweet she dips,
   Close to his ear, to soothe and murmur there;
" O Nino, I was hid so long from thee,
That much I doubted what thy love might be.

"And though 'twas cruel hard for me to try
  Thy faithful heart with such a fearful test,
Yet now thou canst be happy, sweet, as I
  Am wondrous happy in thy truth confessed.
To haggard death indeed thou needst not fly
  To find the softness of thy lady's breast;
For such a gift was never death's to give,
But thou shalt have me for thy love, and live.

" Dost see these cheeks, my Nino? they're so thin,
  Not round and soft, as when thou touched them
      last:
So long with bitter rage they pent me in,
  Like some poor thief in lonely dungeon cast;
Only this night through every bolt and gin
  By cunning stealth I wrought my way at last.
Straight to thine heart I fled, unfaltering,
Like homeward pigeon with uncagèd wing.

" Nay, Nino, kneel not; let me hear thee speak.
  We must not tarry long; the dawn is nigh."
So rises he for very gladness weak;
  But half in fear that yet the dream may fly,
He touches mutely mouth and brow and cheek;
  Till in his ear she 'gins to plead and sigh:
" Dear love, forgive me for that cruel tale,
That stung thine heart and made thy lips so pale."

And so he folds her softly with quick sighs,
  And both with murmurs warm and musical
Talk and retalk, with dim or smiling eyes,
  Of old delights and sweeter days to fall:

And yet not long, for, ere the starlit skies
  Grow pale above the city's eastern wall,
They rise, with lips and happy hands withdrawn,
And pass out softly into the dawn.

For Nino knows the captain of a ship,
  The friend of many journeys, who maybe
This very morn will let his cables slip
  For the warm coast of sunny Sicily.
There in Palermo, at the harbour's lip,
  A brother lives, of tried fidelity:
So to the quays by hidden ways they wend
In the pale morn, nor do they miss their friend.

And ere the shadow of another night
  Hath darkened Pisa, many a foe shall stray
Through Nino's home, with eyes malignly bright
  In wolfish quest, but shall not find his prey:
The while those lovers in their white-winged flight
  Shall see far out upon the twilight gray,
Behind, the glimmer of the sea, before
The dusky outlines of a kindlier shore.

THE CHILD'S MUSIC LESSON

Why weep ye in your innocent toil at all?
  Sweet little hands, why halt and tremble so?
Full many a wrong note falls, but let it fall!
  Each note to me is like a golden glow;

Each broken cadence like a morning call;
   Nay, clear and smooth I would not have you go,
Soft little hands upon the curtained threshold set
Of this long life of labour, and unrestful fret.

Soft sunlight flickers on the checkered green:
   Warm winds are stirring round my dreaming seat:
Among the yellow pumpkin blooms, that lean
   Their crumpled rims beneath the heavy heat,
The stripèd bees in lazy labour glean
   From bell to bell with golden-feathered feet;
Yet even here the voices of hard life go by;
Outside, the city strains with its eternal cry.

Here, as I sit—the sunlight on my face,
   And shadows of green leaves upon mine eyes—
My heart, a garden in a hidden place,
   Is full of folded buds of memories.
Stray hither then with all your old time grace,
   Child-voices, trembling from the uncertain keys;
Play on, ye little fingers, touch the settled gloom,
And quickly, one by one, my waiting buds will
     bloom.

Ah me, I may not set my feet again
   In any part of that old garden dear,
Or pluck one widening blossom, for my pain;
   But only at the wicket gaze I here:
Old scents creep into mine inactive brain,
   Smooth scents of things I may not come anear;
I see, far off, old beaten pathways they adorn;
I cannot feel with hands the blossom or the thorn.

Toil on sweet hands; once more I see the child;
  The little child, that was myself, appears,
And all the old time beauties, undefiled,
  Shine back to me across the opening years,
Quick griefs, that made the tender bosom wild,
  Short blinding gusts, that died in passionate tears,
Sweet life, with all its change, that now so happy
    seems,
With all its child-heart glories, and untutored
    dreams.

Play on into the golden sunshine so,
  Sweeter than all great artists' labouring:
  I too was like you once, an age ago:
  God keep you, dimpled fingers, for you bring
Quiet gliding ghosts to me of joy and woe,
  No certain things at all that thrill or sting,
But only sounds and scents and savours of things
    bright,
No joy or aching pain; but only dim delight.

AN ATHENIAN REVERIE

How the returning days, one after one,
Come ever in their rhythmic round, unchanged,
Yet from each loopèd robe for every man
Some new thing falls. Happy is he
Who fronts them without fear, and like the gods
Looks out unanxiously on each day's gift
With calmly curious eye. How many things
Even in a little space both good and ill,

Have fallen on me, and yet in all of them
The keen experience or the smooth remembrance
Hath found some sweet.   It scarcely seems a month
Since we saw Crete; so swiftly sped the days,
Borne onward with how many changing scenes,
Filled with how many crowding memories.
Not soon shall I forget them, the stout ship,
All the tense labour with the windy sea,
The cloud-wrapped heights of Crete, beheld far off,
And white Cytæon with its stormy pier,
The fruitful valleys, the wild mountain road,
And thòse long days of ever-vigilant toil,
Scarcely with sleepless craft and unmoved front
Escaping robbers, that quiet restful eve
At rich Gortyna, where we lay and watched
The dripping foliage, and the darkening fields,
And over all huge-browed above the night
Ida's great summit with its fiery crown;
And then once more the stormy treacherous sea,
The noisy ship, the seamen's vehement cries,
That battled with the whistling wind, the feet
Reeling upon the swaying deck, and eyes
Strained anxiously toward land; ah, with what joy
At last the busy pier at Nauplia,
Rest and firm shelter for our racking brains:
Most sweet of all, most dear to memory
That journey with Euktemon through the hills
By fair Cleonæ and the lofty pass;
Then Corinth with its riotous jollity,
Remembered like a reeling dream; and here
Good Theron's wedding, and this festal day;
And I chief helper in its various rites,

Not least, commissioned through these wakeful
      hours
To dream before the quiet thalamos,
Unsleeping, like some full-grown bearded Eros,
The guardian of love's sweetest mysteries.
To-morrow I shall hear again the din
Of the loosed cables, and the rowers' chaunt,
The rattled cordage and the plunging oars.
Once more the bending sail shall bear us on
Across the level of the laughing sea.
Ere mid-day we shall see far off behind us,
Faint as the summit of a sultry cloud,
The white Acropolis. Past Sunium
With rushing keel, the long Eubœan strand,
Hymettus and the pine-dark hills shall fade
Into the dusk : at Andros we shall water,
And ere another starlight hush the shores
From seaward valleys catch upon the wind
The fragrance of old Chian vintages.
At Chios many things shall fall, but none
Can trace the future ; rather let me dream
Of what is now, and what hath been, for both
Are fraught with life.

              Here the unbroken silence
Awakens thought and makes remembrance sweet.
How solidly the brilliant moonlight shines
Into the courts ; beneath the colonnades
How dense the shadows. I can scarcely see
Yon painted Dian on the darkened wall ;
Yet how the gloom hath made her real. What sound,
Piercing the leafy covert of her couch,

Hath startled her.   Perchance some prowling wolf,
Or luckless footsteps of the stealthy Pan,
Creeping at night among the noiseless steeps
And hollows of the Erymanthian woods,
Roused her from sleep.   With listening head,
Snatched bow, and quiver lightly slung, she stands,
And peers across that dim and motionless glade,
Beckoning about her heels the wakeful dogs ;
Yet Dian, thus alert, is but a dream,
Making more real this brooding quietness.
How strong and wonderful is night !   Mankind
Has yielded all to one sweet helplessness :
Thought, labour, strife and all activities
Have ebbed like fever.   The smooth tide of sleep,
Rolling across the fields of Attica,
Hath covered all the labouring villages.
Even great Athens with her busy hands
And busier tongues lies quiet beneath its waves.
Only a steady murmur seems to come
Up from her silentness, as if the land
Were breathing heavily in dreams.   Abroad
No creature stirs, not even the reveller,
Staggering, unlanterned, from the cool Piræus,
With drunken shout.   The remnants of the feast,
The crumpled cushions and the broken wreathes,
Lie scattered in yon shadowy court, whose stones
Through the warm hours drink up the staining wine.
The bridal oxen in their well-filled stalls
Sleep, mindless of the happy weight they drew.
The torch is charred ; the garlands at the door,
So gay at morning with their bright festoons,
Hang limp and withered ; and the joyous flutes

Are empty of all sound. Only my brain
Holds now in its remote unsleeping depths
The echo of the tender hymenæos
And memory of the modest lips that sang it.
Within the silent thalamos the queen,
The sea-sprung radiant Cytherean reigns,
And with her smiling lips and fathomless eyes
Regards the lovers, knowing that this hour
Is theirs once only. Earth and thought and time
Lie far beyond them, a great gulf of joy,
Absorbing fear, regret and every grief,
A warm eternity: or now perchance
Night and the very weight of happiness,
Unsought, have turned upon their tremulous eyes
The mindless stream of sleep; nor do they care
If dawn should never come.

         How joyously
These hours have gone with all their pictured scenes,
A string of golden beads for memory
To finger over in her moods, or stay
The hunger of some wakeful hour like this,
The flowers, the myrtles, the gay bridal train,
The flutes and pensive voices, the white robes,
The shower of sweetmeats, and the jovial feast,
The bride cakes, and the teeming merriment,
Most beautiful of all, most sweet to name,
The good Lysippe with her down-cast eyes,
Touched with soft fear, half scared at all the noise.
Whose tears were ready as her laughter, fresh,
And modest as some pink anemone.
How young she looked, and how her smiling lips

Betrayed her happiness. Ah, who can tell,
How often, when no watchful eye was near,
Her eager fingers, trembling and ashamed,
Essayed the apple-pips, or strewed the floor
With broken poppy petals. Next to her,
Theron himself the gladdest goodliest figure,
His honest face ruddy with health and joy,
And smiling like the Ægean, when the sun
Hangs high in heaven, and the freshening wind
Comes in from Melos, rippling all its floor :
And there was Manto too, the good old crone,
So dear to children with her store of tales,
Warmed with new life: how to her old gray face
And withered limbs the very dance of youth
Seemed to return, and in her aged eyes
The waning fire rekindled: little Mæon,
That mischievous satyr with his tipsy wreath,
Who kept us laughing at his pranks, and made
Old Pyrrho angry. Him too sleep hath bound
Upon his rough-hewn couch with subtle thong,
Crowding his brain with odd fantastic shapes.
Even in sleep his little limbs, I think,
Twitch restlessly, and still his tongue gibes on
With inarticulate murmur. Ah, quaint Mæon!
And Manto, poor old Manto, what dim dreams
Of darkly-moving chaos and slow shapes
Of things that creep encumbered with huge burdens
Gloom and infest her through these dragging hours,
Haunting the wavering soul, so near the grave?
But all things journey to the same quiet end
At last, life, joy and every form of motion.
Nothing stands still. Not least inevitable,

The sad recession of this passionate love,
Whose panting fires, so soon and with such grief,
Burn down to ash.

             Ai! Ai! 'tis a strange madness
To give up thought, ambition, liberty,
And all the rooted custom of our days,
Even life itself for one all pampering dream,
That withers like those garlands at the door;
And yet I have seen many excellent men
Besotted thus, and some that bore till death,
In the crook'd vision and embittered tongue,
The effect of this strange poison, like a scar,
An ineradicable hurt; but Fate,
Who deals more wondrously in this disease
Even than in others, yet doth sometimes will
To make the same thing unto different men
Evil or good.   Was not Demetrios happy,
Who wore his fetters with such grace, and spent
On Chione, the Naxian, that shrewd girl,
His fortune and his youth, yet, while she lived,
Enjoyed the rich reward?   He seemed like one,
That trod on wind, and I remember well,
How when she died in that remorseless plague,
And I alone stood with him at the pyre,
He shook me with his helpless passionate grief.
And honest Agathon, the married man,
Whose boyish fondness for his pretty wife
We smiled at, and yet envied; at the close
Of each day's labour how he posted home,
And thence no bait, however plumed, could draw
    him.

We laughed, but envied him.   How sweet she
    looked
That morning at the Dionysia,
With her rare eyes and modest girlish grace,
Leading her two small children by the palm.
I too might marry if the faithful gods
Would promise me such joy as Agathon's.
Perhaps some day—but no, I am not one
To clip my wings, and wind about my feet
A net whose self-made meshes are as stern
As they are soft.   To me is ever present
The outer world with its untravelled paths,
The wanderer's dream, the itch to see new things.
A single tie could never bind me fast,
For life, this joyous, busy, ever-changing life,
Is only dear to me with liberty,
With space of earth for feet to travel in
And space of mind for thought.

            Not so for all;
To most men life is but a common thing,
The hours a sort of coin to barter with,
Whose worth is reckoned by the sum they buy
In gold, or power, or pleasure; each short day
That brings not these deemed fruitless as dry sand.
Their lives are but a blind activity,
And death to them is but the end of motion,
Gray children who have madly eat and drunk,
Won the high seats or filled their chests with gold,
And yet for all their years have never seen
The picture of their lives, or how life looks
To him who hath the deep uneager eye,
    7

How sweet and large and beautiful it was,
How strange the part they played. Like him who
    sits
Beneath some mighty tree, with half-closed eyes,
At ease rejoicing in its murmurous shade,
Yet never once awakes from his dull dream
To mark with curious joy the kingly trunk,
The sweeping boughs and tower of leaves that gave
    it:
Even so the most of men; they take the gift,
And care not for the giver. Strange indeed
Are they, and pitiable beyond measure,
Who, thus unmindful of their wretchedness,
Crowd at life's bountiful gates, like fattening
    beggars,
Greedy and blind. For see how rich a thing
Life is to him who sees, to whom each hour
Brings some fresh wonder to be brooded on,
Adds some new group or studied history
To that wrought sculpture, that our watchful dreams
Cast up upon the broad expanse of time,
As in a never-finished frieze, not less
The little things that most men pass unmarked
Than those that shake mankind. Happy is he,
Who, as a watcher, stands apart from life,
From all life and his own, and thus from all,
Each thought, each deed, and each hour's brief event,
Draws the full beauty, sucks its meaning dry.
For him this life shall be a tranquil joy.
He shall be quiet and free. To him shall come
No gnawing hunger for the coarser touch,

No mad ambition with its fateful grasp;
Sorrow itself shall sway him like a dream.

How full life is; how many memories
Flash, and shine out, when thought is sharply stirred;
How the mind works, when once the wheels are
    loosed,
How nimbly, with what swift activity.
I think, 'tis strange that men should ever sleep,
There are so many things to think upon,
So many deeds, so many thoughts to weigh,
To pierce, and plumb them to the silent depth.
Yet in that thought I do rebuke myself,
Too little given to probe the inner heart,
But rather wont, with the luxurious eye,
To catch from life its outer loveliness,
Such things as do but store the joyous memory
With food for solace rather than for thought,
Like light-lined figures on a painted jar.
I wonder where Euktemon is to-night,
Euktemon with his rough and fitful talk,
His moody gesture and defiant stride;
How strange, how bleak and unapproachable;
And yet I liked him from the first.   How soon
We know our friends through all disguise of mood,
Discerning by a subtle touch of spirit
The honest heart within.   Euktemon's glance
Betrayed him with it's gusty friendliness,
Flashing at moments from the clouded brow,
Like brave warm sunshine, and his laughter too,
So rare, so sudden, so contagious,
How at some merry scene, some well-told tale,

Or swift invention of the wingèd wit,
It broke like thunderous water, rolling out
In shaken peals on the delighted ear.
Yet no man would have dreamed, who saw us two
That first gray morning on the pier at Crete,
That friendship could have forged thus easily
A bond so subtle and so sure between us;
He, gloomy and austere; I, full of thought
As he, yet in an adverse mood, at ease,
Lifting with lighter hands the lids of life,
Untortured by its riddles; he, whose smiles
Were rare and sudden as the autumn sun;
I, to whom smiles are ever near the lip.
And yet I think he loved me too; my mood
Was not unpleasant to him, though I know
At times I teased him with my flickering talk.
How self-immured he was; for all our converse
I gathered little, little, of his life,
A bitter trial to me, who love to learn
The changes of men's outer circumstance,
The strokes that fate has shaped them with, and so,
Fitting to these their present speech and favour,
Discern the thought within.   From him I gleaned
Nothing.   At the least word, however guarded,
That sought to try the fastenings of his life,
With prying hands, how mute and dark he grew,
And like the cautious tortoise at a touch
Drew in beneath his shell.

                    But ah, how sweet
The memory of that long untroubled day,
To me so joyous, and so free from care,

Spent as I love on foot, our first together,
When fate and the reluctant sea at last
Had given us safely to dry land; the tramp
From gray Mycenæ by the pass to Corinth,
The smooth white road, the soft caressing air,
Full of the scent of blossoms, the clear sky,
Strewn lightly with the little tardy clouds,
Old Helios' scattered flock, the low-branched oaks
And fountained resting-places, the cool nooks,
Where eyes less darkened with life's use than mine
Perchance had caught the Naiads in their dreams,
Or won white glimpses of their flying heels.
How light our feet were: with what rhythmic strides
We left the long blue gulf behind us, sown
Far out with snowy sails; and how our hearts
Rose with the growth of morning, till we reached
That moss-hung fountain on the hillside near
Cleonæ, where the dark anemones
Cover the ground, and make it red like fire.
Could ever grief, I wonder, or fixed care,
Or even the lingering twilight of old age,
Divest for me such memories of their sweet?
Even Euktemon's obdurate mood broke down.
The odorous stillness, the serene bright air,
The leafy shadows, the warm blossoming earth,
Drew near with their voluptuous eloquence,
And melted him. Ah, what a talk we had!
How eagerly our nimble tongues ran on,
With linkèd wit in joyous sympathy.
Such hours, I think, are better than long years
Of brooding loneliness, mind touching mind
To leaping life, and thought sustaining thought,

Till even the darkest chambers of gray time,
His ancient seats, and bolted mysteries,
Open their hoary doors, and at a look
Lay all their treasures bare.   How, when our thought
Wheeling on ever bolder wings at last
Grew as it seemed too large for utterance,
We both fell silent, striving to recall
And grasp such things as in our daring mood
We had but glimpsed and leaped at; yet how long
We studied thus with absent eyes, I know not;
Our thought died slowly out; the busy road,
The voices of the passers-by, the change
Of garb and feature, and the various tongues
Absorbed us.   Ah, how clearly I recall them!
For in these silent wakeful hours the mind
Is strangely swift.   With what sharp lines
The shapes of things that even years have buried
Shine out upon the rapid memory,
Moving and warm like life.   I can see now
The form of that tall peddler, whose strange wares,
Outlandish dialect and impudent gait
Awoke Euktemon's laughter.   In mine ear
Is echoing still the cracking string of gibes
They flung at one another.   I remember too
The gray-haired merchant with his bold black eyes
And brace of slaves, the old ship captain tanned
With sweeping sea-winds and the pitiless sun,
But best of all that dainty amorous pair,
Whose youthful spirit neither heat nor toil
Could conquer. What a charming group they made!
The creaking litter and the long brown poles,
The sinewy bearers with their cat-like stride,
Dripping with sweat, that merry dark-eyed girl,

Whose sudden beauty shook us from our dreams,
And chained our eyes. How beautiful she was!
Half-hid among the gay Miletian cushions,
The lovely laughing face, the gracious form,
The fragrant, lightly-knotted hair, and eyes
Full of the dancing fire of wanton Corinth.
That happy stripling, whose delighted feet
Swung at her side, whose tongue ran on so gaily,
Is it for him alone she wreathes those smiles,
And tunes so musically that flexile voice,
Soft as the Lydian flute? Surely his gait
Proclaimed the lover, and his well-filled girdle
Not less the lover's strength. How joyously
He strode, unmindful of his ruffled curls,
Whose perfumes still went wide upon the wind,
His dust-stained robe unheeded, and the stones
Whose ragged edges frayed his delicate shoes.
How radiant, how full of hope he was!
What pleasant memories, how many things
Rose up again before me, as I lay
Half-stretched among the crushed anemones,
And watched them, till a far off jutting ledge
Precluded sight, still listening till mine ears
Caught the last vanishing murmur of their talk.

Only a little longer; then we rose
With limbs refreshed, and kept a swinging pace
Toward Corinth; but our talk, I know not why,
Fell for that day. I wonder what there was
About those dainty lovers or their speech,
That changed Euktemon's mood; for all the way
From high Cleonæ to the city gates,

Till sunset found us loitering without aim,
Half lost among the dusky-moving crowds,
I could get nothing from him but dark looks,
Short answers and the old defiant stride.
Some memory pricked him. It may be, perchance,
A woman's treachery, some luckless passion,
In former days endured, hath seared his blood,
And dowered him with that cureless bitter humour.
To him solitude and the wanderer's life
Alone are sweet; the tumults of this world
A thing unworthy of the wise man's touch,
Its joys and sorrows to be met alike
With broad-browed scorn.   One quality at least
We have in common: we are idlers both,
Shifters and wanderers through this sleepless world,
Albeit in different moods.   'Tis that, I think,
That knit us, and the universal need
For near companionship. Howe'er it be,
There is no hand that I would gladlier grasp,
Either on earth or in the nether gloom,
When the gray keel shall grind the Stygian strand,
Than stern Euktemon's.

LOVE-DOUBT

Yearning upon the faint rose-curves that flit
   About her child-sweet mouth and innocent cheek,
   And in her eyes watching with eyes all meek
The light and shadow of laughter, I would sit
Mute, knowing our two souls might never knit;
   As if a pale proud lily-flower should seek

The love of some red rose, but could not speak
One word of her blithe tongue to tell of it.
For oh, my Love was sunny-lipped and stirred
　　With all swift light and sound and gloom not long
Retained; I, with dreams weighed, that ever heard
　　Sad burdens echoing through the loudest throng;
She, the wild song of some May-merry bird;
　　I, but the listening maker of a song.

PERFECT LOVE

Belovèd, those who moan of love's brief day
　　Shall find but little grace with me, I guess,
　　Who know too well this passion's tenderness
To deem that it shall lightly pass away,
A moment's interlude in life's dull play;
　　Though many loves have lingered to distress,
　　So shall not ours, sweet Lady, ne'ertheless,
But deepen with us till both heads be gray.
For perfect love is like a fair green plant,
　　That fades not with its blossoms, but lives on,
And gentle lovers shall not come to want,
　　Though fancy with its first mad dream be gone;
Sweet is the flower, whose radiant glory flies,
But sweeter still the green that never dies.

LOVE-WONDER

Or whether sad or joyous be her hours,
   Yet ever is she good and ever fair.
   If she be glad, 'tis like a child's wild air,
Who claps her hands above a heap of flowers;
And if she's sad, it is no cloud that lowers,
   Rather a saint's pale grace, whose golden hair
   Gleams like a crown, whose eyes are like a prayer
From some quiet window under minster towers.
But ah, Belovèd, how shall I be taught
   To tell this truth in any rhymèd line?
For words and woven phrases fall to naught,
   Lost in the silence of one dream divine.
Wrapped in the beating wonder of this thought:
   Even thou, who art so precious, thou art mine!

COMFORT

Comfort the sorrowful with watchful eyes
   In silence, for the tongue cannot avail.
   Vex not his wounds with rhetoric, nor the stale
Worn truths, that are but maddening mockeries
To him whose grief outmasters all replies.
   Only watch near him gently; do but bring
   The piteous help of silent ministering,
Watchful and tender.   This alone is wise.
So shall thy presence and thine every motion,
The grateful knowledge of thy sad devotion,

Melt out the passionate hardness of his grief,
And break the flood-gates of the pent-up soul.
He shall bow down beneath thy mute control,
   And take thine hands, and weep, and find relief.

DESPONDENCY

Slow figures in some live remorseless frieze,
   The approaching days escapeless and unguessed,
   With mask and shroud impenetrably dressed;
Time, whose inexorable destinies
Bear down upon us like impending seas;
   And the huge presence of this world, at best
   A sightless giant wandering without rest,
Agèd and mad with many miseries.
The weight and measure of these things who knows?
   Resting at times beside life's thought-swept stream,
Sobered and stunned with unexpected blows,
   We scarcely hear the uproar; life doth seem,
Save for the certain nearness of its woes,
   Vain and phantasmal as a sick man's dream.

OUTLOOK

Not to be conquered by these headlong days,
   But to stand free: to keep the mind at brood
   On life's deep meaning, nature's altitude
Of loveliness, and time's mysterious ways;

At every thought and deed to clear the haze
   Out of our eyes, considering only this,
   What man, what life, what love, what beauty is,
This is to live, and win the final praise.
Though strife, ill fortune and harsh human need
   Beat down the soul, at moments blind and dumb
   With agony; yet, patience—there shall come
      Many great voices from life's outer sea,
Hours of strange triumph, and, when few men heed,
   Murmurs and glimpses of eternity.

GENTLENESS

Blind multitudes that jar confusèdly
   At strife, earth's children, will ye never rest
   From toils made hateful here, and dawns distressed
With ravelling self-engendered misery?
And will ye never know, till sleep shall see
   Your graves, how dreadful and how dark indeed
   Are pride, self-will, and blind-voiced anger, greed,
And malice with its subtle cruelty?
How beautiful is gentleness, whose face
   Like April sunshine, or the summer rain,
   Swells everywhere the buds of generous thought;
So easy, and so sweet it is; its grace
   Smoothes out so soon the tangled knots of pain.
   Can ye not learn it? will ye not be taught?

A PRAYER

O Earth, O dewy mother, breathe on us
  Something of all thy beauty and thy might,
  Us that are part of day, but most of night,
Not strong like thee, but ever burdened thus
With glooms and cares, things pale and dolorous
  Whose gladdest moments are not wholly bright;
  Something of all thy freshness and thy light,
O Earth, O mighty mother, breathe on us.
O mother, who wast long before our day,
  And after us full many an age shalt be,
Careworn and blind, we wander from thy way:
  Born of thy strength, yet weak and halt are we;
Grant us O mother, therefore, us who pray,
  Some little of thy light and majesty.

MUSIC

Move on, light hands, so strongly tenderly,
  Now with dropped calm and yearning undersong,
  Now swift and loud, tumultuously strong,
And I in darkness, sitting near to thee,
Shall only hear, and feel, but shall not see,
  One hour made passionately bright with dreams,
  Keen glimpses of life's splendour, dashing gleams
Of what we would, and what we cannot be.
Surely not painful ever, yet not glad,
  Shall such hours be to me, but blindly sweet,

Sharp with all yearning and all fact at strife,
Dreams that shine by with unremembered feet,
And tones that like far distance make this life
Spectral and wonderful and strangely sad.

KNOWLEDGE

What is more large than knowledge and more sweet;
Knowledge of thoughts and deeds, of rights and
wrongs,
Of passions and of beauties and of songs;
Knowledge of life; to feel its great heart beat
Through all the soul upon her crystal seat;
To see, to feel, and evermore to know;
To till the old world's wisdom till it grow
A garden for the wandering of our feet.
Oh for a life of leisure and broad hours,
To think and dream, to put away small things,
This world's perpetual leaguer of dull naughts;
To wander like the bee among the flowers
Till old age find us weary, feet and wings
Grown heavy with the gold of many thoughts

SIGHT

The world is bright with beauty, and its days
Are filled with music; could we only know
True ends from false, and lofty things from low;
Could we but tear away the walls that graze

Our very elbows in life's frosty ways;
  Behold the width beyond us with its flow,
  Its knowledge and its murmur and its glow,
Where doubt itself is but a golden haze.
Ah brothers, still upon our pathway lies
  The shadow of dim weariness and fear,
Yet if we could but lift our earthward eyes
  To see, and open our dull ears to hear,
  Then should the wonder of this world draw near
And life's innumerable harmonies.

AN OLD LESSON FROM THE FIELDS

Even as I watched the daylight how it sped
  From noon till eve, and saw the light wind pass
  In long pale waves across the flashing grass,
And heard through all my dreams, wherever led,
The thin cicada singing overhead,
  I felt what joyance all this nature has,
  And saw myself made clear as in a glass,
How that my soul was for the most part dead.
O light, I cried, and heaven, with all your blue,
  O earth, with all your sunny fruitfulness,
  And ye, tall lilies, of the wind-vexed field,
  What power and beauty life indeed might yield,
  Could we but cast away its conscious stress,
Simple of heart becoming even as you.

WINTER-THOUGHT

The wind-swayed daisies, that on every side
   Throng the wide fields in whispering companies,
   Serene and gently smiling like the eyes
Of tender children long beatified,
The delicate thought-wrapped buttercups that glide
   Like sparks of fire above the wavering grass,
   And swing and toss with all the airs that pass,
Yet seem so peaceful, so preoccupied;
These are the emblems of pure pleasures flown,
   I scarce can think of pleasure without these.
Even to dream of them is to disown
   The cold forlorn midwinter reveries,
Lulled with the perfume of old hopes new-blown,
No longer dreams, but dear realities.

DEEDS

'Tis well with words, O masters, ye have sought
   To turn men's yearning to the great and true,
   Yet first take heed to what your own hands do;
By deeds not words the souls of men are taught;
Good lives alone are fruitful; they are caught
   Into the fountain of all life (wherethrough
   Men's souls that drink are broken or made new)
Like drops of heavenly elixir, fraught
   With the clear essence of eternal youth.
   Even one little deed of weak untruth
     Is like a drop of quenchless venom cast,

A liquid thread into life's feeding stream,
Woven for ever with its crystal gleam,
   Bearing the seed of death and woe at last.

ASPIRATION

O deep-eyed brothers, was there ever here,
   Or is there now, or shall there sometime be
   Harbour or any rest for such as we,
Lone thin-cheeked mariners, that aye must steer
Our whispering barks with such keen hope and fear
   Toward misty bournes across that coastless sea,
   Whose winds are songs that ever gust and flee,
Whose shores are dreams that tower but come not
     near.
Yet we perchance, for all that flesh and mind
   Of many ills be marked with many a trace,
Shall find this life more sweet more strangely kind
   Than they of that dim-hearted earthly race
   Who creep firm-nailed upon the earth's hard face,
And hear nor see not, being deaf and blind.

THE POETS

Half god, half brute, within the self-same shell,
   Changers with every hour from dawn till even,
   Who dream with angels in the gate of heaven,
And skirt with curious eyes the brinks of hell,
8

Children of Pan, whom some, the few, love well,
   But most draw back, and know not what to say,
   Poor shining angels, whom the hoofs betray,
Whose pinions frighten with their goatish smell.
Half brutish, half divine, but all of earth,
   Half-way 'twixt hell and heaven, near to man,
   The whole world's tangle gathered in one span,
Full of this human torture and this mirth:
   Life with its hope and error, toil and bliss,
   Earth-born, earth-reared, ye know it as it is.

THE TRUTH

Friend, though thy soul should burn thee, yet be still.
   Thoughts were not meant for strife, nor tongues
      for swords.
   He that sees clear is gentlest of his words,
And that's not truth that hath the heart to kill.
The whole world's thought shall not one truth fulfil.
   Dull in our age, and passionate in youth,
   No mind of man hath found the perfect truth,
Nor shalt thou find it; therefore, friend, be still.
Watch and be still, nor hearken to the fool,
The babbler of consistency and rule:
   Wisest is he, who, never quite secure,
      Changes his thoughts for better day by day:
   To-morrow some new light will shine, be sure,
      And thou shalt see thy thought another way.

THE MARTYRS

O ye, who found in men's brief ways no sign
   Of strength or help, so cast them forth, and threw
   Your whole souls up to one ye deemed most true,
Nor failed nor doubted but held fast your line,
Seeing before you that divine face shine;
   Shall we not mourn, when yours are now so few,
   Those sterner days, when all men yearned to you,
White souls whose beauty made their world divine:
Yet still across life's tangled storms we see,
   Following the cross, your pale procession led,
     One hope, one end, all others sacrificed,
Self-abnegation, love, humility,
   Your faces shining toward the bended head,
     The wounded hands and patient feet of Christ.

A NIGHT OF STORM

O city, whom gray stormy hands have sown
   With restless drift, scarce broken now of any,
   Out of the dark thy windows dim and many
Gleam red across the storm.   Sound is there none,
Save evermore the fierce wind's sweep and moan,
   From whose gray hands the keen white snow is
      shaken
   In desperate gusts, that fitfully lull and waken,
Dense as night's darkness round thy towers of stone.
Darkling and strange art thou thus vexed and
     chidden;
   More dark and strange thy veilèd agony,

City of storm, in whose gray heart are hidden
  What stormier woes, what lives that groan and
    beat,
  Stern and thin-cheeked, against time's heavier
    sleet,
  Rude fates, hard hearts, and prisoning poverty.

THE RAILWAY STATION

The darkness brings no quiet here, the light
  No waking: ever on my blinded brain
  The flare of lights, the rush, and cry, and strain,
The engines' scream, the hiss and thunder smite:
I see the hurrying crowds, the clasp, the flight,
  Faces that touch, eyes that are dim with pain:
  I see the hoarse wheels turn, and the great train
Move labouring out into the bourneless night.
So many souls within its dim recesses,
  So many bright, so many mournful eyes:
Mine eyes that watch grow fixed with dreams and
    guesses;
  What threads of life, what hidden histories,
What sweet or passionate dreams and dark distresses,
  What unknown thoughts, what various agonies!

A FORECAST

What days await this woman, whose strange feet
  Breathe spells, whose presence makes men dream
    like wine,

Tall, free and slender as the forest pine,
Whose form is moulded music, through whose sweet
Frank eyes I feel the very heart's least beat,
   Keen, passionate, full of dreams and fire:
   How in the end, and to what man's desire
Shall all this yield, whose lips shall these lips meet?
One thing I know: if he be great and pure,
This love, this fire, this beauty shall endure;
   Triumph and hope shall lead him by the palm:
But if not this, some differing thing he be,
That dream shall break in terror; he shall see
   The whirlwind ripen, where he sowed the calm.

IN NOVEMBER

The hills and leafless forests slowly yield
   To the thick-driving snow. A little while
   And night shall darken down. In shouting file
The woodmen's carts go by me homeward-wheeled,
Past the thin fading stubbles, half concealed,
   Now golden-gray, sowed softly through with snow,
   Where the last 'ploughman follows still his row,
Turning black furrows through the whitening field.
Far off the village lamps begin to gleam,
   Fast drives the snow, and no man comes this way;
     The hills grow wintry white, and bleak winds
      moan
     About the naked uplands. I alone
   Am neither sad, nor shelterless, nor gray,
Wrapped round with thought, content to watch and
     dream.

THE CITY

Beyond the dusky cornfields, towards the west,
  Dotted with farms, beyond the shallow stream,
  Through drifts of elm with quiet peep and gleam,
Curved white and slender as a lady's wrist,
Faint and far off out of the autumn mist,
  Even as a pointed jewel softly set
  In clouds of colour warmer, deeper yet,
Crimson and gold and rose and amethyst,
Toward dayset, where the journeying sun grown old
Hangs lowly westward darker now than gold,
With the soft sun-touch of the yellowing hours
  Made lovelier, I see with dreaming eyes,
  Even as a dream out of a dream, arise
The bell-tongued city with its glorious towers.

MIDSUMMER NIGHT

Mother of balms and soothings manifold,
  Quiet-breathèd night whose brooding hours are
      seven,
  To whom the voices of all rest are given,
And those few stars whose scattered names are told,
Far off beyond the westward hills outrolled,
  Darker than thou, more still, more dreamy even,
  The golden moon leans in the dusky heaven,
And under her one star—a point of gold:
And all go slowly lingering toward the west,
As we go down forgetfully to our rest,

Weary of daytime, tired of noise and light:
Ah, it was time that thou should'st come; for we
Were sore athirst, and had great need of thee,
　　Thou sweet physician, balmy-bosomed night.

THE LOONS

Once ye were happy, once by many a shore,
　　Wherever Glooscap's gentle feet might stray,
　　Lulled by his presence like a dream, ye lay
Floating at rest; but that was long of yore.
He was too good for earthly men; he bore
　　Their bitter deeds for many a patient day,
　　And then at last he took his unseen way.
He was your friend, and ye might rest no more:
And now, though many hundred altering years
Have passed, among the desolate northern meres
　　Still must ye search and wander querulously,
　　　Crying for Glooscap, still bemoan the light
　　With weird entreaties, and in agony
　　　With awful laughter pierce the lonely night.

MARCH

Over the dripping roofs and sunk snow-barrows,
　　The bells are ringing loud and strangely near,
　　The shout of children dins upon mine ear
Shrilly, and like a flight of silvery arrows
Showers the sweet gossip of the British sparrows,
　　Gathered in noisy knots of one or two,

To joke and chatter just as mortals do
Over the day's long tale of joys and sorrows;
Talk before bed-time of bold deeds together,
Of theft and fights, of hard-times and the weather,
  Till sleep disarm them, to each little brain
    Bringing tucked wings and many a blissful
      dream,
    Visions of wind and sun, of field and stream,
And busy barnyards with their scattered grain.

SOLITUDE

How still it is here in the woods.   The trees
  Stand motionless, as if they did not dare
  To stir, lest it should break the spell.   The air
Hangs quiet as spaces in a marble frieze.
Even this little brook, that runs at ease,
  Whispering and gurgling in its knotted bed,
  Seems but to deepen, with its curling thread
Of sound, the shadowy sun-pierced silences.
Sometimes a hawk screams or a woodpecker
  Startles the stillness from its fixèd mood
With his loud careless tap.   Sometimes I hear
    The dreamy white-throat from some far off tree
  Pipe slowly on the listening solitude,
    His five pure notes succeeding pensively.

AUTUMN MAPLES

The thoughts of all the maples who shall name,
  When the sad landscape turns to cold and gray?

Yet some for very ruth and sheer dismay,
Hearing the northwind pipe the winter's name,
Have fired the hills with beaconing clouds of flame;
  And some with softer woe that day by day,
  So sweet and brief, should go the westward way,
Have yearned upon the sunset with such shame
    That all their cheeks have turned to tremulous
      rose;
    Others for wrath have turned a rusty red,
    And some that knew not either grief or dread,
  Ere the old year should find its iron close,
Have gathered down the sun's last smiles acold,
Deep, deep, into their luminous hearts of gold.

THE DOG

" Grotesque!" we said, the moment we espied him,
  For there he stood, supreme in his conceit,
  With short ears close together and queer feet
Planted irregularly: first we tried him
With jokes, but they were lost; we then defied him
  With bantering questions and loose criticism:
  He did not like, I'm sure, our catechism,
But whisked and snuffed a little as we eyed him.
Then flung we balls, and out and clear away,
  Up the white slope, across the crusted snow,
To where a broken fence stands in the way,
    Against the sky-line, a mere row of pegs,
  Quicker than thought we saw him flash and go,
    A straight mad scuttling of four crookèd legs.

LYRICS OF EARTH

TO MY MOTHER

Mother, to whose valiant will
  Battling long ago,
What the heaping years fulfil,
  Light and song, I owe;
Send my little book afield,
  Fronting praise or blame
With the shining flag and shield
  Of your name.

THE SWEETNESS OF LIFE

It fell on a day I was happy,
  And the winds, the concave sky,
The flowers and the beasts in the meadow
  Seemed happy even as I;
And I stretched my hands to the meadow,
  To the bird, the beast, the tree:
" Why are ye all so happy?"
  I cried, and they answered me.

What sayst thou, O meadow,
  That stretchest so wide, so far,
That none can say how many
  Thy misty marguerites are?
And what say ye, red roses,
  That o'er the sun-blanched wall
From your high black-shadowed trellis
  Like flame or blood-drops fall?
    " We are born, we are reared, and we
        linger
      A various space and die;
    We dream, and are bright and happy,
      But we cannot answer why."

What sayest thou, O shadow,
  That from the dreaming hill

All down the broadening valley
  Liest so sharp and still?
And thou, O murmuring brooklet,
  Whereby in the noonday gleam
The loosestrife burns like ruby,
  And the branchèd asters dream?
    " We are born, we are reared, and we
        linger
      A various space and die;
    We dream and are very happy,
      But we cannot answer why."

And then of myself I questioned,
  That like a ghost the while
Stood from me and calmly answered,
  With slow and curious smile:
" Thou art born as the flowers, and wilt
    linger
  Thine own short space and die;
Thou dream'st and art strangely happy,
  But thou canst not answer why."

GODSPEED TO THE SNOW

March is slain; the keen winds fly;
Nothing more is thine to do;
April kisses thee good-bye;
Thou must haste and follow too;
Silent friend that guarded well
Withered things to make us glad,
Shyest friend that could not tell

Half the kindly thought he had.
Haste thee, speed thee, O kind snow;
Down the dripping valleys go,
From the fields and gleaming meadows,
Where the slaying hours behold thee,
From the forests whose slim shadows,
Brown and leafless cannot fold thee,
Through the cedar lands aflame
With gold light that cleaves and quivers,
Songs that winter may not tame,
Drone of pines and laugh of rivers.
May thy passing joyous be
To thy father, the great sea,
For the sun is getting stronger;
Earth hath need of thee no longer;
Go, kind snow, Godspeed to thee!

APRIL IN THE HILLS

To-day the world is wide and fair
  With sunny fields of lucid air,
And waters dancing everywhere;
  The snow is almost gone;
The noon is builded high with light,
And over heaven's liquid height,
In steady fleets serene and white,
  The happy clouds go on.

The channels run, the bare earth steams,
And every hollow rings and gleams
With jetting falls and dashing streams;
  The rivers burst and fill;

The fields are full of little lakes,
And when the romping wind awakes
The water ruffles blue and shakes,
   And the pines roar on the hill.

The crows go by, a noisy throng;
About the meadows all day long
The shore-lark drops his brittle song;
   And up the leafless tree
The nut-hatch runs, and nods, and clings;
The bluebird dips with flashing wings,
The robin flutes, the sparrow sings,
   And the swallows float and flee.

I break the spirit's cloudy bands,
A wanderer in enchanted lands,
I feel the sun upon my hands;
   And far from care and strife
The broad earth bids me forth. I rise
With lifted brow and upward eyes.
I bathe my spirit in blue skies,
   And taste the springs of life.

I feel the tumult of new birth;
I waken with the wakening earth;
I match the bluebird in her mirth;
   And wild with wind and sun,
A treasurer of immortal days,
I roam the glorious world with praise,
The hillsides and the woodland ways,
   Till earth and I are one.

FOREST MOODS

There is singing of birds in the deep wet woods,
In the heart of the listening solitudes,
Peewees, and thrushes, and sparrows, not few,
And all the notes of their throats are true.

The thrush from the innermost ash takes on
A tender dream of the treasured and gone;
But the sparrow singeth with pride and cheer
Of the might and light of the present and here.

There is shining of flowers in the deep wet woods,
In the heart of the sensitive solitudes,
The roseate bell and the lily are there,
And every leaf of their sheaf is fair.

Careless and bold, without dream of woe,
The trilliums scatter their flags of snow;
But the pale wood-daffodil covers her face,
Agloom with the doom of a sorrowful race.

THE RETURN OF THE YEAR

Again the warm bare earth, the noon
    That hangs upon her healing scars,
The midnight round, the great red moon,
    The mother with her brood of stars,

The mist-rack and the wakening rain
    Blown soft in many a forest way,
9

The yellowing elm-trees, and again
  The blood-root in its sheath of gray.

The vesper-sparrow's song, the stress
  Of yearning notes that gush and stream,
The lyric joy, the tenderness,
  And once again the dream! the dream!

A touch of far-off joy and power,
  A something it is life to learn,
Comes back to earth, and one short hour
  The glamours of the gods return.

This life's old mood and cult of care
  Falls smitten by an older truth,
And the gray world wins back to her
  The rapture of her vanished youth.

Dead thoughts revive, and he that heeds
  Shall hear, as by a spirit led,
A song among the golden reeds:
  " The gods are vanished but not dead!"

For one short hour, unseen yet near,
  They haunt us, a forgotten mood,
A glory upon mead and mere,
  A magic in the leafless wood.

At morning we shall catch the glow
  Of Dian's quiver on the hill,
And somewhere in the glades I know
  That Pan is at his piping still.

FAVORITES OF PAN

Once, long ago, before the gods
   Had left this earth, by stream and forest glade,
Where the first plough upturned the clinging sods,
   Or the lost shepherd strayed,

Often to the tired listener's ear
   There came at noonday or beneath the stars
A sound, he knew not whence, so sweet and clear,
   That all his aches and scars

And every brooded bitterness,
   Fallen asunder from his soul, took flight,
Like mist or darkness yielding to the press
   Of an unnamed delight,—

A sudden brightness of the heart,
   A magic fire drawn down from Paradise,
That rent the cloud with golden gleam apart,—
   And far before his eyes

The loveliness and calm of earth
   Lay like a limitless dream remote and strange,
The joy, the strife, the triumph and the mirth,
   And the enchanted change;

And so he followed the sweet sound,
   Till faith had traversed her appointed span,
And murmured as he pressed the sacred ground:
   " It is the note of Pan!"

Now though no more by marsh or stream
  Or dewy forest sounds the secret reed—
For Pan is gone—ah yet, the infinite dream
  Still lives for them that heed.

In April, when the turning year
  Regains its pensive youth, and a soft breath
And amorous influence over marsh and mere
  Dissolves the grasp of death,

To them that are in love with life,
  Wandering like children with untroubled eyes,
Far from the noise of cities and the strife,
  Strange flute-like voices rise

At noon and in the quiet of the night
  From every watery waste; and in that hour
The same strange spell, the same unnamed delight,
  Enfolds them in its power.

An old-world joyousness supreme,
  The warmth and glow of an immortal balm,
The mood-touch of the gods, the endless dream,
  The high lethean calm.

They see, wide on the eternal way,
  The services of earth, the life of man;
And, listening to the magic cry they say:
  " It is the note of Pan!"

For, long ago, when the new strains
  Of hostile hymns and conquering faiths grew
  keen,

And the old gods from their deserted fanes,
  Fled silent and unseen,

So, too, the goat-foot Pan, not less
  Sadly obedient to the mightier hand,
Cut him new reeds, and in a sore distress
  Passed out from land to land;

And lingering by each haunt he knew,
  Of fount or sinuous stream or grassy marge,
He set the syrinx to his lips, and blew
  A note divinely large;

And all around him on the wet
  Cool earth the frogs came up, and with a smile
He took them in his hairy hands, and set
  His mouth to theirs awhile,

And blew into their velvet throats;
  And ever from that hour the frogs repeat
The murmur of Pan's pipes, the notes,
  And answers strange and sweet;

And they that hear them are renewed
  By knowledge in some god-like touch conveyed,
Entering again into the eternal mood
  Wherein the world was made.

THE MEADOW

Here when the cloudless April days begin,
    And the quaint crows flock thicker day by
        day,
Filling the forests with a pleasant din,
    And the soiled snow creeps secretly away,
Comes the small busy sparrow, primed with glee,
        First preacher in the naked wilderness,
        Piping an end to all the long distress
From every fence and every leafless tree.

Now with soft slight and viewless artifice
        Winter's iron work is wondrously undone;
In all the little hollows cored with ice
        The clear brown pools stand simmering in
            the sun,
Frail lucid worlds, upon whose tremulous floors
        All day the wandering water-bugs at will,
        Shy mariners whose oars are never still,
Voyage and dream about the heightening shores.

The bluebird, peeping from the gnarlèd thorn,
        Prattles upon his frolic flute, or flings,
In bounding flight across the golden morn,
        An azure gleam from off his splendid wings.
Here the slim-pinioned swallows sweep and pass
        Down to the far-off river; the black crow
        With wise and wary visage to and fro
Settles and stalks about the withered grass.

Here, when the murmurous May-day is half gone,
　　The watchful lark before my feet takes flight,
And wheeling to some lonelier field far on,
　　　　Drops with obstreperous cry; and here at
　　　　night,
When the first star precedes the great red moon,
　　The shore-lark tinkles from the darkening field,
　　Somewhere, we know not, in the dusk
　　　　concealed,
His little creakling and continuous tune.

Here, too, the robins, lusty as of old,
　　Hunt the waste grass for forage, or prolong
From every quarter of these fields the bold
　　Blithe phrases of their never-finished song,
The white-throat's distant descant with slow stress
　　Note after note upon the noonday falls,
　　Filling the leisured air at intervals
With his own mood of piercing pensiveness.

How often from this windy upland perch,
　　Mine eyes have seen the forest break in bloom,
The rose-red maple and the golden birch,
　　The dusty yellow of the elms, the gloom
Of the tall poplar hung with tasseled black;
　　Ah, I have watched till eye and ear and brain
　　Grew full of dreams as they, the moated plain,
The sun-steeped wood, the marsh-land at its back,

The valley where the river wheels and fills,
　　Yon city glimmering in its smoky shroud,

And out at the last misty rim the hills
    Blue and far off and mounded like a cloud,
And here the noisy rutted road that goes
    Down the slope yonder, flanked on either side
    With the smooth-furrowed fields flung black
        and wide,
Patched with pale water sleeping in the rows.

So as I watched the crowded leaves expand,
    The bloom break sheath, the summer's
        strength uprear,
In earth's great mother heart already planned
    The heaped and burgeoned plenty of the year,
Even as she from out her wintry cell
    My spirit also sprang to life anew,
    And day by day as the spring's bounty grew,
Its conquering joy possessed me like a spell.

In reverie by day and midnight dream
    I sought these upland fields and walked apart,
Musing on Nature, till my thought did seem
    To read the very secrets of her heart;
In mooded moments earnest and sublime
    I stored the themes of many a future song,
    Whose substance should be Nature's, clear and
        strong,
Bound in a casket of majestic rhyme.

Brave bud-like plans that never reached the fruit,
    Like hers our mother's who with every hour,
Easily replenished from the sleepless root,
    Covers her bosom with fresh bud and flower;

Yet I was happy as young lovers be,
    Who in the season of their passion's birth
    Deem that they have their utmost worship's
       worth,
If love be near them, just to hear and see.

IN MAY

  Grief was my master yesternight;
    To-morrow I may grieve again;
    But now along the windy plain
      The clouds have taken flight.

  The sowers in the furrows go;
    The lusty river brimmeth on;
    The curtains from the hills are gone;
      The leaves are out; and lo,

  The silvery distance of the day,
    The light horizons, and between
    The glory of the perfect green,
      The tumult of the May.

  The bob-o-links at noonday sing
    More softly than the softest flute,
    And lightlier than the lightest lute
      Their fairy tambours ring.

  The roads far off are towered with dust;
    The cherry-blooms are swept and thinned;
    In yonder swaying elms the wind
      Is charging gust on gust.

But here there is no stir at all;
    The ministers of sun and shadow
    Hoard all the perfumes of the meadow
        Behind a grassy wall.

An infant rivulet wind-free
    Adown the guarded hollow sets,
    Over whose brink the violets
        Are nodding peacefully.

From pool to pool it prattles by;
    The flashing swallows dip and pass,
    Above the tufted marish grass,
        And here at rest am I.

I care not for the old distress,
    Nor if to-morrow bid me moan;
    To-day is mine, and I have known
        An hour of blessedness.

LIFE AND NATURE

I passed through the gates of the city,
    The streets were strange and still,
Through the doors of the open churches
    The organs were moaning shrill.

Through the doors and the great high windows
    I heard the murmur of prayer,
And the sound of their solemn singing
    Streamed out on the sunlit air;

A sound of some great burden
    That lay on the world's dark breast,
Of the old, and the sick, and the lonely,
    And the weary that cried for rest.

I strayed through the midst of the city
    Like one distracted or mad.
"O Life! O Life!" I kept saying,
    And the very word seemed sad.

I passed through the gates of the city,
    And I heard the small birds sing,
I laid me down in the meadows
    Afar from the bell-ringing.

In the depth and the bloom of the meadows
    I lay on the earth's quiet breast,
The poplar fanned me with shadows,
    And the veery sang me to rest.

Blue, blue was the heaven above me,
    And the earth green at my feet;
"O Life! O Life!" I kept saying,
    And the very word seemed sweet.

WITH THE NIGHT

O doubts, dull passions, and base fears,
    That harassed and oppressed the day,
Ye poor remorses and vain tears,
    That shook this house of clay;

All heaven to the western bars
   Is glittering with the darker dawn;
Here, with the earth, the night, the stars,
   Ye have no place: begone!

JUNE

Long, long ago, it seems, this summer morn
   That pale-browed April passed with pensive tread
   Through the frore woods, and from its frost-
      bound bed
Woke the arbutus with her silver horn;
   And now May, too, is fled,
The flower-crowned month, the merry laughing May,
   With rosy feet and fingers dewy wet,
Leaving the woods and all cool gardens gay
   With tulips and the scented violet.

Gone are the wind-flower and the adder-tongue
   And the sad drooping bellwort, and no more
   The snowy trilliums crowd the forest's floor;
The purpling grasses are no longer young,
     And summer's wide-set door
O'er the thronged hills and the broad panting earth
   Lets in the torrent of the later bloom,
Haytime, and harvest, and the after mirth,
   The slow soft rain, the rushing thunder plume.

All day in garden alleys moist and dim,
   The humid air is burdened with the rose;

In moss-deep woods the creamy orchid blows;
And now the vesper-sparrows' pealing hymn
　　　From every orchard close
At eve comes flooding rich and silvery;
　　　The daisies in great meadows swing and shine;
And with the wind a sound as of the sea
　　　Roars in the maples and the topmost pine.

High in the hills the solitary thrush
　　　Tunes magically his music of fine dreams,
　　　In briary dells, by boulder-broken streams;
And wide and far on nebulous fields aflush
　　　The mellow morning gleams.
The orange cone-flowers purple-bossed are there,
　　　The meadow's bold-eyed gypsies deep of hue,
And slender hawkweed tall and softly fair,
　　　And rosy tops of fleabane veiled with dew.

So with thronged voices and unhasting flight
　　　The fervid hours with long return go by;
　　　The far-heard hylas piping shrill and high
Tell the slow moments of the solemn night
　　　With unremitting cry;
Lustrous and large out of the gathering drouth
　　　The planets gleam; the baleful Scorpion
Trails his dim fires along the drousèd south;
　　　The silent world-incrusted round moves on.

And all the dim night long the moon's white beams
　　　Nestle deep down in every brooding tree,
　　　And sleeping birds, touched with a silly glee,
Waken at midnight from their blissful dreams,
　　　And carol brokenly.

Dim surging motions and uneasy dreads
    Scare the light slumber from men's busy eyes,
And parted lovers on their restless beds
    Toss and yearn out, and cannot sleep for sighs.

Oft have I striven, sweet month, to figure thee,
    As dreamers of old time were wont to feign,
    In living form of flesh, and striven in vain;
Yet when some sudden old-world mystery
    Of passion fired my brain,
Thy shape hath flashed upon me like no dream,
    Wandering with scented curls that heaped the
      breeze,
Or by the hollow of some reeded stream
    Sitting waist-deep in white anemones;

And even as I glimpsed thee thou wert gone,
    A dream for mortal eyes too proudly coy,
    Yet in thy place for subtle thoughts' employ
The golden magic clung, a light that shone
    And filled me with thy joy.
Before me like a mist that streamed and fell
    All names and shapes of antique beauty passed
In garlanded procession with the swell
    Of flutes between the beechen stems; and last,

I saw the Arcadian valley, the loved wood,
    Alpheus stream divine, the sighing shore,
    And through the cool green glades, awake once
      more,
Psyche, the white-limbed goddess, still pursued,
    Fleet-footed as of yore,

The noonday ringing with her frighted peals,
   Down the bright sward and through the reeds she
     ran,
Urged by the mountain echoes, at her heels
   The hot-blown cheeks and trampling feet of Pan.

DISTANCE

To the distance! ah, the distance!
   Blue and broad and dim!
Peace is not in burgh or meadow
   But beyond the rim.

Aye, beyond it, far beyond it;
   Follow still my soul,
Till this earth is lost in heaven,
   And thou feel'st the whole.

THE BIRD AND THE HOUR

The sun looks over a little hill
   And floods the valley with gold—
     A torrent of gold;
And the hither field is green and still;
   Beyond it a cloud outrolled,
   Is glowing molten and bright;
And soon the hill, and the valley and all,
     With a quiet fall,
   Shall be gathered into the night.
   And yet a moment more,

Out of the silent wood,
As if from the closing door
Of another world and another lovelier mood,
Hear'st thou the hermit pour—
So sweet! so magical!—
His golden music, ghostly beautiful.

AFTER RAIN

For three whole days across the sky,
In sullen packs that loomed and broke,
With flying fringes dim as smoke,
The columns of the rain went by;
At every hour the wind awoke;
The darkness passed upon the plain;
The great drops rattled at the pane.

Now piped the wind, or far aloof
Fell to a sough remote and dull;
And all night long with rush and lull
The rain kept drumming on the roof:
I heard till ear and sense were full
The clash or silence of the leaves,
The gurgle in the creaking eaves.

But when the fourth day came—at noon,
The darkness and the rain were by;
The sunward roofs were steaming dry;
And all the world was flecked and strewn
With shadows from a fleecy sky.
The haymakers were forth and gone,
And every rillet laughed and shone.

Then, too, on me that loved so well
The world, despairing in her blight,
Uplifted with her least delight,
On me, as on the earth, there fell
New happiness of mirth and might;
    I strode the valleys pied and still;
    I climbed upon the breezy hill.

I watched the gray hawk wheel and drop,
Sole shadow on the shining world;
I saw the mountains clothed and curled,
With forest ruffling to the top;
I saw the river's length unfurled,
    Pale silver down the fruited plain,
    Grown great and stately with the rain.

Through miles of shadow and soft heat,
Where field and fallow, fence and tree,
Were all one world of greenery,
I hear the robin ringing sweet,
The sparrow piping silverly,
    The thrushes at the forest's hem;
    And as I went I sang with them.

CLOUD-BREAK

With a turn of his magical rod,
That extended and suddenly shone,
From the round of his glory some god
Looks forth and is gone.
  10

To the summit of heaven the clouds
Are rolling aloft like steam;
There's a break in their infinite shrouds,
And below it a gleam.
O'er the drift of the river a whiff
Comes out from the blossoming shore;
And the meadows are greening, as if
They never were green before.

The islands are kindled with gold
And russet and emerald dye;
And the interval waters outrolled
Are more blue than the sky.
From my feet to the heart of the hills
The spirits of May intervene,
And a vapour of azure distills
Like a breath on the opaline green.

Only a moment!—and then
The chill and the shadow decline
On the eyes of rejuvenate men
That wére wide and divine.

THE MOON-PATH

The full, clear moon uprose and spread
    Her cold, pale splendour o'er the sea;
A light-strewn path that seemed to lead
    Outward into eternity.

Betweeen the darkness and the gleam
    An old-world spell encompassed me:
Methought that in a godlike dream
    I trod upon the sea.

And lo! upon that glimmering road,
    In shining companies unfurled,
The trains of many a primal god,
    The monsters of the elder world;
Strange creatures that, with silver wings,
    Scarce touched the ocean's thronging floor,
The phantoms of old tales, and things
    Whose shapes are known no more.

Giants and demi-gods who once
    Were dwellers of the earth and sea,
And they who from Deucalion's stones,
    Rose men without an infancy;
Beings on whose majestic lids
    Time's solemn secrets seemed to dwell,
Tritons and pale-limbed Nereids,
    And forms of heaven and hell.

Some who were heroes long of yore,
    When the great world was hale and young;
And some whose marble lips yet pour
    The murmur of an antique tongue;
Sad queens, whose names are like soft moans,
    Whose griefs were written up in gold;
And some who on their silver thrones
    Were goddesses of old.

As if I had been dead indeed,
  And come into some after-land,
I saw them pass me, and take heed,
  And touch me with each mighty hand;
And evermore a murmurous stream,
  So beautiful they seemed to me,
Not less than in a godlike dream
  I trod the shining sea.

COMFORT OF THE FIELDS

What would'st thou have for easement after grief,
  When the rude world hath used thee with despite,
  And care sits at thine elbow day and night,
Filching thy pleasures like a subtle thief?
To me, when life besets me in such wise,
'Tis sweetest to break forth, to drop the chain,
  And grasp the freedom of this pleasant earth,
    To roam in idleness and sober mirth,
Through summer airs and summer lands, and drain
The comfort of wide fields unto tired eyes.

By hills and waters, farms and solitudes,
  To wander by the day with wilful feet;
  Through fielded valleys wide with yellowing wheat;
Along gray roads that run between deep woods,
Murmurous and cool; through hallowed slopes of
      pine,
    Where the long daylight dreams, unpierced,
      unstirred,
  And only the rich-throated thrush is heard;

By lonely forest brooks that froth and shine
  In bouldered crannies buried in the hills;
By broken beeches tangled with wild vine,
  And log-strewn rivers murmurous with mills.

In upland pastures, sown with gold, and sweet
  With the keen perfume of the ripening grass,
  Where wings of birds and filmy shadows pass,
Spread thick as stars with shining marguerite;
To haunt old fences overgrown with brier,
  Muffled in vines, and hawthorns, and wild cherries,
  Rank poisonous ivies, red-bunched elder-berries,
And pièd blossoms to the heart's desire,
  Gray mullein towering into yellow bloom,
  Pink-tasseled milkweed, breathing dense perfume,
And swarthy vervain, tipped with violet fire.

To hear at eve the bleating of far flocks,
  The mud-hen's whistle from the marsh at morn;
  To skirt with deafened ears and brain o'erborne
Some foam-filled rapid charging down its rocks
With iron roar of waters; far away
  Across wide-reeded meres, pensive with noon,
  To hear the querulous outcry of the loon;
To lie among deep rocks, and watch all day
  On liquid heights the snowy clouds melt by;
Or hear from wood-capped mountain-brows the jay
  Pierce the bright morning with his jibing cry.

To feast on summer sounds; the jolted wains,
  The thresher humming from the farm near by,
  The prattling cricket's intermittent cry,
The locust's rattle from the sultry lanes;

Or in the shadow of some oaken spray,
  To watch, as through a mist of light and dreams,
  The far-off hayfields, where the dusty teams
Drive round and round the lessening squares of hay,
  And hear upon the wind, now loud, now low,
With drowsy cadence half a summer's day,
  The clatter of the reapers come and go.

Far violet hills, horizons filmed with showers,
  The murmur of cool streams, the forest's gloom,
  The voices of the breathing grass, the hum
Of ancient gardens overbanked with flowers:
Thus, with a smile as golden as the dawn,
  And cool fair fingers radiantly divine,
  The mighty mother brings us in her hand,
For all tired eyes and foreheads pinched and wan,
Her restful cup, her beaker of bright wine:
  Drink, and be filled, and ye shall understand!

AT THE FERRY

On such a day the shrunken stream
  Spends its last water and runs dry;
Clouds like far turrets in a dream
  Stand baseless in the burning sky.
On such a day at every rod
  The toilers in the hayfield halt,
With dripping brows, and the parched sod
  Yields to the crushing foot like salt.

But here a little wind astir,
   Seen waterward in jetting lines,
From yonder hillside topped with fir
   Comes pungent with the breath of pines;
And here when all the noon hangs still,
   White-hot upon the city tiles,
A perfume and a wintry chill
   Breathe from the yellow lumber-piles.

And all day long there falls a blur
   Of noises upon listless ears,
The rumble of the trams, the stir
   Of barges at the clacking piers;
The champ of wheels, the crash of steam,
   And ever, without change or stay,
The drone, as through a troubled dream,
   Of waters falling far away.

A tug-boat up the farther shore
   Half pants, half whistles, in her draught;
The cadence of a creaking oar
   Falls drowsily; a corded raft
Creeps slowly in the noonday gleam,
   And wheresoe'er a shadow sleeps
The men lie by, or half adream,
   Stand leaning at the idle sweeps.

And all day long in the quiet bay
   The eddying amber depths retard,
And hold, as in a ring, at play,
   The heavy saw-logs notched and scarred;

And yonder between cape and shoal,
  Where the long currents swing and shift,
An aged punt-man with his pole
  Is searching in the parted drift.

At moments from the distant glare
  The murmur of a railway steals,
Round yonder jutting point the air
  Is beaten with the puff of wheels;
And here at hand an open mill,
  Strong clamour at perpetual drive,
With changing chant, now hoarse, now shrill
  Keeps dinning like a mighty hive.

A furnace over field and mead,
  The rounding noon hangs hard and white;
Into the gathering heats recede
  The hollows of the Chelsea height;
But under all to one quiet tune,
  A spirit in cool depths withdrawn,
With logs, and dust, and wrack bestrewn,
  The stately river journeys on.

I watch the swinging currents go
  Far down to where, enclosed and piled,
The logs crowd, and the Gatineau
  Comes rushing from the northern wild.
I see the long low point, where close
  The shore-lines, and the waters end,
I watch the barges pass in rows
  That vanish at the tapering bend.

I see as at the noon's pale core—
   A shadow that lifts clear and floats—
The cabin'd village round the shore,
   The landing and the fringe of boats;
Faint films of smoke that curl and wreathe;
   And upward with the like desire
The vast gray church that seems to breathe
   In heaven with its dreaming spire.

And there the last blue boundaries rise,
   That guard within their compass furled
This plot of earth: beyond them lies
   The mystery of the echoing world;
And still my thought goes on, and yields
   New vision and new joy to me,
Far peopled hills, and ancient fields,
   And cities by the crested sea.

I see no more the barges pass,
   Nor mark the ripple round the pier,
And all the uproar, mass on mass,
   Falls dead upon a vacant ear.
Beyond the tumult of the mills,
   And all the city's sound and strife,
Beyond the waste, beyond the hills,
   I look far out and dream of life.

SEPTEMBER

Now hath the summer reached her golden close,
 And lost, amid her cornfields, bright of soul,
Scarcely perceives from her divine repose
 How near, how swift, the inevitable goal:
Still, still, she smiles, though from her careless feet
 The bounty and the fruitful strength are gone,
 And through the soft long wondering days goes on
The silent sere decadence sad and sweet.

The kingbird and the pensive thrush are fled,
 Children of light, too fearful of the gloom;
The sun falls low, the secret word is said,
 The mouldering woods grow silent as the tomb;
Even the fields have lost their sovereign grace,
 The cone-flower and the marguerite; and no more.
 Across the river's shadow-haunted floor,
The paths of skimming swallows interlace.

Already in the outland wilderness
 The forests echo with unwonted dins;
In clamorous gangs the gathering woodmen press
 Northward, and the stern winter's toil begins.
Around the long low shanties, whose rough lines
 Break the sealed dreams of many an unnamed lake,
 Already in the frost-clear morns awake
The crash and thunder of the falling pines.

Where the tilled earth, with all its fields set free,
 Naked and yellow from the harvest lies,
By many a loft and busy granary,
 The hum and tumult of the threshers rise ;

There the tanned farmers labour without slack,
  Till twilight deepens round the spouting mill,
  Feeding the loosened sheaves, or with fierce will,
Pitching waist-deep upon the dusty stack.

Still a brief while, ere the old year quite pass,
  Our wandering steps and wistful eyes shall greet
The leaf, the water, the belovéd grass;
  Still from these haunts and this accustomed seat
I see the wood-wrapt city, swept with light,
  The blue long-shadowed distance, and, between,
  The dotted farm-lands with tneir parcelled green,
The dark pine forest and the watchful height.

I see the broad rough meadow stretched away
  Into the crystal sunshine, wastes of sod,
Acres of withered vervain, purple-gray,
  Branches of aster, groves of goldenrod;
And yonder, toward the sunlit summit, strewn
  With shadowy boulders, crowned and swathed with
      weed,
  Stand ranks of silken thistles, blown to seed,
Long silver fleeces shining like the noon.

In far-off russet cornfields, where the dry
  Gray shocks stand peaked and withering, half
      concealed
In the rough earth, the orange pumpkins lie,
  Full-ribbed; and in the windless pasture-field
The sleek red horses o'er the sun-warmed ground
  Stand pensively about in companies,

While all around them from the motionless trees
The long clean shadows sleep without a sound.

Under cool elm-trees floats the distant stream,
    Moveless as air; and o'er the vast warm earth
The fathomless daylight seems to stand and dream,
    A liquid cool elixir—all its girth
Bound with faint haze, a frail transparency,
    Whose lucid purple barely veils and fills
    The utmost valleys and the thin last hills,
Nor mars one whit their perfect clarity.

Thus without grief the golden days go by,
    So soft we scarcely notice how they wend,
And like a smile half happy, or a sigh,
    The summer passes to her quiet end;
And soon, too soon, around the cumbered eaves
    Sly frosts shall take the creepers by surprise,
    And through the wind-touched reddening woods
        shall rise
October with the rain of ruined leaves.

A RE-ASSURANCE

With what doubting eyes, O sparrow,
    Thou regardest me,
Underneath yon spray of yarrow,
    Dipping cautiously.

Fear me not, O little sparrow,
    Bathe and never fear,
For to me both pool and yarrow
    And thyself are dear.

THE POET'S POSSESSION

Think not, O master of the well-tilled field,
This earth is only thine; for after thee,
When all is sown and gathered and put by,
Comes the grave poet with creative eye,
And from these silent acres and clean plots,
Bids with his wand the fancied after-yield
A second tilth and second harvest be,
The crop of images and curious thoughts.

AN AUTUMN LANDSCAPE

No wind there is that either pipes or moans;
  The fields are cold and still; the sky
    Is covered with a blue-gray sheet
    Of motionless cloud; and at my feet
  The river, curling softly by,
Whispers and dimples round its quiet gray stones.

Along the chill green slope that dips and heaves
  The road runs rough and silent, lined
    With plum-trees, misty and blue-gray,
    And poplars pallid as the day,
  In masses spectral, undefined,
Pale greenish stems half hid in dry gray leaves.

And on beside the river's sober edge
  A long fresh field lies black.   Beyond,
    Low thickets gray and reddish stand,
    Stroked white with birch; and near at hand,

Over a little steel-smooth pond,
Hang multitudes of thin and withering sedge.

Across a waste and solitary rise
  A ploughman urges his dull team,
    A stooped gray figure with prone brow
    That plunges bending to the plough
  With strong, uneven steps.   The stream
Rings and re-echoes with his furious cries.

Sometimes the lowing of a cow, long-drawn,
  Comes from far off; and crows in strings
    Pass on the upper silences.
    A flock of small gray goldfinches,
  Flown down with silvery twitterings,
Rustle among the birch-cones and are gone.

This day the season seems like one that heeds,
  With fixèd ear and lifted hand,
    All moods that yet are known on earth,
    All motions that have faintest birth,
  If haply she may understand
The utmost inward sense of all her deeds.

IN NOVEMBER

With loitering step and quiet eye,
Beneath the low November sky,
I wandered in the woods, and found
A clearing, where the broken ground

Was scattered with black stumps and briers,
And the old wreck of forest fires.
It was a bleak and sandy spot,
And, all about, the vacant plot,
Was peopled and inhabited
By scores of mulleins long since dead.
A silent and forsaken brood
In that mute opening of the wood,
So shrivelled and so thin they were,
So gray, so haggard, and austere,
Not plants at all they seemed to me,
But rather some spare company
Of hermit folk, who long ago,
Wandering in bodies to and fro,
Had chanced upon this lonely way,
And rested thus, till death one day
Surprised them at their compline prayer,
And left them standing lifeless there.

There was no sound about the wood
Save the wind's secret stir. I stood
Among the mullein-stalks as still
As if myself had grown to be
One of their sombre company,
A body without wish or will.
And as I stood, quite suddenly,
Down from a furrow in the sky
The sun shone out a little space
Across that silent sober place,
Over the sand heaps and brown sod,
The mulleins and dead goldenrod,
And passed beyond the thickets gray,

And lit the fallen leaves that lay,
Level and deep within the wood,
A rustling yellow multitude.

And all around me the thin light,
So sere, so melancholy bright,
Fell like the half-reflected gleam
Or shadow of some former dream;
A moment's golden reverie
Poured out on every plant and tree
A semblance of weird joy, or less,
A sort of spectral happiness;
And I, too, standing idly there,
With muffled hands in the chill air,
Felt the warm glow about my feet,
And shuddering betwixt cold and heat,
Drew my thoughts closer, like a cloak,
While something in my blood awoke,
A nameless and unnatural cheer,
A pleasure secret and austere.

BY AN AUTUMN STREAM

Now overhead,
Where the rivulet loiters and stops,
The bittersweet hangs from the tops
Of the alders and cherries
Its bunches of beautiful berries,
Orange and red.

And the snowbirds flee,
Tossing up on the far brown field,

Now flashing and now concealed,
Like fringes of spray
That vanish and gleam on the gray
Field of the sea.

Flickering light,
Come the last of the leaves down borne,
And patches of pale white corn
In the wind complain,
Like the slow rustle of rain
Noticed by night.

Withered and thinned,
The sentinel mullein looms,
With the pale gray shadowy plumes
Of the goldenrod;
And the milkweed opens its pod,
Tempting the wind.

Aloft on the hill,
A cloudrift opens and shines
Through a break in its gorget of pines,
And it dreams at my feet
In a sad, silvery sheet,
Utterly still.

All things that be
Seem plunged into silence, distraught,
By some stern, some necessitous thought:
It wraps and enthralls
Marsh, meadow, and forest; and falls
Also on me.
11

SNOWBIRDS

Along the narrow sandy height
    I watch them swiftly come and go,
        Or round the leafless wood,
    Like flurries of wind-driven snow,
Revolving in perpetual flight,
        A changing multitude.

Nearer and nearer still they sway,
    And, scattering in a circled sweep,
        Rush down without a sound;
    And now I see them peer and peep,
Across yon level bleak and gray,
        Searching the frozen ground,—

Until a little wind upheaves,
    And makes a sudden rustling there,
        And then they drop their play,
    Flash up into the sunless air,
And like a flight of silver leaves
        Swirl round and sweep away.

SNOW

White are the far-off plains, and white
        The fading forests grow;
    The wind dies out along the height,
        And denser still the snow,
    A gathering weight on roof and tree,
        Falls down scarce audibly.

The road before me smoothes and fills
    Apace, and all about
The fences dwindle, and the hills
    Are blotted slowly out;
The naked trees loom spectrally
    Into the dim white sky.

The meadows and far-sheeted streams
    Lie still without a sound;
Like some soft minister of dreams
    The snow-fall hoods me round;
In wood and water, earth and air,
    A silence everywhere.

Save when at lonely intervals
    Some farmer's sleigh urged on,
With rustling runners and sharp bells,
    Swings by me and is gone;
Or from the empty waste I hear
    A sound remote and clear;

The barking of a dog, or call
    To cattle, sharply pealed,
Borne echoing from some wayside stall
    Or barnyard far afield;
Then all is silent, and the snow
    Falls, settling soft and slow.

The evening deepens, and the gray
    Folds closer earth and sky;

The world seems shrouded far away;
   Its noises sleep, and I,
As secret as yon buried stream,
   Plod dumbly on, and dream.

SUNSET

From this windy bridge at rest,
In some former curious hour,
We have watched the city's hue,
All along the orange west,
Cupola and pointed tower,
Darken into solid blue.

Tho' the biting north wind breaks
Full across this drifted hold,
Let us stand with icèd cheeks
Watching westward as of old;

Past the violet mountain-head
To the farthest fringe of pine,
Where far off the purple-red
Narrows to a dusky line,
And the last pale splendours die
Slowly from the olive sky;

Till the thin clouds wear away
Into threads of purple-gray,
And the sudden stars between
Brighten in the pallid green;

Till above the spacious east,
Slow returnèd one by one,
Like pale prisoners released
From the dungeons of the sun,
Capella and her train appear
In the glittering Charioteer;

Till the rounded moon shall grow
Great above the eastern snow,
Shining into burnished gold;
And the silver earth outrolled,
In the misty yellow light,
Shall take on the width of night.

WINTER-STORE

Subtly conscious, all awake,
Let us clear our eyes, and break
Through the cloudy chrysalis,
See the wonder as it is.
Down a narrow alley, blind,
Touch and vision, heart and mind,
Turned sharply inward, still we plod,
Till the calmly smiling god
Leaves us, and our spirits grow
More thin, more acrid, as we go.
Creeping by the sullen wall,
We forego the power to see
The threads that bind us to the All,
God or the Immensity;

Whereof on the eternal road
Man is but a passing mode.

Too blind we are, too little see
Of the magic pageantry,
Every minute, every hour,
From the cloudflake to the flower,
For ever old, for ever strange,
Issuing in perpetual change
From the rainbow gates of Time.

But he who through this common air
Surely knows the great and fair,
What is lovely, what sublime,
Becomes, in an increasing span,
One with earth and one with man,
One, despite these mortal scars,
With the planets and the stars;
And Nature from her holy place,
Bending with unveilèd face,
Fills him in her divine employ
With her own majestic joy.

Up the fieldèd slopes at morn,
Where light wefts of shadow pass,
Films upon the bending corn,
I shall sweep the purple grass.
Sun-crowned heights and mossy woods,
And the outer solitudes,
Mountain-valleys, dim with pine,
Shall be home and haunt of mine.
I shall search in crannied hollows,
Where the sunlight scarcely follows,

And the secret forest brook
Murmurs, and from nook to nook
For ever downward curls and cools,
Frothing in the bouldered pools.

Many a noon shall find me laid
In the pungent balsam shade,
Where sharp breezes spring and shiver
On some deep rough-coasted river,
And the plangent waters come,
Amber-hued and streaked with foam;
Where beneath the sunburnt hills
All day long the crowded mills
With remorseless champ and scream
Overlord the sluicing stream,
And the rapids' iron roar
Hammers at the forest's core;
Where corded rafts creep slowly on,
Glittering in the noonday sun,
And the tawny river-dogs,
Shepherding the branded logs,
Bind and heave with cadenced cry;
Where the blackened tugs go by,
Panting hard and straining slow,
Labouring at the weighty tow,
Flat-nosed barges all in trim,
Creeping in long cumbrous line,
Loaded to the water's brim
With the clean, cool-scented pine.

Perhaps in some low meadow land,
Stretching wide on either hand,

I shall see the belted bees
Rocking with the tricksy breeze
In the spirèd meadow-sweet,
Or with eager trampling feet
Burrowing in the boneset blooms,
Treading out the dry perfumes.
Where sun-hot hayfields newly mown
Climb the hillside ruddy brown,
I shall see the haymakers,
While the noonday scarcely stirs,
Brown of neck and booted gray,
Tossing up the rustling hay,
While the hay-racks bend and rock,
As they take each scented cock,
Jolting over dip and rise;
And the wavering butterflies
O'er the spaces brown and bare
Light and wander here and there.

I shall stray by many a stream,
Where the half-shut lilies gleam,
Napping out the sultry days
In the quiet secluded bays;
Where the tasseled rushes tower
O'er the purple pickerel-flower,
And the floating dragon-fly—
Azure glint and crystal gleam—
Watches o'er the burnished stream
With his eye of ebony;
Where the bull-frog lolls at rest
On his float of lily-leaves,
That the swaying water weaves,

And distends his yellow breast,
Lowing out from shore to shore
With a hollow vibrant roar;
Where the softest wind that blows,
As it lightly comes and goes,
O'er the jungled river meads,
Stirs a whisper in the reeds,
And wakes the crowded bull-rushes
From their stately reveries,
Flashing through their long-leaved hordes
Like a brandishing of swords;
There, too, the frost-like arrow flowers
Tremble to the golden core,
Children of enchanted hours,
Whom the rustling river bore
In the night's bewildered noon,
Woven of water and the moon.

I shall hear the grasshoppers
From the parchèd grass rehearse,
And with drowsy note prolong
Evermore the same thin song.
I shall hear the crickets tell
Stories by the humming well,
And mark the locust, with quaint eyes,
Caper in his cloak of gray
Like a jester in disguise
Rattling by the dusty way.

I shall dream by upland fences,
Where the season's wealth condenses
Over a many weedy wreck,

Wild, uncared-for, desert places,
That sovereign Beauty loves to deck
With her softest, dearest graces,
There the long year dreams in quiet,
And the summer's strength runs riot.
Shall I not remember these,
Deep in winter reveries?
Berried brier and thistle-bloom,
And milk-weed with its dense perfume;
Slender vervain towering up
In a many-branchèd cup,
Like a candlestick each spire
Kindled with a violet fire;
Matted creepers and wild cherries,
Purple-bunchèd elderberries,
And on scanty plots of sod
Groves of branchy goldenrod.

What though autumn mornings now,
Winterward with glittering brow,
Stiffen in the silver grass;
And what though robins flock and pass,
With subdued and sober call,
To the old year's funeral;
Though October's crimson leaves
Rustle at the gusty door,
And the tempest round the eaves
Alternates with pipe and roar;
I sit, as erst, unharmed, secure,
Conscious that my store is sure,
Whatsoe'er the fencèd fields,
Or the untilled forest yields

Of unhurt remembrances,
Of thoughts, far-glimpsed, half-followed, these
I have reaped and laid away,
A treasure of unwinnowed grain,
To the garner packed and gray
Gathered without toil or strain.

And when the darker days shall come.
And the fields are white and dumb;
When our fires are half in vain,
And the crystal starlight weaves
Mockeries of summer leaves,
Pictured on the icy pane;
When the high Aurora gleams
Far above the Arctic streams
Like a line of shifting spears,
And the broad pine-circled meres,
Glimmering in that spectral light,
Thunder through the northern night;
Then within the bolted door
I shall con my summer store;
Though the fences scarcely show
Black above the drifted snow,
Though the icy sweeping wind
Whistle in the empty tree,
Safe within the sheltered mind,
I shall feed on memory.

Yet across the windy night
Comes upon its wings a cry;
Fashioned forms and modes take flight,
And a vision sad and high

Of the labouring world down there,
Where the lights burn red and warm,
Pricks my soul with sudden stare,
Glowing through the veils of storm.
In the city yonder sleep
Those who smile and those who weep,
Those whose lips are set with care,
Those whose brows are smooth and fair;
Mourners whom the dawning light
Shall grapple with an old distress;
Lovers folded at midnight
In their bridal happiness;
Pale watchers by belovèd beds,
Fallen adrowse with nodding heads,
Whom sleep captured by surprise,
With the circles round their eyes;
Maidens with quiet-taken breath,
Dreaming of enchanted bowers;
Old men with the mask of death;
Little children soft as flowers;
Those who wake wild-eyed and start
In some madness of the heart;
Those whose lips and brows of stone
Evil thoughts have graven upon,
Shade by shade and line by line,
Refashioning what was once divine.

All these sleep, and through the night,
Comes a passion and a cry,
With a blind sorrow and a might,
I know not whence, I know not why,
A something I cannot control,

A nameless hunger of the soul.
It holds me fast.   In vain, in vain,
I remember how of old
I saw the ruddy race of men,
Through the glittering world outrolled,
A gay-smiling multitude,
All immortal, all divine,
Treading in a wreathèd line
By a pathway through a wood.

THE SUN CUP

The earth is the cup of the sun,
That he filleth at morning with wine,
With the warm, strong wine of his might
From the vintage of gold and of light,
Fills it, and makes it divine.

And at night when his journey is done,
At the gate of his radiant hall,
He setteth his lips to the brim,
With a long last look of his eye,
And lifts it and draineth it dry,
Drains till he leaveth it all
Empty and hollow and dim.

And then as he passes to sleep,
Still full of the feats that he did
Long ago in Olympian wars,
He closes it down with the sweep

Of its slow-turning luminous lid,
Its cover of darkness and stars,
Wrought once by Hephæstus of old
With violet and vastness and gold.

ALCYONE

TO THE MEMORY OF

MY FATHER

HIMSELF A POET

WHO FIRST INSTRUCTED ME

IN THE ART

OF VERSE

ALCYONE

In the silent depth of space,
Immeasurably old, immeasurably far,
Glittering with a silver flame
Through eternity,
Rolls a great and burning star,
With a noble name,
    Alcyone!

In the glorious chart of heaven
It is marked the first of seven;
'Tis a Pleiad:
And a hundred years of earth
With their long-forgotten deeds have come and
    gone,
Since that tiny point of light,
Once a splendour fierce and bright,
Had its birth
In the star we gaze upon.
It has travelled all that time—
Thought has not a swifter flight—
Through a region where no faintest gust
Of life comes ever, but the power of night
Dwells stupendous and sublime,
Limitless and void and lonely,
    12

A region mute with age, and peopled only
With the dead and ruined dust
Of worlds that lived eternities ago.
Man! when thou dost think of this,
And what our earth and its existence is,
The half-blind toils since life began,
The little aims, the little span,
With what passion and what pride,
And what hunger fierce and wide,
Thou dost break beyond it all,
Seeking for the spirit unconfined
In the clear abyss of mind
A shelter and a peace majestical.
For what is life to thee,
Turning toward the primal light,
With that stern and silent face,
If thou canst not be
Something radiant and august as night,
Something wide as space?
Therefore with a love and gratitude divine
Thou shalt cherish in thine heart for sign
A vision of the great and burning star,
Immeasurably old, immeasurably far,
Surging forth its silver flame
Through eternity;
And thine inner heart shall ring and cry
With the music strange and high,
The grandeur of its name
    Alcyone!

IN MARCH

The sun falls warm : the southern winds awake :
The air seethes upwards with a steamy shiver :
Each dip of the road is now a crystal lake,
And every rut a little dancing river.
Through great soft clouds that sunder overhead
The deep sky breaks as pearly blue as summer :
Out of a cleft beside the river's bed
Flaps the black crow, the first demure newcomer.
The last seared drifts are eating fast away
With glassy tinkle into glittering laces :
Dogs lie asleep, and little children play
With tops and marbles in the sun-bare places ;
And I that stroll with many a thoughtful pause
Almost forget that winter ever was.

THE CITY OF THE END OF THINGS

Beside the pounding cataracts
Of midnight streams unknown to us
'Tis builded in the leafless tracts
And valleys huge of Tartarus.
Lurid and lofty and vast it seems ;
It hath no rounded name that rings,
But I have heard it called in dreams
The City of the End of Things.

Its roofs and iron towers have grown
None knoweth how high within the night,

But in its murky streets far down
A flaming terrible and bright
Shakes all the stalking shadows there,
Across the walls, across the floors,
And shifts upon the upper air
From out a thousand furnace doors;
And all the while an awful sound
Keeps roaring on continually,
And crashes in the ceaseless round
Of a gigantic harmony.
Through its grim depths re-echoing
And all its weary height of walls,
With measured roar and iron ring,
The inhuman music lifts and falls.
Where no thing rests and no man is,
And only fire and night hold sway;
The beat, the thunder and the hiss
Cease not, and change not, night nor day.
And moving at unheard commands,
The abysses and vast fires between,
Flit figures that with clanking hands
Obey a hideous routine;
They are not flesh, they are not bone,
They see not with the human eye,
And from their iron lips is blown
A dreadful and monotonous cry;
And whoso of our mortal race
Should find that city unaware,
Lean Death would smite him face to face,
And blanch him with its venomed air:
Or caught by the terrific spell,
Each thread of memory snapt and cut,

His soul would shrivel and its shell
Go rattling like an empty nut.

It was not always so, but once,
In days that no man thinks upon,
Fair voices echoed from its stones,
The light above it leaped and shone:
Once there were multitudes of men,
That built that city in their pride,
Until its might was made, and then
They withered age by age and died.
But now of that prodigious race,
Three only in an iron tower,
Set like carved idols face to face,
Remain the masters of its power;
And at the city gate a fourth,
Gigantic and with dreadful eyes,
Sits looking toward the lightless north,
Beyond the reach of memories;
Fast rooted to the lurid floor,
A bulk that never moves a jot,
In his pale body dwells no more,
Or mind or soul,—an idiot!
But sometime in the end those three
Shall perish and their hands be still,
And with the master's touch shall flee
Their incommunicable skill.
A stillness absolute as death
Along the slacking wheels shall lie,
And, flagging at a single breath,
The fires that moulder out and die.
The roar shall vanish at its height,

And over that tremendous town
The silence of eternal night
Shall gather close and settle down.
All its grim grandeur, tower and hall,
Shall be abandoned utterly,
And into rust and dust shall fall
From century to century;
Nor ever living thing shall grow,
Nor trunk of tree, nor blade of grass;
No drop shall fall, no wind shall blow,
Nor sound of any foot shall pass:
Alone of its accursèd state,
One thing the hand of Time shall spare,
For the grim Idiot at the gate
Is deathless and eternal there.

THE SONG SPARROW

Fair little scout, that when the iron year
    Changes, and the first fleecy clouds deploy,
    Comest with such a sudden burst of joy,
Lifting on winter's doomed and broken rear
That song of silvery triumph blithe and clear;
    Not yet quite conscious of the happy glow,
    We hungered for some surer touch, and lo!
One morning we awake and thou art here.
And thousands of frail-stemmed hepaticas,
    With their crisp leaves and pure and perfect hues,
    Light sleepers, ready for the golden news,
Spring at thy note beside the forest ways—
    Next to thy song, the first to deck the hour—
    The classic lyrist and the classic flower.

INTER VIAS

'Tis a land where no hurricane falls,
But the infinite azure regards
Its waters for ever, its walls·
Of granite, its limitless swards;
Where the fens to their innermost pool
With the chorus of May are aring,
And the glades are wind-winnowed and cool
    With perpetual spring.

Where folded and half-withdrawn
The delicate wind-flowers blow,
And the blood-root kindles at dawn
Her spiritual taper of snow;
Where the limits are met and spanned
By a waste that no husbandman tills,
And the earth-old pine forests stand
    In the hollows of hills.

'Tis the land that our babies behold,
Deep gazing when none are aware;
And the great-hearted seers of old
And the poets have known it, and there
Made halt by the well-heads of truth
On their difficult pilgrimage
From the rose-ruddy gardens of youth
    To the summits of age.

Now too, as of old, it is sweet
With a presence remote and serene;

Still its byways are pressed by the feet
Of the mother immortal, its queen:
The huntress whose tresses flung free,
And her fillets of gold, upon earth,
They only have honour to see
        Who are dreamers from birth.

In her calm and her beauty supreme,
They have found her at dawn or at eve,
By the marge of some motionless stream,
Or where shadows rebuild or unweave
In a murmurous alley of pine,
Looking upward in silent surprise,
A figure, slow-moving, divine,
        With inscrutable eyes.

REFUGE

Where swallows and wheatfields are,
    O hamlet brown and still,
O river that shineth far,
    By meadow, pier, and mill:

O endless sunsteeped plain,
    With forests in dim blue shrouds,
And little wisps of rain,
    Falling from far-off clouds:

I come from the choking air
    Of passion, doubt, and strife,

With a spirit and mind laid bare
    To your healing breadth of life:

O fruitful and sacred ground,
    O sunlight and summer sky,
Absorb me and fold me round,
    For broken and tired am I.

APRIL NIGHT

How deep the April night is in its noon,
The hopeful, solemn, many-murmured night!
The earth lies hushed with expectation; bright
Above the world's dark border burns the moon,
Yellow and large; from forest floorways, strewn
With flowers, and fields that tingle with new birth,
The moist smell of the unimprisoned earth
Comes up, a sigh, a haunting promise. Soon,
Ah, soon, the teeming triumph! At my feet
The river with its stately sweep and wheel
Moves on slow-motioned, luminous, gray like steel.
From fields far off whose watery hollows gleam,
Aye with blown throats that make the long hours
        sweet,
The sleepless toads are murmuring in their dreams.

PERSONALITY

O differing human heart,
Why is it that I tremble when thine eyes,
Thy human eyes and beautiful human speech,
Draw me, and stir within my soul

That subtle ineradicable longing
For tender comradeship?
It is because I cannot all at once,
Through the half-lights and phantom-haunted mists
That separate and enshroud us life from life,
Discern the nearness or the strangeness of thy paths,
Nor plumb thy depths.
I am like one that comes alone at night
To a strange stream, and by an unknown ford
Stands, and for a moment yearns and shrinks,
Being ignorant of the water, though so quiet it is,
So softly murmurous,
So silvered by the familiar moon.

TO MY DAUGHTER

O little one, daughter, my dearest,
  With your smiles and your beautiful curls,
And your laughter, the brightest and clearest,
  O gravest and gayest of girls;

With your hands that are softer than roses,
  And your lips that are lighter than flowers,
And that innocent brow that discloses
  A wisdom more lovely than ours;

With your locks that encumber, or scatter
  In a thousand mercurial gleams,
And those feet whose impetuous patter
  I hear and remember in dreams;

With your manner of motherly duty,
    When you play with your dolls and are wise;
With your wonders of speech, and the beauty
    In your little imperious eyes;

When I hear you so silverly ringing
    Your welcome from chamber or stair,
When you run to me kissing and clinging,
    So radiant, so rosily fair;

I bend like an ogre above you;
    I bury my face in your curls;
I fold you, I clasp you, I love you,
    O baby, queen-blossom of girls!

CHIONE

Scarcely a breath about the rocky stair
Moved, but the growing tide from verge to verge,
Heaving salt fragrance on the midnight air,
Climbed with a murmurous and fitful surge.
A hoary mist rose up and slowly sheathed
The dripping walls and portal granite-stepped,
And sank into the inner court, and crept
From column unto column thickly wreathed.

In that dead hour of darkness before dawn,
When hearts beat fainter and the hands of death
Are strengthened, with lips white and drawn
And feverish lids and scarcely moving breath

The hapless mother, tender Chione,
Beside the earth-cold figure of her child,
After long bursts of weeping sharp and wild
Lay broken, silent in her agony.

At first in waking horror racked and bound
She lay, and then a gradual stupor grew
About her soul and wrapped her round and round
Like death, and then she sprang to life anew
Out of a darkness clammy as the tomb;
And, touched by memory or some spirit hand,
She seemed to keep a pathway down a land
Of monstrous shadow and Cimmerian gloom.

A waste of cloudy and perpetual night—
And yet there seemed a teeming presence there
Of life that gathered onward in thick flight,
Unseen, but multitudinous.   Aware
Of something also on her path she was
That drew her heart forth with a tender cry.
She hurried with drooped ear and eager eye,
And called on the foul shapes to let her pass.

For down the sloping darkness far ahead
She saw a little figure slight and small,
With yearning arms and shadowy curls outspread,
Running at frightened speed; and it would fall
And rise, sobbing; and through the ghostly sleet
The cry came: 'Mother! Mother!' and she wist
The tender eyes were blinded by the mist,
And the rough stones were bruising the small feet.

And when she lifted a keen cry and clave
Forthright the gathering horror of the place,
Mad with her love and pity, a dark wave
Of clapping shadows swept about her face,
And beat her back, and when she gained her breath,
Athwart an awful vale a grizzled steam
Was rising from a mute and murky stream,
As cold and cavernous as the eye of death.

And near the ripple stood the little shade,
And many hovering ghosts drew near him, some
That seemed to peer out of the mist and fade
With eyes of soft and shadowing pity, dumb;
But others closed him round with eager sighs
And sweet insistence, striving to caress
And comfort him; but grieving none the less,
He reached her heartstrings with his tender cries.

And silently across the horrid flow,
The shapeless bark and pallid chalklike arms
Of him that oared it, dumbly to and fro,
Went gliding, and the struggling ghosts in swarms
Leaped in and passed, but myriads more behind
Crowded the dismal beaches. One might hear
A tumult of entreaty thin and clear
Rise like the whistle of a winter wind.

And still the little figure stood beside
The hideous stream, and toward the whispering prow
Held forth his tender tremulous hands, and cried,
Now to the awful ferryman, and now

To her that battled with the shades in vain.
Sometimes impending over all her sight
The spongy dark and the phantasmal flight
Of things half-shapen passed and hid the plain.

And sometimes in a gust a sort of wind
Drove by, and where its power was hurled,
She saw across the twilight, jarred and thinned,
Those gloomy meadows of the under world,
Where never sunlight was, nor grass, nor trees,
And the dim pathways from the Stygian shore,
Sombre and swart and barren, wandered o'er
By countless melancholy companies.

And farther still upon the utmost rim
Of the drear waste, whereto the roadways led,
She saw in piling outline, huge and dim,
The walled and towerèd dwellings of the dead
And the grim house of Hades.   Then she broke
Once more fierce-footed through the noisome press;
But ere she reached the goal of her distress,
Her pierced heart seemed to shatter, and she woke.

It seemed as she had been entombed for years,
And came again to living with a start.
There was an awful echoing in her ears
And a great deadness pressing at her heart.
She shuddered and with terror seemed to freeze,
Lip-shrunken and wide-eyed a moment's space,
And then she touched the little lifeless face,
And kissed it and rose up upon her knees.

And round her still the silence seemed to teem
With the foul shadows of her dream beguiled—
No dream, she thought; it could not be a dream,
But her child called for her; her child, her child!—
She clasped her quivering fingers white and spare,
And knelt low down, and bending her fair head
Unto the lower gods who rule the dead,
Touched them with tender homage and this prayer:

O gloomy masters of the dark demesne,
Hades, and thou whom the dread deity
Bore once from earthly Enna for his queen,
Beloved of Demeter, pale Persephone,
Grant me one boon;
'Tis not for life I pray,
Not life, but quiet death; and that soon, soon!
Loose from my soul this heavy weight of clay,
This net of useless woe.
O mournful mother, sad Persephone,
Be mindful, let me go!

How shall he journey to the dismal beach,
Or win the ear of Charon, without one
To keep him and stand by him, sure of speech?
He is so little, and has just begun
To use his feet
And speak a few small words,
And all his daily usage has been sweet
As the soft nesting ways of tender birds.
How shall he fare at all
Across that grim inhospitable land,

If I too be not by to hold his hand,
And help him if he fall?

And then before the gloomy judges set,
How shall he answer?   Oh, I cannot bear
To see his tender cheeks with weeping wet,
Or hear the sobbing cry of his despair!
I could not rest,
Nor live with patient mind,
Though knowing what is fated must be best;
But surely thou art more than mortal kind,
And thou canst feel my woe,
All-pitying, all-observant, all-divine;
He is so little, mother Proserpine,
He needs me, let me go!

Thus far she prayed, and then she lost her way,
And left the half of all her heart unsaid,
And a great languor seized her, and she lay,
Soft fallen, by the little silent head.
Her numbèd lips had passed beyond control,
Her mind could neither plan nor reason more,
She saw dark waters and an unknown shore,
And the gray shadows crept about her soul.

Again through darkness on an evil land
She seemed to enter but without distress.
A little spirit led her by the hand
And her wide heart was warm with tenderness.
Her lips, still moving, conscious of one care,
Murmured a moment in soft mother tones,
And so fell silent.   From their sombre thrones
Already the grim gods had heard her prayer.

TO THE CRICKET

Didst thou not tease and fret me to and fro,
Sweet spirit of this summer-circled field,
With that quiet voice of thine that would not yield
Its meaning, though I mused and sought it so?
But now I am content to let it go,
To lie at length and watch the swallows pass,
As blithe and restful as this quiet grass,
Content only to listen and to know
That years shall turn, and summers yet shall shine,
And I shall lie beneath these swaying trees,
Still listening thus; haply at last to seize,
And render in some happier verse divine
That friendly, homely, haunting speech of thine,
That perfect utterance of content and ease.

THE SONG OF PAN

Mad with love and laden
    With immortal pain,
Pan pursued a maiden—
    Pan, the god—in vain.

For when Pan had nearly
    Touched her, wild to plead,
She was gone—and clearly
    In her place a reed!
13

Long the god, unwitting,
  Through the valley strayed;
Then at last submitting,
  Cut the reed, and made,

Deftly fashioned, seven
  Pipes, and poured his pain
Unto earth and heaven
  In a piercing strain.

So with god and poet;
  Beauty lures them on,
Flies, and ere they know it
  Like a wraith is gone.

Then they seek to borrow
  Pleasure still from wrong,
And with smiling sorrow
  Turn it to a song.

THE ISLET AND THE PALM

O gentle sister spirit, when you smile
My soul is like a gentle coral isle,
An islet shadowed by a single palm,
Ringed round with reef and foam, but inly calm.

And all day long I listen to the speech
Of wind and water on my charmèd beach:
I see far off beyond mine outer shore
The ocean flash, and hear his harmless roar.

And in the night-time when the glorious sun,
With all his life and all his light, is done,
The wind still murmurs in my slender tree,
And shakes the moonlight on the silver sea.

A VISION OF TWILIGHT

By a void and soundless river
    On the outer edge of space,
Where the body comes not ever,
    But the absent dream hath place,
Stands a city tall and quiet,
    And its air is sweet and dim;
Never sound of grief or riot
    Makes it mad, or makes it grim.

And the tender skies thereover
    Neither sun, nor star, behold—
Only dusk it hath for cover,—
    But a glamour soft with gold,
Through a mist of dreamier essence
    Than the dew of twilight, smiles
On strange shafts and domes and crescents,
    Lifting into eerie piles.

In its courts and hallowed places
    Dreams of distant worlds arise,
Shadows of transfigured faces,
    Glimpses of immortal eyes,

Echoes of serenest pleasure,
　　Notes of perfect speech that fall,
Through an air of endless leisure,
　　Marvellously musical.

And I wander there at even,
　　Sometimes when my heart is clear,
When a wider round of heaven
　　And a vaster world are near,
When from many a shadow steeple
　　Sounds of dreamy bells begin,
And I love the gentle people
　　That my spirit finds therein.

Men of a diviner making
　　Than the sons of pride and strife,
Quick with love and pity, breaking
　　From a knowledge old as life;
Women of a spiritual rareness,
　　Whom old passion and old woe
Moulded to a slenderer fairness
　　Than the dearest shapes we know.

In its domed and towerèd centre
　　Lies a garden wide and fair,
Open for the soul to enter,
　　And the watchful townsmen there
Greet the stranger gloomed and fretting
　　From this world of stormy hands,
With a look that deals forgetting
　　And a touch that understands.

For they see with power, not borrowed
  From a record taught or told,
But they loved and laughed and sorrowed
  In a thousand worlds of old;
Now they rest and dream for ever,
  And with hearts serene and whole
See the struggle, the old fever,
  Clear as on a painted scroll.

Wandering by that gray and solemn
  Water, with its ghostly quays—
Vistas of vast arch and column,
  Shadowed by unearthly trees—
Biddings of sweet power compel me,
  And I go with bated breath,
Listening to the tales they tell me,
  Parables of Life and Death.

In a tongue that once was spoken,
  Ere the world was cooled by Time
When the spirit flowed unbroken
  Through the flesh, and the Sublime
Made the eyes of men far-seeing,
  And their souls as pure as rain,
They declare the ends of being,
  And the sacred need of pain.

For they know the sweetest reasons
  For the products most malign—
They can tell the paths and seasons
  Of the farthest suns that shine.

How the moth-wing's iridescence
  By an inward plan was wrought,
And they read me curious lessons
  In the secret ways of thought.

When day turns, and over heaven
  To the balmy western verge
Sail the victor fleets of even,
  And the pilot stars emerge,
Then my city rounds and rises,
  Like a vapour formed afar,
And its sudden girth surprises,
  And its shadowy gates unbar.

Dreamy crowds are moving yonder
  In a faint and phantom blue;
Through the dusk I lean, and wonder
  If their winsome shapes are true;
But in veiling indecision
  Comes my question back again—
Which is real? The fleeting vision?
  Or the fleeting world of men?

EVENING

From upland slopes I see the cows file by,
Lowing, great-chested, down the homeward trail,
By dusking fields and meadows shining pale
With moon-tipped dandelions. Flickering high,
A peevish night-hawk in the western sky
Beats up into the lucent solitudes,

Or drops with griding wing.   The stilly woods
Grow dark and deep and gloom mysteriously.
Cool night winds creep, and whisper in mine ear.
The homely cricket gossips at my feet.
From far-off pools and wastes of reeds I hear,
Clear and soft-piped, the chanting frogs break sweet
In full Pandean chorus.   One by one
Shine out the stars, and the great night comes on.

THE CLEARER SELF

Before me grew the human soul,
    And after I am dead and gone,
Through grades of effort and control
    The marvellous work shall still go on.

Each mortal in his little span
    Hath only lived, if he have shown
What greatness there can be in man
    Above the measured and the known;

How through the ancient layers of night,
    In gradual victory secure,
Grows ever with increasing light
    The Energy serene and pure:

The Soul that from a monstrous past,
    From age to age, from hour to hour,
Feels upward to some height at last
    Of unimagined grace and power.

Though yet the sacred fire be dull,
  In folds of thwarting matter furled,
Ere death be nigh, while life is full,
  O Master Spirit of the world,

Grant me to know, to seek, to find,
  In some small measure though it be,
Emerging from the waste and blind,
  The clearer self, the grander me!

TO THE PROPHETIC SOUL

What are these bustlers at the gate
  Of now or yesterday,
These playthings in the hand of Fate,
  That pass, and point no way;

These clinging bubbles whose mock fires
  For ever dance and gleam,
Vain foam that gathers and expires
  Upon the world's dark stream;

These gropers betwixt right and wrong,
  That seek an unknown goal,
Most ignorant when they seem most strong;
  What are they, then, O Soul,

That thou shouldst covet overmuch
  A tenderer range of heart,
And yet at every dreamed-of touch
  So tremulously start?

Thou with that hatred ever new
   Of the world's base control,
That vision of the large and true,
   That quickness of the soul;

Nay, for they are not of thy kind,
   But in a rarer clay
God dowered thee with an alien mind;
   Thou canst not be as they.

Be strong, therefore; resume thy load,
   And forward stone by stone
Go singing, though the glorious road
   Thou travellest alone.

THE LAND OF PALLAS

Methought I journeyed along ways that led for ever
   Throughout a happy land where strife and care
   were dead,
And life went flowing by me like a placid river
   Past sandy eyots where the shifting shoals make
   head.

A land where beauty dwelt supreme, and right, the
   donor
   Of peaceful days; a land of equal gifts and deeds,
Of limitless fair fields and plenty had with honour;
   A land of kindly tillage and untroubled meads,

Of gardens, and great fields, and dreaming rose-
    wreathed alleys,
    Wherein at dawn and dusk the vesper sparrows
      sang;
Of cities set far off on hills down vista'd valleys,
    And floods so vast and old, men wist not whence
      they sprang,

Of groves, and forest depths, and fountains softly
    welling,
    And roads that ran soft-shadowed past the open
      doors,
Of mighty palaces and many a lofty dwelling,
    Where all men entered and no master trod their
      floors.

A land of lovely speech, where every tone was
    fashioned
    By generations of emotion high and sweet,
Of thought and deed and bearing lofty and impas-
    sioned;
    A land of golden calm, grave forms, and fretless
      feet.

And every mode and saying of that land gave token
    Of limits where no death or evil fortune fell,
And men lived out long lives in proud content
    unbroken,
    For there no man was rich, none poor, but all were
      well.

And all the earth was common, and no base con-
    triving
  Of money of coined gold was needed there or
    known,
But all men wrought together without greed or
    striving,
  And all the store of all to each man was his own.

From all that busy land, gray town, and peaceful
    village,
  Where never jar was heard, nor wail nor cry of
    strife,
From every laden stream and all the fields of tillage,
  Arose the murmur and the kindly hum of life.

At morning to the fields came forth the men, each
    neighbour
  Hand-linked to other, crowned, with wreaths upon
    their hair,
And all day long with joy they gave their hands to
    labour,
  Moving at will, unhastened, each man to his share.

At noon the women came, the tall fair women,
    bearing
  Baskets of wicker in their ample hands for each,
And learned the day's brief tale, and how the fields
    were faring,
  And blessed them with their lofty beauty and
    blithe speech.

And when the great day's toil was over, and the
    shadows

Grew with the flocking stars, the sound of festival
Rose in each city square, and all the country
  meadows,
 Palace, and paven court, and every rustic hall.

Beside smooth streams, where alleys and green gar-
  dens meeting
  Ran downward to the flood with marble steps, a
   throng
Came forth of all the folk, at even, gaily greeting,
  With echo of sweet converse, jest, and stately
   song.

In all their great fair cities there was neither seeking
  For power of gold, nor greed of lust, nor
   desperate pain
Of multitudes that starve, or in hoarse anger
  breaking,
  Beat at the doors of princes, break and fall in vain.

But all the children of that peaceful land, like
  brothers,
  Lofty of spirit, wise, and ever set to learn
The chart of neighbouring souls, the bent and need
  of others,
  Thought only of good deeds, sweet speech, and
   just return.

And there there was no prison, power of arms, nor
  palace,
  Where prince or judge held sway, for none was
   needed there;

Long ages since the very names of fraud and malice
  Had vanished from men's tongues, and died from
    all men's care.

And there there were no bonds of contract, deed or
    marriage,
  No oath, nor any form, to make the word more
    sure,
For no man dreamed of hurt, dishonour, or mis-
    carriage,
  Where every thought was truth, and every heart
    was pure.

There were no castes of rich or poor, of slave or
    master,
  Where all were brothers, and the curse of gold was
    dead,
But all that wise fair race to kindlier ends and vaster
  Moved on together with the same majestic tread.

And all the men and women of that land were fairer
  Than even the mightiest of our meaner race can
    be ;
The men like gentle children, great of limb, yet rarer
  For wisdom and high thought, like kings for
    majesty.

And all the women through great ages of bright
    living,
  Grown goodlier of stature, strong, and subtly wise,

Stood equal with the men, calm counsellors, ever
  giving
  The fire and succour of proud faith and dauntless
  eyes.

And as I journeyed in that land I reached a ruin,
  A gateway of a lonely and secluded waste,
A phantom of forgotten time and ancient doing,
  Eaten by age and violence, crumbled and defaced.

On its grim outer walls the ancient world's sad
  glories
  Were recorded in fire; upon its inner stone,
Drawn by dead hands, I saw, in tales and tragic
  stories,
  The woe and sickness of an age of fear made
  known.

And lo, in that gray storehouse, fallen to dust and
  rotten,
  Lay piled the traps and engines of forgotten greed,
The tomes of codes and canons, long disused, for-
  gotten,
  The robes and sacred books of many a vanished
  creed.

An old grave man I found, white-haired and gently
  spoken,
  Who, as I questioned, answered with a smile
  benign,
'Long years have come and gone since these poor
  gauds were broken,
  Broken and banished from a life made more divine.

'But still we keep them stored as once our sires
    deemed fitting,
  The symbol of dark days and lives remote and
    strange,
Lest o'er the minds of any there should come
    unwitting
  The thought of some new order and the lust of
    change.

'If any grow disturbed, we bring them gently hither,
  To read the world's grim record and the sombre
    lore
Massed in these pitiless vaults, and they returning
    thither,
  Bear with them quieter thoughts, and make for
    change no more.'

And thence I journeyed on by one broad way that
    bore me
  Out of that waste, and as I passed by tower and
    town
I saw amid the limitless plain far out before me
  A long low mountain, blue as beryl, and its crown

Was capped by marble roofs that shone like snow for
    whiteness,
  Its foot was deep in gardens, and that blossoming
    plain
Seemed in the radiant shower of its majestic
    brightness
  A land for gods to dwell in, free from care and
    pain.

And to and forth from that fair mountain like a river
  Ran many a dim gray road, and on them I could
    see
A multitude of stately forms that seemed for ever
  Going and coming in bright bands; and near to me

Was one that in his journey seemed to dream and
    linger,
  Walking at whiles with kingly step, then standing
    still,
And him I met and asked him, pointing with my
    finger,
  The meaning of the palace and the lofty hill.

Whereto the dreamer: 'Art thou of this land, my
    brother,
  And knowest not the mountain and its crest of
    walls,
Where dwells the priestless worship of the all-wise
    mother?
  That is the hill of Pallas; those her marble halls!

'There dwell the lords of knowledge and of thought
    increasing,
  And they whom insight and the gleams of song
    uplift;
And thence as by a hundred conduits flows unceasing
  The spring of power and beauty, an eternal gift.

Still I passed on until I reached at length, not
    knowing
  Whither the tangled and diverging paths might
    lead,

A land of baser men, whose coming and whose going
  Were urged by fear, and hunger, and the curse of
    greed.

I saw the proud and fortunate go by me, faring
  In fatness and fine robes, the poor oppressed and
    slow,
The faces of bowed men, and piteous women bearing
  The burden of perpetual sorrow and the stamp of
    woe.

And tides of deep solicitude and wondering pity
  Possessed me, and with eager and uplifted hands
I drew the crowd about me in a mighty city,
  And taught the message of those other kindlier
    lands.

I preached the rule of Faith and brotherly Com-
    munion,
  The law of Peace and Beauty and the death of
    Strife,
And painted in great words the horror of disunion,
  The vainness of self-worship, and the waste of life.

I preached but fruitlessly; the powerful from their
    stations
  Rebuked me as an anarch, envious and bad,
And they that served them with lean hands and bitter
    patience
  Smiled only out of hollow orbs, and deemed me
    mad.
        14

And still I preached, and wrought, and still I bore
    my message,
  For well I knew that on and upward without cease
The spirit works for ever, and by Faith and Presage
    That somehow yet the end of human life is Peace.

AMONG THE ORCHARDS

Already in the dew-wrapped vineyards dry
Dense weights of heat press down. The large bright
    drops
Shrink in the leaves. From dark acacia tops
The nut-hatch flings his short reiterate cry;
And ever as the sun mounts hot and high
Thin voices crowd the grass. In soft long strokes
The wind goes murmuring through the mountain
    oaks.
Faint wefts creep out along the blue and die.
I hear far in among the motionless trees—
Shadows that sleep upon the shaven sod—
The thud of dropping apples. Reach on reach
Stretch plots of perfumed orchard, where the bees
Murmur among the full-fringed goldenrod
Or cling half-drunken to the rotting peach.

THE POET'S SONG

  There came no change from week to week
    On all the land, but all one way,
  Like ghosts that cannot touch or speak,
    Day followed day.

Within the palace court the rounds
  Of glare and shadow, day and night,
Went ever with the same dull sounds,
  The same dull flight:

The motion of slow forms of state,
  The far-off murmur of the street,
The din of couriers at the gate,
  Half-mad with heat:

Sometimes a distant shout of boys
  At play upon the terrace walk,
The shutting of great doors, and noise
  Of muttered talk.

In one red corner of the wall,
  That fronted with its granite stain
The town, the palms, and beyond all,
  The burning plain,

As listless as the hour, alone,
  The poet by his broken lute
Sat like a figure in the stone,
  Dark-browed and mute.

He saw the heat on the thin grass
  Fall till it withered joint by joint,
The shadow on the dial pass
  From point to point.

He saw the midnight bright and bare
  Fill with its quietude of stars

The silence that no human prayer
   Attains or mars.

He heard the hours divide, and still
   The sentry on the outer wall
Make the night wearier with his shrill
   Monotonous call.

He watched the lizard where it lay,
   Impassive as the watcher's face;
And only once in the long day
   It changed its place.

Sometimes with clank of hoofs and cries
   The noon through all its trance was stirred:
The poet sat with half-shut eyes,
   Nor saw, nor heard.

And once across the heated close
   Light laughter in a silver shower
Fell from fair lips: the poet rose
   And cursed the hour.

Men paled and sickened; half in fear,
   There came to him at dusk of eve
One who but murmured in his ear
   And plucked his sleeve:

'The king is filled with irks, distressed,
   And bids thee hasten to his side;
For thou alone canst give him rest.'
   The poet cried:

'Go show the king this broken lute!
   Even as it is, so am I!
The tree is perished to its root,
    The fountain dry.

'What seeks he of the leafless tree,
   The broken lute, the empty spring?
Yea, tho' he gave his crown to me,
    I cannot sing!'

II

That night there came from either hand
A sense of change upon the land;
A brooding stillness rustled through
With creeping winds that hardly blew;
A shadow from the looming west,
A stir of leaves, a dim unrest;
It seemed as if a spell had broke.

And then the poet turned and woke
As from the darkness of a dream,
And with a smile divine supreme
Drew up his mantle fold on fold,
And strung his lute with strings of gold,
And bound the sandals to his feet,
And strode into the darkling street.

Through crowds of murmuring men he hied,
With working lips and swinging stride,
And gleaming eyes and brow bent down:
Out of the great gate of the town

He hastened ever and passed on,
And ere the darkness came, was gone,
A mote beyond the western swell.

And then the storm arose and fell
From wheeling shadows black with rain
That drowned the hills and strode the plain;
Round the grim mountain-heads it passed,
Down whistling valleys blast on blast,
Surged in upon the snapping trees,
And swept the shuddering villages.

That night, when the fierce hours grew long,
Once more the monarch, old and gray,
Called for the poet and his song,
And called in vain. But far away,
By the wild mountain-gorges, stirred,
The shepherds in their watches heard,
Above the torrent's charge and clang,
The cleaving chant of one that sang.

A THUNDERSTORM

A moment the wild swallows like a flight
Of withered gust-caught leaves, serenely high,
Toss in the windrack up the muttering sky.
The leaves hang still. Above the weird twilight,
The hurrying centres of the storm unite
And spreading with huge trunk and rolling fringe,
Each wheeled upon its own tremendous hinge.

Tower darkening on. And now from heaven's
    height,
With the long roar of elm-trees swept and swayed,
And pelted waters, on the vanished plain
Plunges the blast. Behind the wild white flash
That splits abroad the pealing thunder-crash,
Over bleared fields and gardens disarrayed,
Column on column comes the drenching rain.

THE CITY

Canst thou not rest, O city,
    That liest so wide and fair;
Shall never an hour bring pity,
    Nor end be found for care?

Thy walls are high in heaven,
    Thy streets are gay and wide,
Beneath thy towers at even
    The dreamy waters glide.

Thou art fair as the hills at morning,
    And the sunshine loveth thee,
But its light is a gloom of warning
    On a soul no longer free.

The curses of gold are about thee,
    And thy sorrow deepeneth still;
One madness within and without thee,
    One battle blind and shrill.

I see the crowds for ever
    Go by with hurrying feet;
Through doors that darken never
    I hear the engines beat.

Through days and nights that follow
    The hidden mill-wheel strains;
In the midnight's windy hollow
    I hear the roar of trains.

And still the day fulfilleth,
    And still the night goes round,
And the guest-hall boometh and shrilleth,
    With the dance's mocking sound.

In chambers of gold elysian,
    The cymbals clash and clang,
But the days are gone like a vision
    When the people wrought and sang.

And toil hath fear for neighbour,
    Where singing lips are dumb,
And life is one long labour,
    Till death or freedom come.

Ah! the crowds that for ever are flowing—
    They neither laugh nor weep—
I see them coming and going,
    Like things that move in sleep:

Gray sires and burdened brothers,
    The old. the young, the fair,

Wan cheeks of pallid mothers,
　And the girls with golden hair.

Care sits in many a fashion,
　Grown gray on many a head,
And lips are turned to ashen
　Whose years have right to red.

Canst thou not rest, O city,
　That liest so wide, so fair;
Shall never an hour bring pity,
　Nor end be found for care?

SAPPHICS

Clothed in splendour, beautifully sad and silent,
Comes the autumn over the woods and highlands,
Golden, rose-red, full of divine remembrance,
　　Full of foreboding.

Soon the maples, soon will the glowing birches,
Stripped of all that summer and love had dowered
　them,
Dream, sad-limbed, beholding their pomp and
　treasure
　　Ruthlessly scattered:

Yet they quail not: Winter with wind and iron
Comes and finds them silent and uncomplaining,
Finds them tameless, beautiful still and gracious,
　　Gravely enduring.

Me too changes, bitter and full of evil,
Dream by dream have plundered and left me naked,
Gray with sorrow.   Even the days before me
          Fade into twilight,

Mute and barren.   Yet will I keep my spirit
Clear and valiant, brother to these my noble
Elms and maples, utterly grave and fearless,
          Grandly ungrieving.

Brief the span is, counting the years of mortals,
Strange and sad; it passes, and then the bright earth,
Careless mother, gleaming with gold and azure,
          Lovely with blossoms—

Shining white anemones, mixed with roses,
Daisies mild-eyed, grasses and honeyed clover—
You and me, and all of us, met and equal,
          Softly shall cover.

VOICES OF EARTH

We have not heard the music of the spheres,
The song of star to star, but there are sounds
More deep than human joy and human tears,
That Nature uses in her common rounds;
The fall of streams, the cry of winds that strain
The oak, the roaring of the sea's surge, might
Of thunder breaking afar off, or rain
That falls by minutes in the summer night.
These are the voices of earth's secret soul,
Uttering the mystery from which she came.

To him who hears them grief beyond control,
Or joy inscrutable without a name,
Wakes in his heart thoughts bedded there,
    impearled,
Before the birth and making of the world.

PECCAVI, DOMINE

O Power to whom this earthly clime
    Is but an atom in the whole,
O Poet-heart of Space and Time,
    O Maker and immortal Soul,
Within whose glowing rings are bound,
    Out of whose sleepless heart had birth
The cloudy blue, the starry round,
    And this small miracle of earth:

Who liv'st in every living thing,
    And all things are thy script and chart,
Who rid'st upon the eagle's wing,
    And yearnest in the human heart;
O Riddle with a single clue,
    Love, deathless, protean, secure,
The ever old the ever new,
    O Energy, serene and pure.

Thou, who art also part of me,
    Whose glory I have sometime seen,
O Vision of the Ought-to-be,
    O Memory of the Might-have-been,

I have had glimpses of thy way,
  And moved with winds and walked with stars,
But, weary, I have fallen astray,
  And, wounded, who shall count my scars?

O Master, all my strength is gone;
  Unto the very earth I bow;
I have no light to lead me on;
  With aching heart and burning brow,
I lie as one that travaileth
  In sorrow more than he can bear;
I sit in darkness as of death,
  And scatter dust upon my hair.

The God within my soul hath slept,
  And I have shamed the nobler rule;
O Master, I have whined and crept;
  O Spirit, I have played the fool.
Like him of old upon whose head
  His follies hung in dark arrears,
I groan and travail in my bed,
  And water it with bitter tears.

I stand upon thy mountain-heads,
  And gaze until mine eyes are dim;
The golden morning glows and spreads;
  The hoary vapours break and swim.
I see thy blossoming fields, divine,
  Thy shining clouds, thy blessèd trees—
And then that broken soul of mine—
  How much less beautiful than these!

O Spirit, passionless, but kind,
   Is there in all the world, I cry,
Another one so base and blind,
   Another one so weak as I?
O Power, unchangeable, but just,
   Impute this one good thing to me,
I sink my spirit to the dust
   In utter dumb humility.

AN ODE TO THE HILLS

" I will lift up mine eyes to the hills, from whence cometh my help."
Psalm cxxi.

Æons ago ye were,
Before the struggling changeful race of men
Wrought into being, ere the tragic stir
Of human toil and deep desire began:
So shall ye still remain,
Lords of an elder and immutable race,
When many a broad metropolis of the plain,
Or thronging port by some renownèd shore,
Is sunk in nameless ruin, and its place
Recalled no more.

Empires have come and gone,
And glorious cities fallen in their prime;
Divine, far-echoing, names once writ in stone
Have vanished in the dust and void of time;
But ye, firm-set, secure,
Like Treasure in the hardness of God's palm,

Are yet the same for ever; ye endure
By virtue of an old slow-ripening word,
In your gray majesty and sovereign calm,
Untouched, unstirred.

Tempest and thunderstroke,
With whirlwinds dipped in midnight at the core,
Have torn strange furrows through your forest cloak,
And made your hollow gorges clash and roar,
And scarred your brows in vain.
Around your barren heads and granite steeps
Tempestuous gray battalions of the rain
Charge and recharge, across the plateaued floors,
Drenching the serried pines; and the hail sweeps
Your pitiless scaurs.

The long midsummer heat
Chars the thin leafage of your rocks in fire:
Autumn with windy robe and ruinous feet
On your wide forests wreaks his fell desire,
Heaping in barbarous wreck
The treasure of your sweet and prosperous days;
And lastly the grim tyrant, at whose beck
Channels are turned to stone and tempests wheel,
On brow and breast and shining shoulder lays
His hand of steel.

And yet not harsh alone,
Nor wild, nor bitter, are your destinies,
O fair and sweet, for all your heart of stone,
Who gather beauty round your Titan knees,
As the lens gathers light.

The dawn gleams rosy on your splendid brows,
The sun at noonday folds you in his might,
And swathes your forehead at his going down,
Last leaving, where he first in pride bestows,
His golden crown.

In unregarded glooms,
Where hardly shall a human footstep pass,
Myriads of ferns and soft maianthemums,
Or lily-breathing slender pyrolas
Distil their hearts for you.
Far in your pine-clad fastnesses ye keep
Coverts the lonely thrush shall wander through,
With echoes that seem ever to recede,
Touching from pine to pine, from steep to steep,
His ghostly reed.

The fierce things of the wild
Find food and shelter in your tenantless rocks.
The eagle on whose wings the dawn hath smiled,
The loon, the wild-cat, and the bright-eyed fox;
For far away indeed
Are all the ominous noises of mankind,
The slaughterer's malice and the trader's greed:
Your rugged haunts endure no slavery:
No treacherous hand is there to crush or bind,
But all are free.

Therefore out of the stir
Of cities and the ever-thickening press
The poet and the worn philosopher
To your bare peaks and radiant loneliness

Escape, and breathe once more
The wind of the Eternal: that clear mood,
Which Nature and the elder ages bore,
Lends them new courage and a second prime,
At rest upon the cool infinitude
Of Space and Time.

The mists of troublous days,
The horror of fierce hands and fraudful lips,
The blindness gathered in Life's aimless ways
Fade from them, and the kind Earth-spirit strips
The bandage from their eyes,
Touches their hearts and bids them feel and see:
Beauty and Knowledge with that rare apprise
Pour over them from some divine abode,
Falling as in a flood of memory,
The bliss of God.

I too perchance some day,
When Love and Life have fallen far apart,
Shall slip the yoke and seek your upward way
And make my dwelling in your changeless heart;
And there in some quiet glade,
Some virgin plot of turf, some innermost dell,
Pure with cool water and inviolate shade,
I'll build a blameless altar to the dear
And kindly gods who guard your haunts so well
From hurt or fear.

There I will dream day-long,
And honour them in many sacred ways,

With hushèd melody and uttered song,
And golden meditation and with praise.
I'll touch them with a prayer,
To clothe my spirit as your might is clad
With all things bountiful, divine, and fair,
Yet inwardly to make me hard and true,
Wide-seeing, passionless, immutably glad,
And strong like you.

INDIAN SUMMER

The old gray year is near his term in sooth,
And now with backward eye and soft-laid palm
Awakens to a golden dream of youth,
A second childhood lovely and most calm,
And the smooth hour about his misty head
An awning of enchanted splendour weaves,
Of maples, amber, purple, and rose-red,
And droop-limbed elms down-dropping golden leaves.
With still half-fallen lids he sits and dreams
Far in a hollow of the sunlit wood,
Lulled by the murmur of thin-threading streams,
Nor sees the polar armies overflood
The darkening barriers of the hills, nor hears
The north-wind ringing with a thousand spears.
15

GOOD SPEECH

Think not, because thine inmost heart means well,
Thou hast the freedom of rude speech: sweet words
Are like the voices of returning birds
Filling the soul with summer, or a bell
That calls the weary and the sick to prayer.
Even as thy thought, so let thy speech be fair.

THE BETTER DAY

Harsh thoughts, blind angers, and fierce hands,
　That keep this restless world at strife,
Mean passions that like choking sands,
　Perplex the stream of life.

Pride and hot envy and cold greed,
　The cankers of the loftier will,
What if ye triumph, and yet bleed?
　Ah, can ye not be still?

Oh, shall there be no space, no time,
　No century of weal in store,
No freedom in a nobler clime,
　Where men shall strive no more?

Where every motion of the heart
　Shall serve the spirit's master-call,
Where self shall be the unseen part,
　And human kindness all?

Or shall we but by fits and gleams
  Sink satisfied, and cease to rave,
Find love but in the rest of dreams,
  And peace but in the grave?

WHITE PANSIES

Day and night pass over, rounding,
  Star and cloud and sun,
Things of drift and shadow, empty
  Of my dearest one.

Soft as slumber was my baby,
  Beaming bright and sweet;
Daintier than bloom or jewel
  Were his hands and feet.

He was mine, mine all, mine only,
  Mine and his the debt;
Earth and Life and Time are changers;
  I shall not forget.

Pansies for my dear one—heartsease—
  Set them gently so;
For his stainless lips and forehead,
  Pansies white as snow.

Would that in the flower-grown little
  Grave they dug so deep,
I might rest beside 'him, dreamless,
  Smile no more, nor weep.

WE TOO SHALL SLEEP

Not, not for thee,
Belovèd child, the burning grasp of life
Shall bruise the tender soul.   The noise, and strife,
And clamour of midday thou shalt not see;
But wrapped for ever in thy quiet grave,
Too little to have known the earthly lot,
Time's clashing hosts above thine innocent head,
Wave upon wave,
Shall break, or pass as with an army's tread,
And harm thee not.

A few short years
We of the living flesh and restless brain
Shall plumb the deeps of life and know the strain,
The fleeting gleams of joy, the fruitless tears;
And then at last when all is touched and tried,
Our own immutable night shall fall, and deep
In the same silent plot, O little friend,
Side by thy side,
In peace that changeth not, nor knoweth end,
We too shall sleep.

THE AUTUMN WASTE

There is no break in all the wide gray sky,
Nor light on any field, and the wind grieves
And talks of death.   Where cold gray waters lie
Round grayer stones, and the new-fallen leaves

Heap the chill hollows of the naked woods,
A lisping moan, an inarticulate cry,
Creeps far among the charnel solitudes,
Numbing the waste with mindless misery.
In these bare paths, these melancholy lands,
What dream, or flesh, could ever have been young?
What lovers have gone forth with linkèd hands?
What flowers could ever have bloomed, what birds
    have sung?
Life, hopes, and human things seem wrapped away,
With shrouds and spectres, in one long decay.

VIVIA PERPETUA

Now being on the eve of death discharged
From every mortal hope and earthly care,
I questioned how my soul might best employ
This hand, and this still wakeful flame of mind
In the brief hours yet left me for their use;
Wherefore have I bethought me of my friend,
Of you Philarchus, and your company,
Yet wavering in the faith and unconfirmed;
Perchance that I may break into thine heart
Some sorrowful channel for the love divine,
I make this simple record of our proof
In divers sufferings for the name of Christ,
Whereof the end already for the most
Is death this day with steadfast faith endured.

We were in prison many days, close-pent
In the black lower dungeon, housed with thieves

And murderers and divers evil men;
So foul a pressure, we had almost died,
Even there, in struggle for the breath of life
Amid the stench and unendurable heat;
Nor could we find each other save by voice
Or touch, to know that we were yet alive,
So terrible was the darkness. Yea, 'twas hard
To keep the sacred courage in our hearts,
When all was blind with that unchanging night,
And foul with death, and on our ears the taunts
And ribald curses of the soldiery
Fell mingled with the prisoners' cries, a load
Sharper to bear, more bitter than their blows.
At first what with that dread of our abode,
Our sudden apprehension, and the threats
Ringing perpetually in our ears, we lost
The living fire of faith, and like poor hinds
Would have denied our Lord and fallen away.
Even Perpetua, whose joyous faith
Was in the later holier days to be
The stay and comfort of our weaker ones,
Was silent for long whiles. Perchance she shrank
In the mere sickness of the flesh, confused
And shaken by our new and horrible plight—
The tender flesh, untempered and untried,
Not quickened yet nor mastered by the soul;
For she was of a fair and delicate make,
Most gently nurtured, to whom stripes and threats
And our foul prison-house were things undreamed.
But little by little as our spirits grew
Inured to suffering, with clasped hands, and tongues
That cheered each other to incessant prayer,

We rose and faced our trouble: we recalled
Our Master's sacred agony and death,
Setting before our eyes the high reward
Of steadfast faith, the martyr's deathless crown.

So passed some days whose length and count we lost,
Our bitterest trial.   Then a respite came.
One who had interest with the governor
Wrought our removal daily for some hours
Into an upper chamber, where we sat
And held each other's hands in childish joy,
Receiving the sweet gift of light and air
With wonder and exceeding thankfulness.
And then began that life of daily growth
In mutual exaltation and sweet help
That bore us as a gently widening stream
Unto the ocean of our martyrdom.
Uniting all our feebler souls in one—
A mightier—we reached forth with this to God.

Perpetua had been troubled for her babe,
Robbed of the breast and now these many days
Wasting for want of food; but when that change
Whereof I spake, of light and liberty
Relieved the horror of our prison gloom,
They brought it to her, and she sat apart,
And nursed and tended it, and soon the child
Would not be parted from her arms, but throve
And fattened, and she kept it night and day.
And always at her side with sleepless care
Hovered the young Felicitas—a slight
And spiritual figure—every touch and tone

Charged with premonitory tenderness,
Herself so near to her own motherhood.
Thus lightened and relieved, Perpetua
Recovered from her silent fit.   Her eyes
Regained their former deep serenity,
Her tongue its gentle daring; for she knew
Her life should not be taken till her babe
Had strengthened and outgrown the need of her.
Daily we were amazed at her soft strength,
Her pliant and untroubled constancy,
Her smiling, soldierly contempt of death,
Her beauty and the sweetness of her voice.

Her father, when our first few bitterest days
Were over like a gust of grief and rage,
Came to her in the prison with wild eyes,
And cried: 'How mean you, daughter, when you say
You are a Christian?   How can any one
Of honoured blood, the child of such as me,
Be Christian?   'Tis an odious name, the badge
Only of outcasts and rebellious slaves!'
And she, grief-touched, but with unyielding gaze,
Showing the fulness of her slender height:
'This vessel, father, being what it is,
An earthen pitcher, would you call it thus?
Or would you name it by some other name?'
'Nay, surely,' said the old man, catching breath,
And pausing, and she answered: 'Nor can I
Call myself aught but what I surely am—
A Christian!' and her father, flashing back
In silent anger, left her for that time.

A special favour to Perpetua
Seemed daily to be given, and her soul
Was made the frequent vessel of God's grace,
Wherefrom we all, less gifted, sore athirst,
Drank courage and fresh joy ; for glowing dreams
Were sent her, full of forms august, and fraught
With signs and symbols of the glorious end
Whereto God's love hath aimed us for Christ's sake.
Once—at what hour I know not, for we lay
In that foul dungeon where all hours were lost,
And day and night were indistinguishable—
We had been sitting a long silent while,
Some lightly sleeping, others bowed in prayer,
When on a sudden, like a voice from God,
Perpetua spake to us and all were roused.
Her voice was rapt and solemn : 'Friends,' she said,
'Some word hath come to me in a dream. I saw
A ladder leading to heaven, all of gold,
Hung up with lances, swords, and hooks. A land
Of darkness and exceeding peril lay
Around it, and a dragon fierce as hell
Guarded its foot. We doubted who should first
Essay it, but you, Saturus, at last—
So God hath marked you for especial grace—
Advancing and against the cruel beast
Aiming the potent weapon of Christ's name—
Mounted, and took me by the hand, and I
The next one following, and so the rest
In order, and we entered with great joy
Into a spacious garden filled with light
And balmy presences of love and rest ;

And there an old man sat, smooth-browed, white-
      haired,
Surrounded by unnumbered myriads
Of spiritual shapes and faces angel-eyed,
Milking his sheep; and lifting up his eyes
He welcomed us in strange and beautiful speech,
Unknown yet comprehended, for it flowed
Not through the ears, but forth-right to the soul,
God's language of pure love.   Between the lips
Of each he placed a morsel of sweet curd,
And while the curd was yet within my mouth,
I woke, and still the taste of it remains,
Through all my body flowing like white flame,
Sweet as of some immaculate spiritual thing.'
And when Perpetua had spoken, all
Were silent in the darkness, pondering,
But Saturus spake gently for the rest:
'How perfect and acceptable must be
Your soul to God, Perpetua, that thus
He bends to you, and through you speaks his will.
We know now that our martyrdom is fixed,
Nor need we vex us further for this life.'

While yet these thoughts were bright upon our souls,
There came the rumour that a day was set
To hear us.   Many of our former friends,
Some with entreaties, some with taunts and threats,
Came to us to pervert us; with the rest
Again Perpetua's father, worn with care,
Nor could we choose but pity his distress,
So miserably, with abject cries and tears,
He fondled her and called her 'Domina,'

And bowed his agèd body at her feet,
Beseeching her by all the names she loved
To think of him, his fostering care, his years,
And also of her babe, whose life, he said,
Would fail without her; but Perpetua,
Sustaining by a gift of strength divine
The fulness of her noble fortitude,
Answered him tenderly: 'Both you and I,
And all of us, my father, at this hour
Are equally in God's hands, and what he wills
Must be'; but when the poor old man was gone
She wept and knelt for many hours in prayer,
Sore tried and troubled by her tender heart.

One day while we were at our midday meal,
Our cell was entered by the soldiery,
And we were seized and borne away for trial.
A surging crowd had gathered, and we passed
From street to street, hemmed in by tossing heads
And faces cold or cruel; yet we caught
At moments from masked lips and furtive eyes
Of friends—some known to us and some unknown—
Many veiled messages of love and praise.
The floorways of the long basilica
Fronted us with an angry multitude;
And scornful eyes and threatening foreheads frowned
In hundreds from the columned galleries.
We were placed all together at the bar,
And though at first unsteadied and confused
By the imperial presence of the law,
The pomp of judgment and the staring crowd,
None failed or faltered; with unshaken tongue

Each met the stern Proconsul's brief demand
In clear profession.   Rapt as in a dream,
Scarce conscious of my turn, nor how I spake,
I watched with wondering eyes the delicate face
And figure of Perpetua; for her
We that were youngest of our company
Loved with a sacred and absorbing love,
A passion that our martyr's brotherly vow
Had purified and made divine.   She stood
In dreamy contemplation, slightly bowed,
A glowing stillness that was near a smile
Upon her soft closed lips.   Her turn had come,
When, like a puppet struggling up the steps,
Her father from the pierced and swaying crowd
Appeared, unveiling in his agèd arms
The smiling visage of her babe.   He grasped
Her robe and strove to draw her down.   All eyes
Were bent upon her.   With a softening glance,
And voice less cold and heavy with death's doom,
The old Proconsul turned to her and said:
'Lady, have pity on your father's age;
Be mindful of your tender babe; this grain
Of harmless incense offer for the peace
And welfare of the Emperor'; but she,
Lifting far forth her large and noteless eyes,
As one that saw a vision only said:
'I cannot sacrifice'; and he, harsh-tongued,
Bending a brow upon her rough as rock,
With eyes that struck like steel, seeking to break
Or snare her with a sudden stroke of fear:
'Art thou a Christian?' and she answered, 'Yea,
I am a Christian!'   In brow-blackening wrath

He motioned a contemptuous hand and bade
The lictors scourge the old man down and forth
With rods, and as the cruel deed was done,
Perpetua stood white with quivering lips,
And her eyes filled with tears. While yet his cries
Were mingling with the curses of the crowd,
Hilarianus, calling name by name,
Gave sentence, and in cold and formal phrase
Condemned us to the beasts, and we returned
Rejoicing to our prison. Then we wished
Our martyrdom could soon have followed, not
As doubting for our constancy, but some
Grew sick under the anxious long suspense.
Perpetua again was weighed upon
By grief and trouble for her babe, whom now
Her father, seeking to depress her will,
Withheld and would not send it; but at length
Word being brought her that the child indeed
No longer suffered, nor desired the breast,
Her peace returned and, giving thanks to God,
All were united in new bonds of hope.
Now being fixed in certitude of death,
We stripped our souls of all their earthly gear,
The useless raiment of this world; and thus,
Striving together with a single will,
In daily increment of faith and power,
We were much comforted by heavenly dreams,
And waking visitations of God's grace.
Visions of light and glory infinite
Were frequent with us, and by day or night
Woke at the very name of Christ the Lord,
Taken at any moment on our lips;

So that we had no longer thought or care
Of life or of the living, but became
As spirits from this earth already freed,
Scarce conscious of the dwindling weight of flesh.
To Saturus appeared in dreams the space
And splendour of the heavenly house of God,
The glowing gardens of eternal joy,
The halls and chambers of the cherubim,
In wreaths of endless myriads involved
The blinding glory of the angel choir,
Rolling through deeps of wheeling cloud and light
The thunder of their vast antiphonies.
The visions of Perpetua not less
Possessed us with their homely tenderness
As one, wherein she saw a rock-set pool
And weeping o'er its rim a little child,
Her brother, long since dead, Dinocrates:
Though sore athirst he could not reach the stream,
Being so small, and her heart grieved thereat.
She looked again, and lo! the pool had risen,
And the child filled his goblet, and drank deep,
And prattling in a tender childish joy
Ran gaily off, as infants do, to play.
By this she knew his soul had found release
From torment and had entered into bliss.

Quickly as by a merciful gift of God,
Our vigil passed unbroken. Yesternight
They moved us to the amphitheatre,
Our final lodging-place on earth, and there
We sat together at our agapè
For the last time. In silence, rapt and pale,

We hearkened to the agèd Saturus,
Whose speech, touched with a ghostly eloquence,
Canvassed the fraud and littleness of life,
God's goodness and the solemn joy of death.
Perpetua was silent, but her eyes
Fell gently upon each of us, suffused
With inward and eradiant light; a smile
Played often upon her lips.   While yet we sat,
A tribune with a band of soldiery
Entered our cell, and would have had us bound
In harsher durance, fearing our escape
By fraud or witchcraft; but Perpetua,
Facing him gently with a noble note
Of wonder in her voice, and on her lips
A lingering smile of mournful irony:
'Sir, are ye not unwise to harass us,
And rob us of our natural food and rest?
Should not ye rather tend us with soft care,
And so provide a comely spectacle?
We shall not honour Cæsar's birthday well,
If we be waste and weak, a piteous crew,
Poor playthings for your proud and pampered
    beasts.'
The noisy tribune, whether touched indeed,
Or by her grave and tender grace abashed,
Muttered and stormed a while, and then withdrew.
The short night passed in wakeful prayer for some,
For others in brief sleep, broken by dreams
And spiritual visitations.   Earliest dawn
Found us arisen, and Perpetua,
Moving about with smiling lips, soft-tongued,
Besought us to take food; lest so, she said,

For all the strength and courage of our hearts
Our bodies should fall faint. We heard without,
Already ere the morning light was full,
The din of preparation, and the hum
Of voices gathering in the upper tiers;
Yet had we seen so often in our thoughts
The picture of this strange and cruel death,
Its festal horror, and its bloody pomp,
The nearness scarcely moved us, and our hands
Met in a steadfast and unshaken clasp.

The day is over. Ah, my friend, how long
With its wild sounds and bloody sights it seemed!
Night comes, and I am still alive—even I,
The least and last—with other two, reserved
To grace to-morrow's second day. The rest
Have suffered and with holy rapture passed
Into their glory. Saturus and the men
Were given to bears and leopards, but the crowd
Feasted their eyes upon no cowering shape,
Nor hue of fear, nor painful cry. They died
Like armèd men, face foremost to the beasts,
With prayers and sacred songs upon their lips.
Perpetua and the frail Felicitas
Were seized before our eyes and roughly stripped,
And shrinking and entreating, not for fear,
Nor hurt, but bitter shame, were borne away
Into the vast arena, and hung up
In nets, naked before the multitude,
For a fierce bull, maddened by goads, to toss.
Some sudden tumult of compassion seized
The crowd, and a great murmur like a wave

Rose at the sight, and grew, and thundered up
From tier to tier, deep and imperious:
So white, so innocent they were, so pure:
Their tender limbs so eloquent of shame;
And so our loved ones were brought back, all faint,
And covered with light raiment, and again
Led forth, and now with smiling lips they passed
Pale, but unbowed, into the awful ring,
Holding each other proudly by the hand.

Perpetua first was tossed, and her robe rent,
But, conscious only of the glaring eyes,
She strove to hide herself as best she could
In the torn remnants of her flimsy robe,
And putting up her hands clasped back her hair,
So that she might not die as one in grief,
Unseemly and dishevelled. Then she turned,
And in her loving arms caressed and raised
The dying, bruised Felicitas. Once more
Gored by the cruel beast, they both were borne
Swooning and mortally stricken from the field.
Perpetua, pale and beautiful, her lips
Parted as in a lingering ecstasy,
Could not believe the end had come, but asked
When they were to be given to the beasts.
The keepers gathered round her—even they—
In wondering pity—while with fearless hand,
Bidding us all be faithful and stand firm,
She bared her breast, and guided to its goal
The gladiator's sword that pierced her heart.
16

The night is passing.　In a few short hours
I too shall suffer for the name of Christ.
A boundless exaltation lifts my soul!
I know that they who left us, Saturus,
Perpetua, and the other blessèd ones,
Await me at the opening gates of heaven.

THE MYSTERY OF A YEAR

A little while, a year agone,
　I knew her for a romping child,
A dimple and a glance that shone
　　With idle mischief when she smiled.

To-day she passed me in the press,
　And turning with a quick surprise
I wondered at her stateliness,
　　I wondered at her altered eyes.

To me the street was just the same,
　The people and the city's stir;
But life had kindled into flame,
　　And all the world was changed for her.

I watched her in the crowded ways,
　A noble form, a queenly head,
With all the woman in her gaze,
　　The conscious woman in her tread.

WINTER EVENING

To-night the very horses springing by
Toss gold from whitened nostrils. In a dream
The streets that narrow to the westward gleam
Like rows of golden palaces; and high
From all the crowded chimneys tower and die
A thousand aureoles. Down in the west
The brimming plains beneath the sunset rest,
One burning sea of gold. Soon, soon shall fly
The glorious vision, and the hours shall feel
A mightier master; soon from height to height,
With silence and the sharp unpitying stars,
Stern creeping frosts, and winds that touch like
    steel,
Out of the depth beyond the eastern bars,
Glittering and still shall come the awful night.

WAR

By the Nile, the sacred river,
  I can see the captive hordes
Strain beneath the lash and quiver
  At the long papyrus cords,
While in granite rapt and solemn,
Rising over roof and column,
  Amen-hotep dreams, or Ramses,
    Lord of Lords.

I can hear the trumpets waken
  For a victory old and far—

Carchemish or Kadesh taken—
　I can see the conquerer's car
Bearing down some Hittite valley,
Where the bowmen break and sally,
　Sargina or Esarhaddon,
　　Grim with war!

From the mountain streams that sweeten
　Indus, to the Spanish foam,
I can feel the broad earth beaten
　By the serried tramp of Rome;
Through whatever foes environ
Onward with the might of iron—
　Veni, vidi; veni, vici—
　　Crashing home!

I can see the kings grow pallid
　With astonished fear and hate,
As the hosts of Amr or Khaled
　On their cities fall like fate;
Like the heat-wind from its prison
In the desert burst and risen—
　La ilaha illah 'llahu—
　　God is great!

I can hear the iron rattle,
　I can see the arrows sting
In some far-off northern battle,
　Where the long swords sweep and swing;
I can hear the scalds declaiming,
I can see their eyeballs flaming,

Gathered in a frenzied circle
  Round the king.

I can hear the horn of Uri
  Roaring in the hills enorm;
Kindled at its brazen fury,
  I can see the clansmen form;
In the dawn in misty masses,
Pouring from the silent passes
  Over Granson or Morgarten
    Like the storm.

On the lurid anvil ringing
  To some slow fantastic plan,
I can hear the sword-smith singing
  In the heart of old Japan—
Till the cunning blade grows tragic
With his malice and his magic—
  Tenka tairan! Tenka tairan!
    War to man!

Where a northern river charges
  By a wild and moonlit glade,
From the murky forest marges,
  Round a broken palisade,
I can see the red men leaping,
See the sword of Daulac sweeping,
  And the ghostly forms of heroes
    Fall and fade.

I can feel the modern thunder
  Of the cannon beat and blaze,

When the lines of men go under
  On your proudest battle-days;
Through the roar I hear the lifting
Of the bloody chorus drifting
    Round the burning mill at Valmy—
      Marseillaise!

I can see the ocean rippled
  With the driving shot like rain,
While the hulls are crushed and crippled,
  And the guns are piled with slain;
O'er the blackened broad sea-meadow
Drifts a tall and titan shadow,
    And the cannon of Trafalgar
      Startle Spain.

Still the tides of fight are booming,
  And the barren blood is spilt;
Still the banners are up-looming,
  And the hands are on the hilt;
But the old world waxes wiser,
    From behind the bolted visor
    It descries at last the horror
      And the guilt.

Yet the eyes are dim, nor wholly
  Open to the golden gleam,
And the brute surrenders slowly
  To the godhead and the dream.
From his cage of bar and girder,
Still at moments mad with murder,

Leaps the tiger, and his demon
　　Rules supreme.

One more war with fire and famine
　　Gathers—I can hear its cries—
And the years of might and Mammon
　　Perish in a world's demise;
When the strength of man is shattered,
And the powers of earth are scattered,
　　From beneath the ghastly ruin
　　　　Peace shall rise!

THE WOODCUTTER'S HUT

Far up in the wild and wintry hills in the heart of the
　　cliff-broken woods,
Where the mounded drifts lie soft and deep in the
　　noiseless solitudes,
The hut of the lonely woodcutter stands, a few rough
　　beams that show
A blunted peak and a low black line, from the glitter-
　　ing waste of snow.
In the frost-still dawn from his roof goes up in the
　　windless, motionless air,
The thin, pink curl of leisurely smoke; through the
　　forest white and bare
The woodcutter follows his narrow trail, and the
　　morning rings and cracks
With the rhythmic jet of his sharp-blown breath and
　　the echoing shout of his axe.

Only the waft of the wind besides, or the stir of some
    hardy bird—
The call of the friendly chickadee, or the pat of the
    nut-hatch—is heard;
Or a rustle comes from a dusky clump, where the
    busy siskins feed,
And scatter the dimpled sheet of the snow with the
    shells of the cedar-seed.
Day after day the woodcutter toils untiring with axe
    and wedge,
Till the jingling teams come up from the road that
    runs by the valley's edge,
With plunging of horses, and hurling of snow, and
    many a shouted word,
And carry away the keen-scented fruit of his cutting,
    cord upon cord.
Not the sound of a living foot comes else, not a
    moving visitant there,
Save the delicate step of some halting doe, or the
    sniff of a prowling bear.
And only the stars are above him at night, and the
    trees that creak and groan,
And the frozen, hard-swept mountain-crests with
    their silent fronts of stone,
As he watches the sinking glow of his fire and the
    wavering flames upcaught,
Cleaning his rifle or mending his moccasins, sleepy
    and slow of thought.
Or when the fierce snow comes, with the rising wind,
    from the gray north-east,
He lies through the leaguering hours in his bunk
    like a winter-hidden beast,

Or sits on the hard-packed earth, and smokes by his
    draught-blown guttering fire,
Without thought or remembrance, hardly awake,
    and waits for the storm to tire.
Scarcely he hears from the rock-rimmed heights to
    the wild ravines below,
Near and far off, the limitless wings of the tempest
    hurl and go
In roaring gusts that plunge through the cracking
    forest, and lull, and lift,
All day without stint and all night long with the
    sweep of the hissing drift.
But winter shall pass ere long with its hills of snow
    and its fettered dreams,
And the forest shall glimmer with living gold, and
    chime with the gushing of streams;
Millions of little points of plants shall prick through
    its matted floor,
And the wind-flower lift and uncurl her silken buds
    by the woodman's door;
The sparrow shall see and exult; but lo! as the
    spring draws gaily on,
The woodcutter's hut is empty and bare, and the
    master that made it is gone.
He is gone where the gathering of valley men
    another labour yields,
To handle the plough and the harrow, and scythe,
    in the heat of the summer fields.
He is gone with his corded arms, and his ruddy face,
    and his moccasined feet,
The animal man in his warmth and vigour, sound,
    and hard, and complete.

And all summer long, round the lonely hut, the black
    earth burgeons and breeds,
Till the spaces are filled with the tall-plumed ferns
    and the triumphing forest-weeds;
The thick wild raspberries hem its walls, and stretch-
    ing on either hand,
The red-ribbed stems and the giant-leaves of the
    sovereign spikenard stand.
So lonely and silent it is, so withered and warped
    with the sun and snow,
You would think it the fruit of some dead man's toil
    a hundred years ago;
And he who finds it suddenly there, as he wanders far
    and alone,
Is touched with a sweet and beautiful sense of some-
    thing tender and gone,
The sense of a struggling life in the waste, and the
    mark of a soul's command,
The going and coming of vanished feet, the touch of
    a human hand.

AMOR VITÆ

I love the warm bare earth and all
    That works and dreams thereon:
I love the seasons yet to fall:
    I love the ages gone,

The valleys with the sheeted grain,
    The river's smiling might,

The merry wind, the rustling rain,
  The vastness of the night.

I love the morning's flame, the steep
  Where down the vapour clings:
I love the clouds that float and sleep,
  And every bird that sings.

I love the purple shower that pours
  On far-off fields at even:
I love the pine-wood dusk whose floors
  Are like the courts of heaven.

I love the heaven's azure span,
  The grass beneath my feet:
I love the face of every man
  Whose thought is swift and sweet.

I let the wrangling world go by,
  And like an idle breath
Its echoes and its phantoms fly:
  I care no jot for death.

Time like a Titan bright and strong
  Spreads one enchanted gleam:
Each hour is but a fluted song,
  And life a lofty dream.

WINTER-BREAK

All day between high-curded clouds the sun
Shone down like summer on the steaming planks.
The long bright icicles in dwindling ranks
Dripped from the murmuring eaves till one by one
They fell. As if the spring had now begun,
The quilted snow, sun-softened to the core,
Loosened and shunted with a sudden roar
From downward roofs. Not even with day done
Had ceased the sound of waters, but all night
I heard it. In my dreams forgetfully bright
Methought I wandered in the April woods,
Where many a silver-piping sparrow was,
By gurgling brooks and sprouting solitudes,
And stooped, and laughed, and plucked hepaticas.

SONNETS

AN INVOCATION

Spirit of joy and that enchanted air
  That feeds the poet's parted lips like wine,
  I dreamed and wandered hand in hand of thine,
How many a blissful day; but doubt and care,
The ghostly masters of this world, did come
  With torturous malady and hid the day,
  A gnawing flame that robbed my songs away,
And bound mine ears, and made me blind and
      dumb.
Master of mine, and Lord of light and ease,
  Return, return, and take me by the hand;
  Lead me again into that pleasant land,
  Whose charmèd eyes and griefless lips adore
  No lord but beauty; let me see once more
The light upon her golden palaces.

A MORNING SUMMONS

Upon the outer verge of sleep I heard
  A little sparrow piping in the morn;
  Unto my very heart the sound was borne;
It seemed to me a something more than bird,

Even Nature's self that touched me with a word:—
  "While thou sleep'st on, I have not done **my**
    duty.
  Awake, O man! Of all this gift of beauty
Lose not one grain. The forest deeps are stirred
With morning, and the brooks are loud aflow."
Perhaps it was a dream, but this I know,
  Behind me, as I passed into the sun,
    Whether to me or each one to his mate,
  I heard the little sparrows one by one
    Piping in triumph at my garden gate.

NESTING TIME

The bees are busy in their murmurous search,
The birds are putting up their woven frames,
And all the twigs and branches of the birch
Are shooting into tiny emerald flames:
The maple leaves are spreading slowly out
Like small red hats, or pointed parasols.
The high-ho flings abroad his merry shout,
The veery from the inner brushwood calls:
The gold-green poplar, jocund as may be,
The sunshine in its laughing heart receives,
And shimmers in the wind innumerably
Through all its host of little lacquered leaves.
And lo! the bob-o-link—he soars and sings,
With all the heart of summer in his wings.

THE SPIRIT OF THE HOUSE

These four gray walls are but the bodily shell,
Whereof my lady of the brave blue eyes
Is the immortal soul. All sweet replies
And viewless records of a touch known well
That like the tone within a golden bell
Pervade them with a gentle atmosphere,
These things are just herself—she being here—
The breath that makes the rose-tree sweet to smell.
Through sunshine, and gray shadow, and through
        gloom,
With mirth and gracious courage for her ways,
And goodness ever forth, but never spent,
She passes with light hands from room to room,
And beauty grows before her, and the days
Are full, and quietly rounded, and content.

APRIL VOICES

To-day all throats are touched with life's full
        treasure;
Even the blackbirds in yon leafless tree,
    Wheezing and squeaking in discordant glee,
Make shift to sing, and full of pensive pleasure
Here the bold robin sits and at his leisure
    Whistles and warbles disconnectedly,
    As if he were too happy and too free
To trim his notes and sing a perfect measure.
Across the steaming meadows all day long,
    I hear the murmur of the frogs. In schools

17

Shy harping lizards pipe about the pools.
   From hedge and roof and many a garden gate,
The cheery sparrow still repeats his song,
   So clear, so silver sweet, and delicate.

BEAUTY

Only the things of Beauty shall endure.
While man goes woeful, wasting his brief day,
From Truth and Love and Nature far astray,
Lo! Beauty, the lost goal, the unsought cure;
For how can he whom Beauty hath made sure,
Who hath her law and sovereign creed by heart,
Be proud, or pitiless, play the tyrant's part,
Be false, or envious, greedy or impure.
Nay! she will gift him with a golden key
To unlock every virtue.   Name not ye,
As once, "the good, the beautiful, the true,"
For these are but three names for one sole thing;
Or rather Beauty is the perfect ring
That circles and includes the other two.

ON THE COMPANIONSHIP WITH NATURE

Let us be much with Nature; not as they
That labour without seeing, that employ
Her unloved forces, blindly without joy;
Nor those whose hands and crude delights obey

The old brute passion to hunt down and slay;
But rather as children of one common birth,
Discerning in each natural fruit of earth
Kinship and bond with this diviner clay.
Let us be with her wholly at all hours,
With the fond lover's zest, who is content
If his ear hears, and if his eye but sees;
So shall we grow like her in mould and bent,
Our bodies stately as her blessèd trees,
Our thoughts as sweet and sumptuous as her
   flowers.

IN THE CITY

I wandered in a city great and old,
At morn, at noon, and when the evening fell,
And round my spirit gathered like a spell
Its splendour and its tumult and its gold,
The mysteries and the memories of its years,
Its victors and fair women, all the life,
The joy, the power, the passion, and the strife,
Its sighs of hand-locked lovers, and its tears.
And whereso in that mighty city, free
And with clear eyes and eager heart I trod,
My thought became a passion high and strong,
And all the spirit of humanity,
Soft as a child and potent as a god,
Drew near to me, and rapt me like a song.

MUSIC

O, take the lute this brooding hour for me—
The golden lute, the hollow crying lute—
Nor call me even with thine eyes; be mute,
And touch the strings; yea, touch them tenderly;
Touch them and dream, till all thine heart in thee
Grow great and passionate and sad and wild.
Then on me, too, as on thine heart, O child,
The marvellous light, the stress divine shall be,
And I shall see, as with enchanted eyes,
The unveiled vision of this world flame by,
Battles and griefs, and storms and phantasies,
The gleaming joy, the ever-seething fire,
The hero's triumph and the martyr's cry,
The pain, the madness, the unsearched desire.

THE PIANO

Low brooding cadences that dream and cry
Life's stress and passion echoing straight and clear;
Wild flights of notes that clamour and beat high
Into the storm and battle, or drop sheer;
Strange majesties of sound beyond all words
Ringing on clouds and thunderous heights
　　　sublime;
Sad detonance of golden tones and chords
That tremble with the secret of all time;
O wrap me round; for one exulting hour
Possess my soul, and I indeed shall know

The wealth of living, the desire, the power,
The tragic sweep, the Apollonian glow;
All life shall stream before me; I shall see,
With eyes unblanched, Time and Eternity.

MAY

The broad earth smiles in open benison,
An emerald sea, whose waves of leaf and shade
On far-off shores of misty turquoise fade;
And all the host of life steers blithely on,
With joy for captain, fancy at the helm:
The woodpecker taps roundly at his tree,
The vaulting high-ho flings abroad his glee
In fluty laughter from the towering elm.
Here at my feet are violets, and below—
A gracile spirit tremulously alive—
Spring water fills a little greenish pool,
Paved all with mottled leaves and crystal cool.
Beyond it stands a plum-tree in full blow,
Creamy with bloom, and humming like a hive.

EUPHRONE

O soft-cheeked mother, O belovèd night,
Dispeller of black thoughts and mortal dreads,
Drowner of sorrows. In how many beds,
Betwixt the evening and the dawning light,
Thy tenderness, thy pity infinite,
Hath it not poured nepenthe, soft as rain,

On thankful lids that have forgotten pain,
Forgotten grief, forgotten care and spite!
How many lovers also side by side,
After long waiting such a weary while,
Now with arms locked, cheeks touching,
    satisfied,
Sleep, and their one great hour returns to thee,
On these too dost thou not incline thy smile,
Tender with welcome, Mother Euphrone?

ACROSS THE PEA-FIELDS

Field upon field to westward hum and shine
  The gray-green sun-drenched mists of blossom-
    ing peas;
  Beyond them are great elms and poplar trees
That guard the noon-stilled farm-yards, groves of
    pine,
And long dark fences muffled thick with vine;
  Then the high city, murmurous with mills;
  And last upon the sultry west blue hills,
Misty, far-lifted, a mere filmy line.
Across these blackening rails into the light
  I lean and listen, lolling drowsily;
On the fence corner, yonder to the right,
  A red squirrel whisks and chatters; nearer by
    A little old brown woman on her knees
    Searches the deep hot grass for strawberries.

NIGHT

Come with thine unveiled worlds, O truth of night,
  Come with thy calm. Adown the shallow day,
  Whose splendours hid the vaster world away,
I wandered on this little plot of light,
A dreamer among dreamers. Veiled or bright,
  Whether the gold shower roofed me or the gray,
  I strove and fretted at life's feverish play,
And dreamed until the dream seemed infinite.

But now the gateway of the All unbars;
  The passions and the cares that beat so shrill,
    The giants of this petty world, disband;
    On the great threshold of the night I stand,
  Once more a soul self-cognizant and still,
Among the wheeling multitude of stars.

SALVATION

Nature hath fixed in each man's life for dower
One root-like gift, one primal energy,
Wherefrom the soul takes growth, as grows a tree,
With sap and fibre, branch and leaf and flower;
But if this seed in its creative hour
Be crushed and stifled, only then the shell
Lifts like a phantom falsely visible,
Wherein is neither growth, nor joy, nor power.
Find thou this germ, and find thou thus thyself,
This one clear meaning of the deathless I,

This bent, this work, this duty—for thereby
God numbers thee, and marks thee for His own:
Careless of hurt, or threat, or praise, or pelf,
Find it and follow it, this, and this alone!

AFTER THE SHOWER

The shower is past, ere it hath well begun.
The enormous clouds are rolling up like steam
Into the illimitable blue.   They gleam
In summits of banked snow against the sun.
The old dry beds begin to laugh and run,
As if 'twere spring.   The trees in the wind's stir
Shower down great drops, and every gossamer
Glitters a net of diamonds fresh-spun.
The happy flowers put on a spritelier grace,
Star-flower and smilacina creamy-hued,
With little spires of honey-scent and light,
And that small, dainty violet, pure and white,
That holds by magic in its twisted face
The heart of all the perfumes of the wood.

IN ABSENCE

My love is far away from me to-night,
O spirits of sweet peace, kind destinies,
Watch over her, and breathe upon her eyes;
Keep near to her in every hurt's despite,

That no rude care or noisome dream affright.
   So let her rest, so let her sink to sleep,
   As little clouds that breast the sunset steep
Merge and melt out into the golden light.
My love is far away and I am grown
   A very child, oppressed with formless glooms,
Some shadowy sadness with a name unknown
   Haunts the chill twilight, and these silent rooms
Seem with vague fears and dim regrets astir,
Lonesome and strange and empty without her.

TO THE WARBLING VIREO

Sweet little prattler, whom the morning sun
   Found singing, and this livelong summer day
   Keeps warbling still: here have I dreamed away
Two bright and happy hours, that passed like one,
Lulled by thy silvery converse, just begun
   And never ended. Thou dost preach to me
   Sweet patience and her guest, reality,
The sense of days, and weeks, and months that run
Scarce altering in their round of happiness,
   And quiet thoughts, and toils that do not kill,
And homely pastimes. Though the old distress
   Loom gray above us both at times, ah, still,
Be constant to thy woodland note, sweet bird;
By me at least thou shalt be loved and heard.

THE PASSING OF THE SPIRIT

The wind—the world-old rhapsodist—goes by,
And the great pines in changeless vesture gloomed,
And all the towering elm-trees thatched and plumed
With green, take up, one after one, the cry,
And as their choral voices swell and die,
Catching the infinite note from tree to tree,
Others far off in long antistrophe
With swaying arms and surging tops reply.
So to men's souls, at sacred intervals,
Out of the dust of life takes wing and calls
A spirit that we know not, nor can trace,
And heart to heart makes answer with strange
    thrill,
It passes, and a moment face to face
We dream ourselves immortal, and are still.

XENOPHANES

While knowledge and high wisdom yet were young,
Through Sicily of old, from tryst to tryst,
Wandered with sad-set brow and eloquent tongue,
The melancholy, austere rhapsodist:
'All my life long,' he cried, 'by many ways
I follow truth where devious footmarks fall;
Now I am old, and still my spirit strays,
Mocked and eluded, lost amid the All.'
That was Mind's youth, and ages long ago,
And still thine hunger, O Xenophanes,

Preys on the hearts of men ; and to and fro,
They probe the same implacable mysteries :
The same vast toils oppress them, and they bear
The same unquenchable hope, the same despair.

IN THE PINE GROVES

I

Here is a quiet place where one may dream
The hours away and be content.   It shines
With many a shadow spot and golden gleam
Under the murmur of these priestly pines.
About the level russet-matted floor,
Each like a star in his appointed station,
The sole-flowered scented pyrolas by the score
Stand with heads drooped in fragrant meditation.
The pensive thrush, the hermit of the wood,
Dreams far within, and piping at his leisure,
Tells to the hills the forest's inmost mood
Of memory and its solitary pleasure.
Earth only and sun are here, and shadow and trees
And thoughts that are eternal even as these.

II

Almost till noon I kept the weary road,
Amid the dust and din of passing teams,
With a soul shaped to its accustomed load
Of silly cares and microscopic dreams :

But here a nobler influence is unfurled;
It is no more the present petty hour,
But Time, and all the pine-groves of the world
Enfold my spirit in their pensive power.
Behold this little speedwell: Time shall flow,
Customs and commonwealths and faiths shall pass,
And be as they had never been; not so
The little pale blue speedwell in the grass,
Whatever change shall fall of good or ill,
Grave eyes shall mark the little speedwell still.

SIRIUS

The old night waned, and all the purple dawn
Grew pale with green and opal.   The wide earth
Lay darkling and strange and silent as at birth,
Save for a single far-off brightness drawn
Of water gray as steel.   The silver bow
Of broad Orion still pursued the night,
And farther down, amid the gathering light,
A great star leaped and smouldered.   Standing so,
I dreamed myself in Denderah by the Nile;
Beyond the hall of columns and the crowd
And the vast pylons, I beheld afar
The goddess gleam, and saw the morning smile,
And lifting both my hands, I cried aloud
In joy to Hathor, smitten by her star!

AT DUSK

Already o'er the west the first star shines,
  And day and dark are imperceptibly linked;
  The fences and pied fields grow indistinct,
Deep beyond deep the living light declines,
Still lingering o'er the westward mountain lines,
  Pallid and clear; and on its silent breast
  A symbol of eternal quiet rest,
Far and black-plumed, the imperturbable pines.
A few thin threads of purple clouds still float
  In the serene ether, and the night wind,
    Wandering in puffs from off the darkening hill,
    Breathes warm or cool; and now the whip-
        poor-will,
  Beyond the river margins glassed and thinned,
Whips the cool hollows with his liquid note.

DEAD CITIES

I

Phantoms of many a dead idolatry,
Dream-rescued from oblivion, in mine ear
Your very names are strange and great to hear,
A sound of ancientness and majesty,
  Memphis and Shushan, Carthage, Meroë,
And crowned, before these ages rose, with fame,
Troja, long vanished in Achæan flame,
On and Cyrene, perished utterly.

Things old and strange and dim to dream upon,
Cumæ and Sardis, cities waste and gone;
And that pale river by whose ghostly strand
Thebes' monstrous tombs and desolate altars
    stand,
Baalbec, and Tyre, and buried Babylon,
And ruined Tadmor in the desert sand.

II

Of Ur and Erech and Accad who shall tell
And Calneh in the land of Shinar. Time
Hath made them but the substance of a rhyme.
And where are Ninus and the towers that fell,
When Jahveh's anger was made visible?
Where now are Sepharvaim and its dead?
Hammath and Arpad? In their ruined stead
The wild ass and the maneless lion dwell.
In Pœstum now the roses bloom no more,
But the wind wails about the barren shore,
An echo in its gloomed and ghostly reeds.
And many a city of an elder age,
Now nameless, fallen in some antique rage,
Lies worn to dust, and none shall know its deeds.

A MIDNIGHT LANDSCAPE

A great black cloud from heaven's midmost height
  Hangs all to eastward roofing half the world,
  Whereunder in vast shadow stretches furled
A waste, meseems, where never leaf nor light

Might be, but only darkness infinite,
   Where the lost heroes of old dreams oppressed
   Might still be wandering on some dolorous quest,
A land of witchcraft and accursed blight.
Lapping the border of that huge distress,
   A pallid stream from valleys gnarled and dim
Comes creeping with a Stygian silentness;
   While yonder southward at the cloud's last rim
      Antares from the Scorpion burns afar,
      With surge and baleful gleam, the fierce red star!

TO CHAUCER

   'Twas high mid-spring, when thou wert here on
      earth,
   Chaucer, and the new world was just begun;
   For thee 'twas pastime and immortal mirth
   To work and dream beneath the pleasant sun,
   Full glorious were the hearty ways of man,
   And God above was great and wise and good,
   Thy soul sufficient for its earthly span,
   Thy body brave and full of dancing blood.
   Such was thy faith, O master! We believe
   Neither in God, humanity, nor self;
   Even the votaries of place and pelf
   Pass by firm-footed, while we build and weave
   With doubt and restless care. Too well we see
   The drop of life lost in eternity.

BY THE SEA

At morn beside the ocean's foamy roar
  I walked soft-shadowed through the luminous mist,
  And saw not clearly, sea or land, nor wist
Where the tide stayed, nor where began the shore.
A gentle seaward wind came down, and bore
  The scent of roses and of bay-berry;
  And through the great gray veil that hid the sea
Broke the pale sun—a silvery warmth—not more.
So through the fogs that cover all this life
  I walk as in a dream 'twixt sea and land—
The meadows of wise thought, the sea of strife—
  And sounds and happy scents from either hand
    Come with vast gleams that spread and softly
    shine.
    The joy of life, the energy divine.

A NIAGARA LANDSCAPE

Heavy with haze that merges and melts free
  Into the measureless depth on either hand,
  The full day rests upon the luminous land
In one long noon of golden reverie.
Now hath the harvest come and gone with glee.
  The shaven fields stretch smooth and clean away,
  Purple and green, and yellow, and soft gray,
Chequered with orchards. Farther still I see
Towns and dim villages, whose roof-tops fill
  The distant mist, yet scarcely catch the view.

Thorold set sultry on its plateau'd hill,
  And far to westward, where yon pointed towers
Rise faint and ruddy from the vaporous blue,
  Saint Catharines, city of the host of flowers.

THE PILOT

The skilful pilot from the windy prow
Watches far off the markings of the sea,
And knows, long-studied in its charactery,
What rocks, what shoals, what currents hide
      below.
This can the skilful pilot do, with brow
Serene and certain; but not so to me
That mouth, those eyes, a subtler mystery,
Yield up the secrets of the heart.   I know,
Poring upon the soul-chart of your face,
That all my searching, all my skill are vain.
I do but follow on some broken trace,
And please myself with guessing.   Joy concurs
With grief, but neither can the script explain,
So veiled and various are the characters.

A SUNSET AT LES EBOULEMENTS

Broad shadows fall.   On all the mountain side
The scythe-swept fields are silent.   Slowly home
By the long beach the high-piled hay-carts come,
Splashing the pale salt shallows.   Over wide
      18

Fawn-coloured wastes of mud the slipping tide,
Round the dun rocks and wattled fisheries,
Creeps murmuring in.   And now by twos and
    threes,
O'er the slow spreading pools with clamorous
    chide,
Belated crows from strip to strip take flight.
Soon will the first star shine; yet ere the night
Reach onward to the pale-green distances,
The sun's last shaft beyond the gray sea-floor
Still dreams upon the Kamouraska shore,
And the long line of golden villages.

THAMYRIS

Œchalian Eurytus in his hall
Held feast; and, charged with triumph and with
    wine,
Wrought to a glowing madness half divine,
The Thracian Thamyris sang, and held in thrall
The kings and leaning heroes, each and all;
And there he challenged, standing with raised head,
The Zeus-born Muses, offering, void of dread,
To meet and match them in the song, nor fall
In aught behind, nor yield the mastery;
But him, when his great spirit seemed most strong,
Leading at cool of dawn their sacred round,
The vengeful daughters of Mnemosyne
In the gray gorges near Eurotas found,
And made him blind, and took away his song.

Now by the gate at Argos, where the way
Brings all the traffic in from Argolis,
Gray-haired and full of grief, sits Thamyris,
Blind; and his numbed and witless fingers stray
Among the broken harp-strings—so men say—
And ever, when feet pass, he lifts his eyes,
Sightless and robbed of all their fire, and cries
With a great warning twenty times a day:
'The proud and boastful man who grasps a crown
For his own greatness, him the gods strike down.
Heroes and Bards know that it is not ye
That make yourselves, but a god gave it you;
Therefore walk heedfully, holding as is due
Your sacred gift with thankful mind in fee.'

THE DEATH OF TENNYSON

They tell that when his final hour drew near,
He whose fair praise the ages shall rehearse,
Whom now the living and the dead hold dear;
Our gray-haired master of immortal verse,
Called for his Shakespeare, and with touch of rue
Turned to that page in stormy Cymbeline
That bears the dirge. Whether he read none knew,
But on the book he laid his hand serene,
And kept it there unshaken, till there fell
The last gray change, and from before his eyes,
This glorious world that Shakespeare loved so well,
Slowly, as at a beck, without surprise—
Its woe, its pride, its passion, and its play—
Like mists and melting shadows passed away.

STORM VOICES

The night grows old; again and yet again
　The tempest wakens round the whistling height,
　And all the winds like loosened hounds take flight
With bay and halloo, and the wintry rain
Sweeps the drenched roof, and blears the narrow
　　　pane.
　There is a surging horror in the night;
　The woods far out are roaring in their might;
The curtains sway; the rafters creak and strain:
And as I dream, o'er all my spirit swims
　　A passion sad and holy as the tomb;
　Strange human voices cry into mine ear;
　Out of the vexèd dark I seem to hear
Vast organ thunders, and a burst of hymns
　　That swell and soar in some cathedral gloom.

TO A MILLIONAIRE

The world in gloom and splendour passes by,
And thou in the midst of it with brows that gleam,
A creature of that old distorted dream
That makes the sound of life an evil cry.
Good men perform just deeds, and brave men die,
And win not honour such as gold can give,
While the vain multitudes plod on, and live,
And serve the curse that pins them down:　But I
Think only of the unnumbered broken hearts,
The hunger and the mortal strife for bread,

Old age and youth alike mistaught, misfed,
By want and rags and homelessness made vile,
The griefs and hates, and all the meaner parts
That balance thy one grim misgotten pile.

THE MODERN POLITICIAN

What manner of soul is his to whom high truth
Is but the plaything of a feverish hour,
A dangling ladder to the ghost of power!
Gone are the grandeurs of the world's iron youth,
When kings were mighty, being made by swords.
Now comes the transit age, the age of brass,
When clowns into the vacant empires pass,
Blinding the multitude with specious words.
To them faith, kinship, truth and verity,
Man's sacred rights and very holiest thing,
Are but the counters at a desperate play,
Flippant and reckless what the end may be,
So that they glitter, each his little day,
The little mimic of a vanished king.

VIRTUE

I deem that virtue but a thing of straw
That is not self-subsistent, needs the press
Of sharp-eyed custom, or the point of law
To teach it honour, justice, gentleness.

His soul is but a shadow who does well
Through lure of gifts or terror of the rod,
Some painted paradise or pictured hell,
Not for the love but for the fear of God.
Him only do I honour in whom right,
Not the sour product of some grudged control,
Flows from a Godlike habit, whose clear soul,
Bathed in the noontide of an inward light,
In its own strength and beauty is secure,
Too proud to lie, too proud to be impure.

FALLING ASLEEP

Slowly my thoughts lost hold on consciousness
    Like waves that urge but cannot reach the shore:
    Once and again I wakened and once more
The wind sighed in, and with a lingering stress
Brushed the loose blinds.   Out of some far recess
    There came the stealthy creaking of a door
    The mice ran scuffling underneath the floor;
And then when all the house stood motionless,
Something dropped sharply overhead; a deep
Dead silence followed; only half aware,
    I groped and strove to waken and fell flat;
    A moment after, step by step, a cat
Came plumping softly down the attic stair;
And then I turned and then I fell asleep.

PASSION

As slowly on a mountain slope toward spring
The soft snows gather week by week, and charge
The peaks and slanted ridges smooth and large
With drifts that hang light-poised and glistening:
Then sharply on the hidden key by chance
An echo strikes, and like a storm unpinned,
Down from a hundred ledges light as wind,
Loosens and shoots the thundering avalanche.
So in the soul our passions year by year
By the cool winds of custom banked and rolled,
Gather and deftly balance, and hang clear;
Then on the inner master-chord one day
Some fateful shock intrudes, and all gives way
In wild descent and ruin manifold.

THE RUIN OF THE YEAR

Along the hills and by the sleeping stream
A warning falls, and all the glorious trees—
Vestures of gold and grand embroideries—
Stand mute, as in a sad and beautiful dream,
Brooding on death and Nature's vast undoing,
And spring that came an age ago and fled,
And summer's splendour long since drawn to head,
And now the fall and all the slow soft ruin:
And soon some day comes by the pillaging wind,
The winter's wild outrider, with harsh roar,

And leaves the meadows sacked and waste and
     thinned,
And strips the forest of its golden store;
Till the grim tyrant comes, and then they sow
The silent wreckage, not with salt, but snow.

THE CUP OF LIFE

One after one the high emotions fade;
   Time's wheeling measure empties and refills
   Year after year; we seek no more the hills
That lured our youth divine and unafraid,
But swarming on some common highway, made
   Beaten and smooth, plod onward with blind feet
   And only where the crowded crossways meet
We halt and question, anxious and dismayed.
Yet can we not escape it; some we know
   Have angered and grown mad, some scornfully
        laughed;
        Yet surely to each lip—to mine to thine—
Comes with strange scent and pallid poisonous
        glow
   The cup of Life, that dull Circean draught,
      That taints us all, and turns the half to swine.

THE MARCH OF WINTER

They that have gone by forest paths shall hear
   The outcry of worn reeds and leaves long shed,

The rise and sound of waters.   Overhead,
Out of the wide northwest, wind-stripped and clear,
Like some great army dense with battle gear,
   All day the columned clouds come marching on,
   Long hastening lines in sombre unison,
Vanguard, and centre, and still deepening rear;
While from the waste beyond the barren verge
   Drives the great wind with hoof and thong set
      free,
And buffets and wields high its whistling scourge
   Around the roofs, or in tempestuous glee,
Over the far-off woods with tramp and surge,
   Huge and deep-tongued, goes roaring like the
      sea.

SORROW

At last I fell· asleep, and a sweet dream,
For respite and for peace, was given to me;
But in the dawn I wakened suddenly,
And like a fiery swift and stinging stream
Returned, with fear and horror, the supreme͵
Remembrance of my sorrow.   All my mind
Grew hot within me.   As one sick and blind,
Round and still round an old and fruitless theme,
I toiled, nor saw the golden morning light,
Nor heard the sparrows singing, but the sweat
Beaded my brow and made my pillow wet.
So seared and withered as a plant with blight,
Eaten by passion, stripped of all my pride,
I wished that somehow then I might have died.

LOVE

How much of wasteful grief, and fruitless sighs,
O Passion, whom men justly name the blind,
How many crimes, how many miseries,
Scored in the tragic story of mankind
Accuse your power! With what strange care you
    bind
And part for ever with your charmèd lies,
Unmated bosoms and unknowing eyes!
How rarely in your barren search you find
The two who in some fair and fortunate hour
Know at a glance each other's absolute power—
A single touch, a single tone, betraying
The truth adorned in ancient song and fable,
And rush into each other's arms, obeying
An impulse perfect and inevitable.

TO DEATH

Methought in dreams I saw my little son—
My little son that in his cradle died;
No more a babe, but all his childhood done,
A full-grown man.   Deep-browed and tender-eyed,
I knew him by the subtle touch of me,
And by his mother's look, and by the eyes
We hold in such remembrance piteously,
And the bright smile so quick for sweet replies.
O Death, I would that from thy front of stone
My grief could wring one word, or my tears draw

On the strange night of life, one single gleam!
Was he whom by the gift of sleep I saw
The living shape of my belovèd gone,
My very son, or but a fleeting dream.

THE VAIN FIGHT

Such a grim fight we fought for thee with death
As never hero in the ancient gloom,
With swollen brows, strained cords, and labouring
        breath,
Fought for Alcestis by the rocky tomb.
In vain.   Thou wert too beautiful, too pure,
Too tender and too frail for earthly life.
Thou wert in love with Death, nor could'st endure
Even the dawnrise of this day of strife.
Ah! thou art gone, who scarcely saw the day,
Fair little comrade of one fleeting while,
And we must travel our appointed space,
Nor ever for the brightening of our way
Behold again on any living face
That matchless kindred look, that touching smile.

EARTH—THE STOIC

Earth, like a goblet empty of delight,
  Empty of summer and balm-breathing hours,
  Empty of music, empty of all flowers,
Now with that other draught of death and night

And loss, and iron bitterness refills.
   The upland rifts are gleaming white with snow
   The north wind pipes, the forest groans below,
The clouds are heaping grandly on the hills.

Yet thou complainest not, O steadfast Earth,
   Beautiful mother with thy stoic fields;
In all the ages since thy fiery birth
   Deep in thine own wide heart thou findest still
Whatever comforts and whatever shields,
   And plannest also for us the same sheer will.

STOIC AND HEDONIST

The cup of knowledge emptied to its lees,
Soft dreamers in a perfumed atmosphere,
Ye turn, and from your luminous reveries
Follow with curious eyes and biting sneer
Yon grave-eyed men, to whom alone are sweet
Strength and self-rule, who move with stately tread,
And reck not if the earth beneath your feet
With bitter herb or blossoming rose be spread.
Ye smile and frown, and yet for all your art,
Supple and shining as the ringèd snake,
And all your knowledge, all your grace of heart,
Is there not one thing missing from your make—
The thing that is life's acme, and its key—
The stoic's grander portion—Dignity.

AVARICE

Beware of avarice! It is the sin
That hath no pardon either in death or here,
For it means cruelty.   Hatred and fear
Enter the soul, and are the lords therein.
The gold that gathers at the rich man's knees
Is stored with curses and with dead men's bones,
And women's cries and little children's moans,
The harvest of ten thousand miseries.
What needs it to be rich—only a soul,
Deaf to the shaken tongue and blind to tears,
The sordid patience of the sightless mole!
Would'st thou thus waste the sacred span of
    years?
Lock up the doors of life and break the key,
The simple heart-touch with humanity?

TO AN ULTRA PROTESTANT

Why rage and fret thee; only let them be:
The monkish rod, the sacerdotal pall,
Council and convent, Pope and Cardinal,
The black priest and his holy wizardry.
Nay dread them not, for thought and liberty
Spread ever faster than the foe can smite,
And these shall vanish as the starless night
Before a morning mightier than the sea.
But what of thee and thine?   That battle cry?
Those forms and dogmas that thou rear'st so high?

Those blasts of doctrine and those vials of wrath?
Thy hell for most and heaven for the few?
That narrow, joyless and ungenerous path?
What then of these?　Ah, they shall vanish too!

A JANUARY MORNING

The glittering roofs are still with frost; each worn
Black chimney builds into the quiet sky
Its curling pile to crumble silently.
Far out to westward on the edge of morn,
The slender misty city towers up-borne
Glimmer faint rose against the pallid blue;
And yonder on those northern hills, the hue
Of amethyst, hang fleeces dull as horn.
And here behind me come the woodmen's sleighs
With shouts and clamorous squeakings; might and
　　main
Up the steep slope the horses stamp and strain,
Urged on by hoarse-tongued drivers—cheeks
　　ablaze,
Iced beards and frozen eyelids—team by team,
With frost-fringed flanks, and nostrils jetting
　　steam.

A FOREST PATH IN WINTER

Along this secret and forgotten road
　　All depths and forest forms, above, below,

Are plumed and draped and hillocked with the
   snow.
A branch cracks now and then, and its soft load
Drifts by me in a thin prismatic shower;
   Else not a sound, but vistas bound and crossed
   With sheeted gleams and sharp blue shadows, frost,
And utter silence. In his glittering power
The master of mid-winter reveries
   Holds all things buried soft and strong and deep.
   The busy squirrel has his hidden lair;
And even the spirits of the stalwart trees
   Have crept into their utmost roots, and there,
Upcoiled in the close earth, lie fast asleep.

AFTER MIST

Last night there was a mist. Pallid and chill
The yellow moon-blue clove the thickening sky,
And all night long a gradual wind crept by,
And froze the fog, and with minutest skill
Fringed it and forked it, adding bead to bead,
In spears, and feathery tufts, and delicate hems
Round windward trunks, and all the topmost stems,
And every bush, and every golden weed;
And now upon the meadows silvered through
And forests frosted to their farthest pines—
A last faint gleam upon the misty blue—
The magic of the morning falls and shines,
A creamy splendour on a dim white world,
Broidered with violet, crystalled and impearled.

DEATH

I like to stretch full-length upon my bed,
 Sometimes, when I am weary body and mind,
 And think that I shall some day lie thus, blind
And cold, and motionless, my last word said.
How grim it were, how piteous to be dead!
 And yet how sweet, to hear no more, nor see,
 Sleeping, past care, through all eternity,
With clay for pillow to the clay-cold head.
And I should seem so absent, so serene:
 They who should see me in that hour would ask
What spirit, or what fire, could ever have been
 Within that yellow and discoloured mask;
For there seems life in lead, or in a stone,
But in a soul's deserted dwelling none.

IN BEECHWOOD CEMETERY

Here the dead sleep—the quiet dead.   No sound
Disturbs them ever, and no storm dismays.
Winter mid snow caresses the tired ground,
And the wind roars about the woodland ways.
Springtime and summer and red autumn pass,
With leaf and bloom and pipe of wind and bird,
And the old earth puts forth her tender grass,
By them unfelt, unheeded and unheard.
Our centuries to them are but as strokes
In the dim gamut of some far-off chime.

Unaltering rest their perfect being cloaks—
A thing too vast to hear or feel or see—
Children of Silence and Eternity,
They know no season but the end of time.

BEFORE THE ROBIN

The noon hangs warm and still.   Only the crow
    Banters and chides with his importunate call
    The world-wide silence resting over all.
Down by the hollow yonder, where the slow
Frail sheets of tremulous pools collect and grow,
    A few bronzed cedars in their fading dress,
    Almost asleep for happy weariness,
Lean their blue shadows on the puckered snow.
    And as I listen, all my sense concealed
In the very core of silence, mirthfully still,
    Where the first grass above the gleeting field
Lies bare and yellow on a tiny hill,
    I hear the shore-lark in his search prolong
    The little lonely welcome of his song.

A MARCH DAY

The wind went by in buffeting gusts that grew
And lulled and gathered.   In the town below
It piled the drifts and drove the powdered snow
In sheets from the roof-edges.   Dim clouds flew
All day across the silvery mist-veiled blue,
And far away between the dark pine-patches
                19

The sun shone out and dimmed again by snatches,
And swept the foothills with long gleams, and threw
A blind white glare upon the buried plain.
Toward night there came a rush of clouds with rain
And sleet driving, and then all passed, and now
Clouds, wind and sunshine, all have sunk to rest.
Slowly athwart the midnight's eastern brow,
The Herdsman mounts: Orion spans the west.

UPLIFTING

We passed heart-weary from the troubled house,
   Where much of care and much of strife had been,
   A jar of tongues upon a petty scene;
And now as from a long and tortured drouse,
The dark returned us to our purer vows:
   The open darkness, like a friendly palm,
   And the great night was round us with her calm:
We felt the large free wind upon our brows,
And suddenly above us saw revealed
   The holy round of heaven— all its rime
      Of suns and planets and its nebulous rust—
Sable and glittering like a mythic shield,
   Sown with the gold of giants and of time,
      The worlds and all their systems but as dust.

A DAWN ON THE LIEVRE

Up the dark-valleyed river stroke by stroke
   We drove the water from the rustling blade;

And when the night was almost gone we made
The Oxbow bend; and there the dawn awoke;
Full on the shrouded night-charged river broke
    The sun, down the long mountain valley rolled,
    A sudden swinging avalanche of gold,
Through mists that sprang and reeled aside like
      smoke.
And lo! before us, toward the east upborne,
    Packed with curled forest, bunched and topped
      with pine,
    Brow beyond brow, drawn deep with shade and
      shine,
    The mount; upon whose golden sunward side,
Still threaded with the melting mist, the morn
    Sat like some glowing conqueror satisfied.

A WINTER-DAWN

Thin clouds are vanishing slowly. Overhead
    The stars melt in the wakening sky; and, lo,
    Far on the blue band of the eastern snow
Sober and still the morning breaks, dull red.
Innumerable smoke wreaths curl and spread
    Up from the snow-capped roofs. From the gray
      north
    A little wind that bites like fire creeps forth.
The purple mists along the south hang dead.
Out of the distance eastward, frosty, still,
    Where soon the gold-shower of the sun shall be,

A file of straggling snowshoers winds aslant,
Across the dull blue river, up the hill,
   Toward the dusk city plodding silently,—
   The jaded enders of some midnight jaunt.

GOLDENROD

Ere the stout year be waxed shrewd and old,
And while the grain upon the well-piled stack
Waits yet unthreshed, by every woodland track,
Low stream, and meadow, and wide waste out-
   rolled,
By every fence that skirts the forest mould,
Sudden and thick, as at the reaper's hail,
They come, companions of the harvest, frail
Green forests yellowing upward into gold.
Lo, where yon shaft of level sunshine gleams
Full on those pendent wreathes, those bounteous
   plumes
So gracious and so golden! Mark them well,
The last and best from summer's empty looms,
Her benedicite, and dream of dreams,
The fulness of her soul made visible.

TEMAGAMI

Far in the grim Northwest beyond the lines
That turn the rivers eastward to the sea,
Set with a thousand islands, crowned with pines,
Lies the deep water, wild Temagami:

Wild for the hunter's roving, and the use
Of trappers in its dark and trackless vales,
Wild with the trampling of the giant moose,
And the weird magic of old Indian tales.
All day with steady paddles toward the west
Our heavy-laden long canoe we pressed:
All day we saw the thunder-travelled sky
Purpled with storm in many a trailing tress,
And saw at eve the broken sunset die
In crimson on the silent wilderness.

ON LAKE TEMISCAMINGUE

A single dreamy elm, that stands between
   The sombre forest and the wan-lit lake,
Halves with its slim gray stem and pendent green
   The shadowed point. Beyond it without break
Bold brows of pine-topped granite bend away,
   Far to the southward, fading off in grand
Soft folds of looming purple. Cool and gray,
   The point runs out, a blade of thinnest sand.
Two rivers meet beyond it: wild and clear,
   Their deepening thunder breaks upon the ear—
The one descending from its forest home
   By many an eddied pool and murmuring fall—
The other cloven through the mountain wall,
   A race of tumbled rocks, a roar of foam.

NIGHT IN THE WILDERNESS

The good fire-ranger is our friend to-night;
We sit before his tent, and watch his fire
Send up its fount of sailing sparks that light
The ruddy pine-stems.   Hands that never tire
Our friend's are, as he spreads his frugal store,
And cooks his bouillon with a hunter's pride,
Till, warm with woodland fare and forest lore
We sink at last to sleep.   On every side,
A grim mysterious presence, vast and old,
The forest stretches leagues on leagues away,
With lonely rivers running dark and cold,
And many a gloomy lake and haunted bay.
The stars above the pines are sharp and still.
The wind scarce moves.   An owl hoots from the
      hill

IN THE WILDS

We run with rushing streams that toss and spume;
We speed or dream upon the open meres;
The pine-woods fold us in their pungent gloom;
The thunder of wild water fills our ears;
The rain we take, we take the beating sun;
The stars are cold above our heads at night;
On the rough earth we lie when day is done,
And slumber even in the storm's despite.
The savage vigour of the forest creeps
Into our veins, and laughs upon our lips;

The warm blood kindles from forgotten deeps,
And surges tingling to the finger tips.
The deep-pent life awakes and bursts its bands;
We feel the strength and goodness of our hands.

AMBITION

I see the world in pride and tumult pass
  Too bright with flame, too dark with phantasy,
Its forces meet and mingle mass in mass,
  A tangle of Desire and Memory.
I see the labours of untiring hands
  Closing at last upon a shadowy prize,
And Glory bear abroad through many lands
  Great names—I watching with unenvious eyes
From other lips let stormy numbers flow:
  By others let great epics be compiled;
For me, the dreamer, 'tis enough to know
  The lyric stress, the fervour sweet and wild:
I sit me in the windy grass and grow
  As wise as age, as joyous as a child.

THE WINTER STARS

Across the iron-bound silence of the night
A keen wind fitfully creeps, and far away
The northern ridges glimmer faintly bright,
Like hills on some dead planet hard and gray.
Divinely from the icy sky look down
The deathless stars that sparkle overhead,

The Wain, the Herdsman, and the Northern
    Crown,
And yonder, westward, large and balefully red,
Arcturus, brooding over fierce resolves:
Like mystic dancers in the Arctic air
The troops of the Aurora shift and spin:
The Dragon strews his bale-fires, and within
His trailing and prodigious loop involves
The lonely Pole Star and the Lesser Bear.

THE PASSING OF SPRING

No longer in the meadow coigns shall blow
    The creamy blood-root in her suit of gray,
    But all the first strange flowers have passed away,
Gone with the childlike dreams that touched us so;
April is spent, and summer soon shall go,
    Swift as a shadow o'er the heads of men,
    And autumn with the painted leaves; and then,
When fires are set, and windows blind with snow,
    We shall remember, with a yearning pang,
    How in the poplars the first robins sang,
The wind-flowers risen from their leafy cots,
    When life was gay and spring was at the helm,
The maple full of little crimson knots,
    And all that delicate blossoming of the elm.

TO THE OTTAWA

Dear dark-brown waters full of all the stain
Of sombre spruce-woods and the forest fens,
Laden with sound from far-off northern glens
Where winds and craggy cataracts complain,
Voices of streams and mountain pines astrain,
The pines that brood above the roaring foam
Of La Montagne or Des Erables; thine home
Is distant yet, a shelter far to gain.
Aye still to eastward, past the shadowy lake
And the long slopes of Rigaud toward the sun,
The mightier stream, thy comrade, waits for thee,
The beryl waters that espouse and take
Thine in their deep embrace, and bear thee on
In that great bridal journey to the sea.

TO THE OTTAWA RIVER

O slave, whom many a cunning master drills
    To lift, or carry, bind, or crush, or churn,
    Whose dammed and parcelled waters drive or turn
The saws and hammers of a hundred mills,
Yet hath thy strength for our rebellious ills
    A counsel brave, a message sweet and stern,
    Uttered for them that have the heart to learn:
Yea to the dwellers in the rocky hills,
The folk of cities, and the farthest tracts,
    There comes above the human cry for gold

The thunder of thy chutes and cataracts:
  And lo! contemptuous of the driver's hold,
Thou movest under all thy servile pacts
  Full-flowing, fair, and stately as of old.

A SUMMER EVENING

The clouds grow clear, the pine-wood glooms and
    stills
With brown reflections in the silent bay,
And far beyond the pale blue-misted hills
The rose and purple evening dreams away.
The thrush, the veery, from mysterious dales
Rings his last round; and outward like a sea
The shining, shadowy heart of heaven unveils—
The starry legend of eternity.
The day's long troubles lose their sting and pass.
Peaceful the world, and peaceful grows my heart.
The gossip cricket from the friendly grass
Talks of old joys and takes the dreamer's part.
Then night, the healer, with unnoticed breath,
And sleep, dark sleep, so near, so like to death.

WAYAGAMACK

Beautiful are thy hills, Wayagamack,
  Thy depths of lonely rock, thine endless piles
  Of grim birch forest and thy spruce-dark isles,
Thy waters fathomless and pure and black,

But golden where the gravel meets the sun,
And beautiful thy twilight solitude,
The gloom that gathers over lake and wood
A weirder silence when the day is done.
For ever wild, too savage for the plough,
Thine austere beauty thou canst never lose.
Change shall not mar thy loneliness, nor tide
Of human trespass trouble thy repose,
The Indian's paddle and the hunter's stride
Shall jar thy dream, and break thy peace enow.

WINTER UPLANDS

The frost that stings like fire upon my cheek,
The loneliness of this forsaken ground,
The long white drift upon whose powdered peak
I sit in the great silence as one bound;
The rippled sheet of snow where the wind blew
Across the open fields for miles ahead;
The far-off city towered and roofed in blue
A tender line upon the western red;
The stars that singly, then in flocks appear,
Like jets of silver from the violet dome,
So wonderful, so many and so near,
And then the golden moon to light me home—
The crunching snowshoes and the stinging air,
And silence, frost and beauty everywhere.

THE LARGEST LIFE

I

I lie upon my bed and hear and see.
The moon is rising through the glistening trees;
And momently a great and sombre breeze,
With a vast voice returning fitfully,
Comes like a deep-toned grief, and stirs in me,
Somehow, by some inexplicable art,
A sense of my soul's strangeness, and its part
In the dark march of human destiny.
What am I, then, and what are they that pass
Yonder, and love and laugh, and mourn and weep?
What shall they know of me, or I, alas!
Of them?　Little.　At times, as if from sleep,
We waken to this yearning passionate mood,
And tremble at our spiritual solitude.

II

Nay, never once to feel we are alone,
While the great human heart around us lies:
To make the smile on other lips our own,
To live upon the light in others' eyes:
To breathe without a doubt the limpid air
Of that most perfect love that knows no pain:
To say—I love you—only, and not care
Whether the love come back to us again,
Divinest self-forgetfulness, at first
A task, and then a tonic, then a need;

To greet with open hands the best and worst,
And only for another's wound to bleed:
This is to see the beauty that God meant,
Wrapped round with life, ineffably content.

III

There is a beauty at the goal of life,
A beauty growing since the world began,
Through every age and race, through lapse and strife
Till the great human soul complete her span.
Beneath the waves of storm that lash and burn,
The currents of blind passion that appall,
To listen and keep watch till we discern
The tide of sovereign truth that guides it all;
So to address our spirits to the height,
And so attune them to the valiant whole,
That the great light be clearer for our light,
And the great soul the stronger for our soul:
To have done this is to have lived, though fame
Remember us with no familiar name.

POEMS AND BALLADS

I kept the pure and glassy floors
Swept clean between the sounding doors :
Through ivied port and window blew,
With gentle voices never done,
A mellow wind that brought the sun :
And always more divinely than I knew
The vistas deepened ; and the years
Brought dreams, and only ghosts of tears
More bright than dew.

THE MINSTREL

Through the wide-set gates of the city, bright-eyed,
Came the minstrel; many a song behind him,
Many still before him, re-echoing strangely,
      Ringing and kindling.

First he stood, bold-browed, in the hall of warriors,
Stood, and struck, and flung from his strings the roar
And sweep of battle, praising the might of foemen,
      Met in the death-grip:

Bugle-voiced, wild-eyed, till the old men, rising,
Gathered all the youth in a ring, and drinking
Deep, acclaimed him, making the walls and roof-tree
      Jar as with thunder.

Then of horse and hound, and the train of huntsmen
Sprang his song, and into the souls of all men
Passed the cheer and heat of the chase, the fiery
      Rush of the falcon.

Singing next of love, in the silken chambers
Sat the minstrel, eloquent, urged by lovely
Eyes of women, sang till the girls, white-handed,
      Gathered, and round him

Leaned, and listened, eager, and flushed, and
    dreaming
Now of things remembered, and now the dearer
Wishes yet unfilled; and they praised and crowned
    him,
        They, the beloved ones.

Gentlest songs he made for the mothers, weaving
Over cradles tissues of softest vision,
Tender cheeks, and exquisite hands, and little
        Feet of their dearest.

Into cloisters also he came, and cells, and
Dwellings, sad and heavy with shadow, making
All his lute-strings bear for the hour their bitter
        Burden of sorrow.

Children gathered, many and bright, around him,
Sweet-eyed, eager, beautiful, fairy-footed,
While with jocund hand upon string and mad notes,
        Full of the frolic,

He rejoicing, followed and led their pastime,
Wilder yet and wilder, till weary, over
All their hearts he murmured a spell, and gently
        Sleep overcame them.

So the minstrel sang with a hundred voices
All day long, and now in the dusk of even
Once again the gates of the city opened,
        Wide for his passing

Forth to dreaming meadows, and fields, and wooded
Hillsides, solemn under the dew and the starlight
There the singer far from the pathways straying,
    Silent and lonely,

Plucked and pressed the fruit of his day's devotion,
Making now a song for the spirit only,
Deeper-toned, more pure, than his soul had fashioned
    Ever aforetime.

Sorrow touched it, travail of spirit, broken
Hopes, and faiths uprooted, and aspirations
Dimmed and soiled, and out of the depth of being
    Limitless hunger.

First his own strange destiny, darkly guided;
Next, the tragic ways of the world and all men,
Caught and foiled for ever among perplexing,
    Endlessly ravelled,

Nets of truth and falsehood, and good, and evil,
Wild of heart, beholding the hands of Beauty
Decking all, he sang with a voice and fingers
    Trembling and shaken.

Then of earth and time, and the pure and painless
Night, serene with numberless worlds inwoven
Scripts and golden traceries, hourly naming
    God, the Eternal,

Sang the minstrel, full of the light and splendour,
Full of power and infinite gift, once only—

Only once—for just as the solemn glory,
　　Flung by the moonshine,

Over folds of hurrying clouds at midnight,
Gleams and passes, so was his song—the noblest—
Once outpoured, and then in the strain and tumult
　　Gone and forgotten.

YARROW

The yarrow's beauty: fools may laugh,
　　And yet the fields without it
Were shorne of half their comfort, half
　　Their magic—who can doubt it?

Yon patches of a milky stain
　　In verdure bright or pallid
Are something like the deep refrain
　　That tunes a perfect ballad.

The meadows by its sober white—
　　Though few would bend to pick it—
Are tempered as the sounds of night
　　Are tempered by the cricket.

It blooms as in the fields of life
　　Those spirits bloom for ever,
Unnamed, unnoted in the strife,
　　Among the great and clever.

Who spread from an unconscious soul
　　An aura pure and tender,

A kindlier background for the whole,
  Between the gloom and splendour.

Let others captivate the mass
  With power and brilliant seeming:
The lily and the rose I pass,
  The yarrow holds me dreaming.

TO A FLOWER

Thou hast no human soul, O flower!
  Thou heedest not if I am near;
But I may come at any hour
  And take thy beauty without fear.

Thou hast no human smile to bless,
  And not with tears thine eyes are wet;
But I may love thee and caress,
  Without reproach, without regret.

SORROW

In the morning early
I became aware
Of the sunlight pouring clearly
On a world so fair,
That from every part
Breathed a single bright good morrow:
And I heard the sparrow sing—
I awakening

With my fiery robe of sorrow,
And my heavy heart.

Then amid the glitter,
Pure on flower and leaf,
Seemed a hundredfold more bitter
Than before my grief:
For the bright and scornful morrow
Pierced me like a dart:
All the singing brilliance and the stir
Made me lonelier,
With my fiery robe of sorrow
And my heavy heart.

PATERNITY

Child, for thy love and for thy beauty's sake,
    My heart hath opened warmlier to the day;
Springs of new joy and deeper tears awake,
    Whose wells were buried in the baser clay.

For thy sake nobler visions are unfurled,
    Vistas of tenderer humanity,
And all the little children of this world
    Are dearer now to me.

PEACE

Him only shall peace find
Who plans no more and long hath ceased to sue

Existent only in the flawless mind,
Accounting nothing as his due:

Whose soul hath set aside
Desire and hope; who lives no more in fee,
But looks far forth and casts his spirit wide
On Nature and Eternity:

Who sees this glorious earth—
An open radiance, a script sublime—
Regarding in her elemental mirth
Not now, nor yesterday, but time:

To whom the marvellous sun,
The dædal spectacle of earth and sky,
In endless forms and beauty never done,
The night's slow-moving majesty:

Life's never-flagging tale,
An infinite pursuit, a vast employ,
In lonely brightness far removed from bale,
Bring wonder and sufficient joy.

This is to live in truth,
To plant against the passions' dark control
The spirit's birth-right of immortal youth,
The simple standard of the soul.

STRIFE AND FREEDOM

The fool impatient of control,
  Must prove himself in every strife;
Age finds him with a withered soul,
  Exhausted in the nets of life.

Not Nature only he defies,
  The forces from of old obeyed,
But ever lifts the bitterest cries
  Against the bonds himself hath made.

The wise man sees in every let
  The purpose of the soul made plain,
A warning and a signal set
  To point it to its own domain.

The wise man storms not nor complains,
  But lets his quiet spirit shine,
And knows himself beyond his chains
  A boundless mood of the divine.

THE PASSING OF AUTUMN

The wizard has woven his ancient scheme;
  A day and a starlit night;
And the world is a shadowy-pencilled dream
  Of colour, haze, and light.

Like something an angel wrought, maybe,
  To answer a fairy's whim,

A fold of an ancient tapestry,
  A phantom rare and dim.

Silent and smooth as the crystal stone
  The river lies serene,
And the fading hills are a jewelled throne
  For the Fall and the Mist, his Queen.

Slim as out of aerial seas,
  The elms and poplars fair
Float like the dainty spirits of trees
  In the mellow dreamlike air.

Silvery-soft by the forest side—
  Wine-red, yellow, rose—
The wizard of Autumn, faint, blue-eyed—
  Swinging his censer, goes.

THE LAKE IN THE FOREST

O Manitou, O Spirit of the earth,
  Maker and monarch of this silent mere,
  These ridges and this lonely atmosphere,
Savage and bright and pure, to whom the dearth
And sickness of the world and men's distress
    Appeal, and thou art kind,
O Spirit of the virgin wilderness,
    O Worker unconfined,
Here in thy fastness and thy dreaming-place,
I feel thy living presence, face to face.

Thy soul is in the splendour of the night,
    When silent shadows darken from the shores,
    And all thy swaying fairies over floors
Of luminous water lying strange and bright,
Are spinning mists of silver in the moon;
        When out of magic bays
The yells and demon laughter of the loon
        Startle the hills and raise
The solitary echoes far away;
Then art thou present, Spirit, wild as they.

O Monarch of the morning, Manitou;
    The sun, thy first-born, from the gleaming hills
    Uptilts the handles of his jar, and fills
This moss-embroidered bowl of rock and dew
With torrent-light and ether.   From his eye,
        Divine and wide with day,
Belated broods of spectres break and fly,
        And cringe, and curl away—
Thin mists—the ferns of midnight, and her bines—
That vanish tangled in the topmost pines.

O Master of the noon; the dusky bass
    Lurk in the chambers of the rocks—the deep
    Cool crypts of amber brown and dark—and sleep,
Dim-shadowed, waiting for the day to pass.
The shy red deer come down by crooked paths,
        Whom countless flies assail,
And splash and wallow in the sandy baths,
        And cry to thee to veil
Thine eye's exceeding brightness and strike dead
The hot cicada singing overhead.

O Spirit of the sunset; in thine hand
  This hollow of the forest brims with fire,
  And piling high to westward builds a pyre
Of sombre spruces and black pines that stand,
Ragged, and grim, and eaten through with gold.
      The archèd east grows sweet
With rose and orange, and the night acold
      Looms, and beneath her feet
Still waters green and purple in strange schemes,
Till twilight wakes the hoot-owl from his dreams.

O Manitou, O Spirit of the spring,
  That hast the wind-flower in thy fertile care;
  Thy footstep falls, and all the forest air
Grows gentle at the whisper of thy wing;
And always with the fifing of the frogs
      The rivers swell, and soon
The shouting woodmen drive the herded logs;
      And ever, night or noon,
Soft violet or unfathomable blue,
The cup is poured, the censer smokes anew.

O Spirit of the Autumn; ah! the trees,
  Thy maskers, that make revel for an hour,
  In gold and ruby, till the blighting power
Strips them, and all their rustling braveries
In urns and earthen caskets lays away;
      But thou, O Spirit, still
Armest thy children for the bitter day;
      The plants observe thy skill,
Whose secret buds in woolly folds abide,
And the fur thickens on the fox's hide.

O Manitou, O Spirit of the snow,
   That buries, each and all, the moose's track,
   The woodman's shanty, and the hunter's shack,
Lord of the hissing winds that plunge and blow,
Till pines and powdered birches are embossed
      With loaded white and gray;
O Manitou, O Master of the frost,
      The frost that hath its way,
The waters are forsaken by the loon,
And the ice roars beneath the winter moon.

Thy soul is in the silence, Manitou,
   The silence of the winter, which is sleep;
   The silence of the midnight made more deep
By the deer's footstep and the loon's halloo,
The lashing wings and laughter of the wild;
      The silence of the Fall,
Windless at even when the logs are piled,
      When every stroke or call
Awakes the fairies from their caves, and thrills
In taunting echoes up the cloven hills.

O Maker of the light and sinewy frame,
   The hunter's iron hands and tireless feet;
   O Breath, whose kindling ether, keen and sweet,
Thickens the thews and fills the blood with flame;
O Manitou, before the mists are drawn,
      The dewy webs unspun,
While yet the smiling pines are soft with dawn,
      My forehead greets the sun;
With lifted heart and hands I take my place.
And feel thy living presence face to face.

DROUGHT

From week to week there came no rain,
  The very birds took flight,
The river shrank within its bed,
The borders of the world grew red
  With woods that flamed by night.

No rest beneath the fearful sun,
  No shelter brought the moon;
Lean cattle on the reeded fen
Searched every hole for drink, and men
  Dropped dead beneath the noon.

And ever as each sun went down
  Beyond the reeling plain,
Into the mocking sky uprist,
Like phantoms from the burning west,
  Dim clouds that brought no rain.

Each root and leaf and living thing
  Fell sicklier day by day,
And I that still must live and see
The agony of plant and tree,
  Grew weary even as they.

But oh, at last the joy, the change;
  With sudden sigh and start
I woke upon the middle night,
And thought that something strange and bright
  Had burst upon my heart.

With surging of great winds, a lull
  And hush upon the plain,
A hollow murmur far aloof,
And then a roar upon the roof,
  Down came the rushing rain.

AFTER SNOW

High to westward lies the city,
  Soft upon the pallid blue,
With the storms of half a winter
  Packed and sifted through and through.

Spire and tower against the azure,
  Deepening as the morning grows,
From the distance faint and slender
  Rising each a shaft of rose.

Icy fringes, violet shadows,
  ` Every roof a creamy sheet,
Ridges of gray broken silver
  Up and down the misty street.

O'er the roofs the smoke in torrents
  Billows like a glimmering sea,
From the city's thousand chimneys
  Rolling out tumultuously.

Down the frozen street to market
  Come the woodmen team by team,

Squeaking runners, jolting cordwood,
　　Frost-fringed horses jetting steam.

Some upon the load, some walking,
　　Down the misty street they come,
With their cheeks as red as flannel,
　　And their beards as white as foam.

And they swing their arms to warm them—
　　Ah, the wind is keen we know—
Beating crosswise round the shoulders
　　Till their fingers sting and glow.

Brothers, let us serve the morning
　　With a worship glad as meet,
Roll the tuque about our foreheads,
　　Bind the snowshoes to our feet.

All along the north the mountains,
　　Hoary with the sifted snow,
Gleaming front and powdered forest,
　　Overlook the sweep below.

Where the frosted creamy splendour
　　Of the morning slants and shines
On smooth fields and sheeted rivers,
　　Stretching to the western pines.

Past the bridge and past the river,
　　Comrades, striding, let us wind,
Over marsh and meadow, leaving
　　Miles of braided track behind.

Praising with deep tongue the season,
  Master in whose caustic ken,
We become this winter morning
  Equal with the lords of men.

THE WIND'S WORD

The wind charged every way and fled
  Across the meadows and the wheat;
It whirled the swallows overhead,
  And swung the daisies at my feet.

As if in mockery of me,
  And all the deadness of my thought,
It mounted to the largest glee,
  And, like a lord that laughed and fought,

Took all the maples by surprise,
  And made the poplars clash and shiver,
And flung my hair about my eyes,
  And sprang and blackened on the river.

And through the elm-tree tops, and round
  The city steeples wild and high,
It floundered with a mighty sound,
  A buoyant voice that seemed to cry:

Behold how grand I am, how free!
  And all the forest bends my way!
I roam the earth, I stalk the sea,
  And make my labour but a play.

BIRD VOICES

The robin and the sparrow awing in silver-throated
    accord;
The low soft breath of a flute, and the deep short pick
    of a chord,
A golden chord and a flute, where the throat of the
    oriole swells
Fieldward, and out of the blue the passing of bob-o-
    link bells.

HEPATICAS

The trees to their innermost marrow
    Are touched by the sun;
The robin is here and the sparrow:
    Spring is begun!

The sleep and the silence are over:
    These petals that rise
Are the eyelids of earth that uncover
    Her numberless eyes.

THE OLD HOUSE

All men love the old house, roofed with brown,
    Rising grayly from its woodland ring,
Over all the valley, ford and town,
    Facing westward like an agèd king:
21

And along the level west are lines
    Of pencilled hills and slender pines.
Bright its gardens are with pipe and carol,
    All its chambers fair with woven dies,
  Lovely forms and beautiful apparel,
    Gentle faces and the kindliest eyes.
          To its ways
            Love belongs;
          All its days
          Are but songs:
And the customs of the house are fair to see,
The master and his noble company.

When the angel of the springtime broods
    O'er the dead leaves and the vanished snow,
Fraught with sunbeams and the scent of woods,
    And the dove-like wind begins to blow;
When the yearning city towers have seen
    The willows spreading golden-green;
Then about the arbours and the eaves
    Sparrows busy with their nesting, meet;
O'er the gray grass and the matted leaves
    Golden-headed, silver-tonguèd, children fleet.
          Shout and song
            Over all,
          Pierce and throng
          Yard and hall;
And with softer brilliance down the ancient walls
The glory of the sunset smiles and falls.

Summer comes; and when the fancied hour
    Fills its gardens and its lawns with light;

When the too great sun forgets his power,
   And the fainting leaves desire the night;
When the few round ringing notes are heard
   That clearly name the oriole bird;
Into silent glades and leafy places
   Footsteps follow where the quiet flies—
Sunlight scattered upon restful faces
   Shadows fallen upon pensive eyes.
          Tongues that keep
            Court and bower
          Murmur deep
            Every hour
Gravely, and the sound of joyous music pours
Flooding at even from the princely doors.

All the golden long October days
   On the gray and orange-stainèd walls
Dripping lengths of scarlet creepers blaze,
   And the warm and misty sunlight falls,
Nestling in the swart and silent cedar screen
   That keeps the lingering lilacs green.
Far within the mute and dreaming garden,
   Pavèd all with red and russet leaves,
Ere the winds of winter lock and harden,
   Nothing jibes and nothing grieves.
          Voices sweet
            Ebb and flow:
          Quiet feet
            Come and go
And among the faded stalks and ruined roses
The easy master of the house reposes.

Often in the winter nights I see
   One or two great stars, that seem to pry
Just above the roof-edge, wonderfully
   Hard and sparkling in the bitter sky.
In the tranquil moonlight droop and curl
   Long icicles that beam like pearl,
Round the gable-ends and steep roof-edges
   Slant the shadows, curve the folds of snow;
Down the crystal paths in crimson wedges
   Firelight flickers from the panes below.
          Onward slips
            Night awhile;
          Kindly lips
            Bend and smile
Yonder, and the magic of the dance illumes
The dreamy faces in the festal rooms.

Open-doored upon its sunny steep
   'Tis a home of friendly pilgrimage:
Softly round it, light of hand like sleep,
   Beauty grows upon its stones with age:
Love, its only master, keeps the hall,
   The surest-sceptered lord of all.
So the old house for its day shall flourish,
   Till the twilight and the dark descend,
And the heart within shall cease to nourish,
   Ending as all mortal things must end;
          Till at last,
            Some dark day,
          All be past,
            Work and play;
And forsaken, deaf to every wind that blows,
The rooms fall silent and the shutters close.

KING OSWALD'S FEAST

The king had laboured all an autumn day
For his folk's good and welfare of the kirk,
And now when eventide was well away,
    And deepest mirk

Lay heavy on York town, he sat at meat,
With his great councillors round him and his kin,
And a blithe face was sat in every seat,
    And far within

The hall was jubilant with banqueting,
The tankards foaming high as they could hold
With mead, the plates well-heaped, and everything
    Was served with gold.

Then came to the king's side the doorkeeper,
And said: "The folk are thronging at the gate,
And flaunt their rags and many plaints prefer,
    And through the grate

"I see that many are ill-clad and lean,
For fields are poor this year, and food hard-won."
And the good king made answer, " 'Twere ill seen
    And foully done,

"Were I to feast, while many starve without;"
And he bade bear the most and best of all
To give the folk; and lo, they raised a shout
    That shook the hall.

And now lean fare for those at board was set,
But came again the doorkeeper and cried:
The folk still hail thee, sir, nor will they yet
        Be satisfied;

"They say they have no surety for their lives,
When winters bring hard nights and heatless suns,
Nor bread, nor raiment have they for their wives
        And little ones."

Then said the king: "It is not well that I
Should eat from gold, when many are so poor,
For he that guards his greatness guards a lie;
        Of that be sure."

And so he bade collect the golden plate,
And all the tankards, and break up, and bear,
And give them to the folk that thronged the gate,
        To each his share.

And the great councillors in cold surprise
Looked on and murmured; but unmindfully
The king sat dreaming with far-fixèd eyes,
        And it may be

He saw some vision of that Holy One
Who knew no rest or shelter for His head,
When self was scorned and brotherhood begun.
        " 'Tis just," he said:

"Henceforward wood shall serve me for my plate,
And earthen cups suffice me for my mead;
With them that joy or travail at my gate
        I laugh or bleed."

SOSTRATUS

Sostratus, son of Laodamas, Prince of Ægina,
Named in the book of Herodotus still shall you find
    him,
He who was first of the Hellenes in trade, and out-
    sailing
All to the westward, returned with the goodliest cargo,
Now in the dusk of the twilight meseemeth I see him,
Straight on the deck of his ship within sight of Ægina,
Borne by the evening wind, with the hold of his vessel
Heavy with amber and pitch and hides from the
    Spanish
Forests, and copper hewed out from the hills of
    Tartessus.
Westward the shores of Kalauria gloom, but the
    golden
Crests of the islands are luminous still with the sunset;
Taut are the sails, and the cordage groans, and the
    plunging
Oars keep time with the tremulous chant of the sailors.
Full of the triumph of life is his strenuous figure;
Bronzed are his cheeks, and toughened his hands, and
    his shining
Eyes are alive with memories, full of the stories
Gathered from wonderful folk on the strands of the
    ocean,
Soon to be rolled from his lips on the listening market
There in Ægina.   Full is his heart too of visions,
Plans for far-venturing trade in the opulent future.
Gone are his figure and face now; gone are his people,
Sostratus, son of Laodamas, Prince of Ægina;

Yet like a gleam out of primitive shadow revealing
Worlds of old joy and wonder of living and effort
Named in the book of Herodotus still shall you find
    him.

PHOKAIA

I will tell you a tale of an ancient city of men,
    Of men that were men in truth:
The world grows wide now; 'twas smaller and
        goodlier then,
    And the busy shores of the little islanded sea
      Were filled with a beautiful folk,
A people of children and sages, untouched by the
        yoke,
    Eager, far-venturing, fearless and free,
      In the pride and glory of youth.

Phokaia the city was named, built on a northern
    strand
Of the old bright-watered, sunny, Ionian land.
For many an age its marts had flourished: the city
    had grown
Famous and rich: and far from the East to the West
The sounds of the sea and the opening waters were
    sown
With their long swift ships. The hands of its sailors
    had pressed,
With venturesome gains and many a toilful escape,
Dreaded Pachynus long since: and its glistening oars,
Farther and farther each year, past the Sicilian cape,

Out from the gates of the ocean, past Tartessus, had
     found
Havens of trade with wonderful men, and the sound
Of unknown waves on unknown measureless shores.
And fair was the city now with an eager and mingled
     throng
Of people and princes, with festival, art, and song;
And busy its workshops were: the fruit of their myriad
     hands
Drew traffic, and praise, and gold out of many lands.

          But life is like the uncertain sea,
          And some day, somewhere, surely falls
          The fierce inevitable storm:
          Thrice-happy in that hour shall be
          The ship whose decks are clear, whose walls
          Of timber are still sound, whose prow
          Is captained by no cowering form,
          But a bright mind and an unflinching brow.

The long fair peace was over. An ominous star
Dawned on the land of the Hellenes, livid with war.
For far away in the East a conquering tyrant rose,
And the lords of the earth were smitten, and laid their
     crowns
At the Great King's feet. Like a pitiless storm-black
     cloud,
Out of the Lydian valleys, sudden and loud,
The foemen gathered with sword and fire and began
     to close
Round the sweet sea-fields and the soft Ionian towns.
          Some held to their own, and fell,

And many fought and surrendered, and left no tale to
        And one that was richly fee'd   [tell;
Purchased a shameful pact by a bloody and impious
    deed.
At last they came to Phokaia, and harried the plain,
And leaguered its walls, and battered its gates in vain,
For the citizens stood to their posts like heroes, and
    fought,
Till the Persian dead were many and no good wrought.
And then, for their strength was needed in other lands,
The foe drew off, and sent a herald, and cried:
"O men of Phokaia, the Persians seek at your hands
Nor service, nor tribute, but only this; tear down,
For a sign of homage and faith to our master's crown,
A single turret of all your walls, and set aside
One roof for the Great King's use in your ample town,
And ye shall possess your city untouched, your gods
    and your laws."
And well the Phokaians knew what the end must be,
For their foes were many as waves on the island sea;
They were alone, alone with a ruined cause.
And so they demanded a day for counsel and choice,
And the people met and cried with a single voice:
"Dear are the seats of our gods, and dear is the name
Of our beautiful land, but we will not hold them with
    shame.
Let us take to the ships, for the shores of the sea are
    wide,
And its waves are free, and wherever our keels shall
    ride,
There are sites for a hundred Phokaias."

                                    Swift as the thought,
They turned like a torrent out of the market, and rolled
Down to the docks, and manned them, a multitude,
      young and old;
And ran the long ships into the sea, and brought
Their wives and little ones down to the shining shore,
And gathered the best of their goods, and the things
      of gold,
And the sacred altars and vessels, a priceless store;
And, moving ever in pride and sorrow silently,
They put them into the ships, and embarked, and
      smote the sea,
Each ship with its fifty glimmering oars, and far
      behind,
In the cooling heart of the dusk and the soft night
      wind,
Left the belovèd docks and the city, proud and fair,
A lonely prey to the Persians empty and bare.

And first they halted at Chios, a people, they thought,
      of friends,
And sought a home at their hands, but the island men,
Looking with crafty eyes to their selfish ends,
And dreading the mighty traders, whose ships in the
      bay
Lay like a glimmering cloud beyond count or ken,
Gave them faint cheer and bade them coldly away.
The grim Phokaians lay for an hour or two on their
      path,
Heavy with grief and heavier still with wrath,
Till the pride of the people sprang forth in a single
      word,

And they turned them back to Phokaia, and fell with
    the sword
On the startled Persian garrison, smitten with dread,
And hewed them down to a man, and left them dead;
And they laid a curse on the city, and sank a weight
Of red-hot hissing iron at the harbour gate,
With a vow to return no more till the time should be,
When the iron, so sunk, should appear red-hot from
    the sea.
And then once more from the desolate harbour mouth
They turned the tall prows round, and headed to west
    and south,
Through many an islanded strait, where the bright sea
    shone,
With bellying sails and plunging oars, and ran
    straight on,
Past Melos and Malea, past the Laconian bay,
Into the open main.
                  On the windy decks all day
The little children played, and the mothers with wistful
    eyes
Looked forth on the crests of the wild and widening
    sea,
Full of regrets and misgivings and tender memories:
But the men stood keen and unanxious, whatever
    might be,
For the heads of the people had gathered and issued
    command:
"We will build us another Phokaia far hence in a land
That is ringed all round with the surf-beaten guardian
    strand

Of the ocean: in Kyrnos, an isle once peopled, for
 there the prince,
Our sire Iolaus, made halt, and settled long since
With the Thespian children of Herakles, founding a
 home,
Crowned with impregnable hills and circled with
 foam."

  For stormy times and ruined plans
  Make keener the determined will,
  And Fate with all its gloomy bans
  Is but the spirit's vassal still:
  And that deep force, that made aspire
  Man from dull matter and the beast,
  Burns sleeplessly a spreading fire,
  By every thrust and wind increased.

And so the Phokaians sailed on,
Through seas rough-laughing in stormy play,
Till many a watchful day,
And many a toil-broken anxious night were gone;
And the ridges of Kyrnos appeared, and they stranded
 the ships,
And set up the shrines of the gods, and with eloquent
 lips
And giftful hands besought them for prosperous days;
  But the land was rough and uncleared,
  And a hostile people dwelt in its bays,
And the old blithe kin, no longer counted or feared,
  Were few and their glorious seed
  Was mixed with a barbarous breed.
  Even the sea was scanned

By the jealous eye of an ancient sea-faring foe,
And so the Phokaians were thwarted, and trouble
    continued to grow,
       And failure was ever at hand.

For five dark years they fought with their fate, and
    then
A famine lay hard on the folk, and their desperate men
       Put forth in the open day
In their long swift ships, and harried the sea for prey:
And a great fleet came from Carthage out of the west,
And fell on the Phokaians, and when the battle was
    done,
The sons of Phokaia stood firm, and the day was won;
But a host of their ships were shattered or sunk, and
    the rest
Lay on the sea, half-manned, like birds with broken
    wings:
And the remnant took counsel again and said:
"The gods are ill-pleased, and their bountiful care has
    ceased;
But ever good at the last our Father Poseidon brings.
Let us choose anew, by a holier guidance led."
And again were the half-built roofs and the luckless
    springs
Forsaken and cursed; and forth in their ships once
    more,
With their wistful wives and their young and their
    dwindled store,
The grim Phokaians sailed: and now they turned to
    the east,

Recalling some ancient oracle; and favoured at last,
With omens and fortunate winds they sped on their
way,
Till the giant forges, the islands of fire, were passed,
    And they came on a day
To a little port on a sunny rock-built shore.
And a beckoning blessing came down, an odorous air,
From hills, far off, that were bright with olive and
vine;
And a god-given spirit of peace, a pleasure divine,
Rose in their hearts, long-troubled and seared with
care,
When they looked on the land and saw that the haven
was fair.
        And the word of the god was true;
        The days of their evil plight
Were broken and ended at last; on a fair new site,
        Afar from the track of their foes,
        A little city upgrew,
With the bloom and the flushing strength of an open-
        Hyele named.   [ing rose,
    And their sea-faring vigour of trade
Returned to the sons of Phokaia, honoured and famed
For daring and skill and endurance: but noblest and
best
In all the old world towns from the east to the west,
The gathering schools of their strenuous city were
made
Famous for knowledge and wisdom, famous for song:
    And humanly sweet and strong,
Over all the world the seed of their teaching was
spread

By the Delphic lips of poets, endless in youth;
    For insight and splendour of mind
Not they that are yielding and lovers of ease shall find,
But only of strength comes wisdom, only of faith
    comes truth.

THE VASE OF IBN MOKBIL

In the house of Ibn Mokbil
    Stands a vase;
        Masters if you ask us
What within its heart is dreaming,
Heart of gold and crystal gleaming,
        We shall answer:
All the riches of Damascus,
    Cairo or Shiraz.

No man—even Ibn Mokbil—
    Ever guessed
        Whence it came—who brought it:
But it stood there one fair morning,
All the simple place adorning
        With its beauty—
People said the Jinn had wrought it—
    Faith is best.

In the house of Ibn Mokbil,
    Till it came,
        There was nothing. Only
His few books and herbs for healing

And his prayer-mat worn with kneeling,
    And the old man,
With his sleepless eyes and lonely
    Heart of flame.

Full of woe was Ibn Mokbil
    To behold
        Brothers overtaken
By misfortune—sitting restless
In his house forlorn and guestless,
        With a larder
Empty, and a purse forsaken
    Of its gold.

For the spirit of the Faquir
    Loved the light
        And the burden weighing,
Deeper still with every morrow,
Of the people's want and sorrow
        Bent and aged him
And his knees were sore with praying,
    Day and night.

Then somehow to Ibn Mokbil
    Came the vase,
        And the tale would task us,
Half to tell what meat and treasure,
Things of help and things of pleasure,
        Overbrimmed it—
All the riches of Damascus,
    Cairo or Shiraz.
        22

Now the door of Ibn Mokbil
    Open wide—
        Moan is heard no longer—
Now the gifts are overflowing;
Coming round the vase and going,
        Crowd the people:
None that ail, and none that hunger
    Are denied.

For the vase, a magic fountain,
    By unseen
        Hands at midnight charging—
Jinn, they say—its store reneweth
Ready for the lip that sueth,
        First at morning,
Heaped about the flashing margin,
    Gold and green.

Yet one law for Ibn Mokbil,
    If he break,
        Spoils and ends the treasure:
Round the vase it runs in letters,
Woven like a wreath of fetters,
        Not one tittle
Must the Faquir for his pleasure
    Touch or take.

Never murmurs Ibn Mokbil,
    Nor complains.
        Though the fierce and greedy
Enter at his gate for plunder

Scattered by no bolt of thunder,
 Yet untroubled,
He a Faquir, poor and needy,
 Still remains.

In the house of Ibn Mokbil
 Nothing stays,
  Of the gifts returning:
All is empty; it is lonely;
Save the books and prayer-mat only,
 And the Faquir
With his gleaming eyes and burning
 Heart of praise.

For the vase beyond the crystal
 To his eyes—
  Now when day is sinking—
Opens like a rift of heaven,
And the things of Allah given—
 Dreams and visions—
Pour upon his spirit drinking
 Paradise.

To the ears of Ibn Mokbil
 Angels tell
  Tales of how the bringer
Of the faith of old still careth
For the foot that strictly fareth.
 As he listens,
Falls a voice divine, the singer,
 Israfel.

BAKI

One day at his door sat Baki,
  With a rapt and absent look,
Poring over old traditions,
  In a dim and ancient book.

Like a shadow came a woman,
  With her eyelids weeping, red;
Breaking from a dream, looked Baki,
  And the woman spake and said:

"Full of care and trouble, Baki,
  Is thy servant; ah, so deep
Is my spirit plunged in sorrow
  That I cannot rest nor sleep.

"For my son, my life, my rosebud,
  He who held me by the hand,
Toils beneath the lash, a captive,
  Fettered in the Christian land.

"How to salve my wound I know not,
  In my weakness and my lack,
How to break the foreign fetters,
  How to win my angel back.

"Hungry for a surer wisdom,
  For a knowledge that can see,
When the ways are dark, O Faquir,
  I have come at last to thee.

"Give me but a moment, Master:
  If I mar thy reading, know,
All things in this world are nothing
  To a mother's sleepless woe."

Brimming with the light of pity,
  Were the eyes of Baki then,
He that had the heart of wisdom.
  He, the holiest of men.

"Woman, leave me for a season;
  I will think, and if I may,
I will help thee;" and the woman,
  Full of comfort, went away.

Long and lean with thinking, Baki,
  To his chamber slowly trod,
And in silence prayed and struggled,
  Lifting up his heart to God.

Weeks had passed: one day at even,
  When the dew had just begun,
Came the woman back, and smiling,
  At her side she brought her son.

"Better than a mint of treasure,
  Baki, was thy potent care;
Here beside me stands my rosebud
  In his beauty tall and fair.

"Better than a sheaf of lances,
  Better than a coat of mail;
Loosen now thy lips, my rosebud,
  Let the Faquir hear the tale."

"Master, I was bound, a captive,
　　Portioned to the Christian king.
Every day I journeyed fieldward,
　　Hurried by the lash's sting.

"Not alone, for we were many,
　　Toiling in the cold and heat,
With the guards and keepers near us,
　　And the fetters round our feet.

"O! the very sun at noontide
　　Seemed a shadow cold and gray,
Till the chosen friend of Allah
　　Sent his succour; and one day

"Unto me, thy slave O Faquir,
　　Came the sense that all was well;
Something touched me as by magic,
　　And my fetters split and fell.

"Round me there were hands and voices,
　　Rough with anger, and forthwith
I was seized anew and fastened,
　　Fettered by their wisest smith.

"But the strength of man is weakness;
　　He is nothing; God is great;
Scarcely were the hammers silent,
　　And the rivets fast as fate,

"When my body leaped and lightened,
　　And I felt my sinews swell,
Quickened by a power I know not,
　　And again the fetters fell.

"O they crossed themselves, our keepers,
   Half in rage and half in fear,
Till the wondering crowd was parted,
   And a white-haired priest drew near.

"Like a voice from God the old man
   Took me gently by the hand:
'Hast thou father, lad, or mother,
   Living in thy Moslem land.'

"Father have I none, I answered,
   But a mother. 'Blessed is she,'
Cried the priest, 'her prayers are granted;'
   And he bade them set me free."

Long as in a dream sat Baki,
   With a rapt and absent look,
As he rolled the leaves together
   Of his dim and ancient book.

"Woman, thou art blest and happy
   In that thou hast got thy son,
And for me the token telleth
   That my sands are nearly run.

"I have thought, and prayed, and fasted,
   Cleaving to the choicer part;
Once I dreamed, but now I know it,
   I am counted pure of heart."

A SPANISH TAUNT

"Now who will carry the gate with me?"
    Fernando del Pulgar cried:
"Carry and hold it safe, while I
    To the church of Mahomet ride?"

Fifteen stalwarts of old Castile
    At the side of the hero strode.
They carried the gate, and in at the gap
    Fernando del Pulgar rode.

He clove and shattered a helm or twain,
    And gathered his reins and sprang,
And far and away in the silent night
    The hoofs of his courser rang.

Fernando del Pulgar, sword and shield,
    Helmet and hauberk too—
Through the startled streets of Mahomet's town
    The sparks from the pavement flew.

On like the hurricane wind he rode,
    With thunder of saddle and steel:
At the front of the proudest mosque drew up
    With a crashing sweep and wheel:

And, "Ave Maria," high aloft
    To the moonlit door, writ plain,
He pinned with his poniard point, and spurred,
    And rode for the gate again.

Back with the thunder of saddle and steel,
   The heart of the hero sprang:
Loud and sharp in the silent night
   The hoofs of his courser rang.

Fernando del Pulgar, sword and shield,
   Helmet and hauberk too;
Back, like the hurricane wind he rode,
   And the sparks from the pavement flew.

With a singing sweep and dint of his sword,
   The blood of the Paynim flowed,
Hurled this way and that, and out of the gate
   Fernando del Pulgar rode.

"I have ridden," he shouted, "Mahomet's town,
   As free as light or wind,
And high to the door of Mahomet's mosque
   The name of the Virgin pinned."

THE VIOLINIST

In Dresden in the square one day,
   His face of parchment, seamed and gray,
With wheezy bow and proffered hat,
   An old blind violinist sat.

Like one from whose worn heart the heat
   Of life had long ago retired,
He played to the unheeding street
   Until the thin old hands were tired.

Few marked the player how he played,
  Or how the child beside his knee
Besought the passers-by for aid
  So softly and so wistfully.

A stranger passed.   The little hand
  Went forth, so often checked and spurned.
The stranger wavered, came to stand,
  Looked round with absent eyes and turned.

He saw the sightless withered face,
  The tired old hands, the whitened hair,
The child with such a mournful grace,
  The little features pinched and spare.

"I have no money, but," said he,
  "Give me the violin and bow.
I'll play a little, we shall see,
  Whether the gold will come or no."

With lifted brow and flashing eyes
  He faced the noisy street and played.
The people turned in quick surprise,
  And every foot drew near and stayed.

First from the shouting bow he sent
  A summons, an impetuous call;
Then some old store of grief long pent
  Broke from his heart and mastered all.

The tumult sank at his command,
  The passing wheels were hushed and stilled;
The burning soul, the sweeping hand
  A sacred ecstasy fulfilled.

The darkness of the outer strife,
  The weariness and want within,
The giant wrongfulness of life,
  Leaped storming from the violin.

The jingling round of pleasure broke,
  Gay carriages were drawn anear,
And all the proud and haughty folk
  Leaned from their cushioned seats to hear.

And then the player changed his tone,
  And wrought another miracle
Of music, half a prayer, half moan,
  A cry exceeding sorrowful.

A strain of pity for the weak,
  The poor that fall without a cry,
The common hearts that never speak,
  But break beneath the press and die.

Throughout the great and silent crowd
  The music fell on human ears,
And many kindly heads were bowed,
  And many eyes were warm with tears.

"And now your gold," the player cried,
  "While love is master of your mood;"
He bowed, and turned, and slipped aside,
  And vanished in the multitude.

And all the people flocked at that,
  The money like a torrent rolled,
Until the gray old battered hat
  Was bursting to the brim with gold.

And loudly as the giving grew,
   The question rose on every part,
If any named or any knew
   The stranger with so great a heart,

Or what the moving wonder meant,
   Such playing never heard before;
A lady from her carriage leant,
   And murmured softly, " It was Spohr."

INGVI AND ALF

Ingvi and Alf, the sons of Alrek, reigned
In Upsala together, kings; and each
Was diverse from the other both in mood
And habit of his hands.   Ingvi was bold,
And great of stature, fair of limb and face,
A man of bountiful ways and winsome speech,
Fond of his sword-play, fierce and fell in fight;
But Alf was dark and dour, a silent man,
Fond of the tillage of his acres, fond
Of thrift and plenty and well ordered rule,
Fond too of song-craft, and of cunning read,
The lore and wisdom of experienced men:
But he was grave and moody as men be
That love much thinking but are slow of heart

Now Ingvi had been gone three summers long
With all his proud sea-dragons and his earls,
And all his berserks, to the Westland borne
By joy of fight and plunder, when King Alf

One shrewd mid-autumn day to Upsala,
Brought home a bride, Queen Bera named of men;
And a great feast was made, and in the hall
Was goodly cheer and revel without stint,
And night-long drinking of the foam-topped mead,
With tale-telling and endless minstrelsy,
And the dark face of Alf was brimmed with joy.

Such love had Alf for Bera, such desire
And passionate worship, that the mood of him
Was changed at that time; his forbidding ways
Were softened in her presence, and his heart,
For some short while forgetful of its gloom,
Gave forth unwonted joyance; yet men's minds
Misgave them, and they deemed the end not well
Of such a mating: "Not for Alf," they said:
"This living light, this summer gladsomeness,
"This mirth was made; not for the night-owl Alf,
"But Ingvi should have had her:" this they said,
And capped it with dark tales of ancient wrongs,
And broken troths and bloody strifes of kin.
For Bera was the comeliest, and thereto
The blithest of all women then on earth,
The fairest shaped, the eagerest of heart;
A spirit fashioned like the running brook
With curve and shadow, fairy-foam, and light;
A face of mirth and morning, and a tongue
So sweet with laughter and so eloquent
In all the bubbling womanly ways of talk
That none had converse with her but his heart,
Though grieved and grimly wrought, forgot its cares.

Long days and busy months were eaten away,
And Alf went to and fro about the stead
A strong and silent figure, with a mind
That settled slowly to its former hue,
And brooded doubtfully on its happiness.
But the slow months were like a wintry dawn,
An endless wintry twilight, to the queen.
The manor hummed with labour, but its rule,
Prim set, and changeless, and of little mirth,
Hung like a damp upon her soul; for Alf
Had laid his mood upon the place, its men,
Rugged and fettered to their ceaseless tasks,
And its bleak laughterless women.   Among these
Bera was like a summer wild-bird caught
And clipped and prisoned out of wind and sun,
Too strange to give her buoyant heart the wing:
And yet she was a dutiful wife, and Alf,
Whose love was rooted large, though scant of leaf,
Observed her gravely, seeming well content:
But sometimes, when she was alone, she fell
Even to weeping, not for any grief,
But a sheer aching emptiness of heart.
The winter passed ; another summer shone
With tilth and bloom ; and in the midst thereof
Came Ingvi with his bruised and sea-worn ships
Home-faring, rich in booty and full-fed
With battle for that tide ; and in the hall
The bronzed sea-rover and his restless carles
Made endless feasting, and sat long anights
Over the mead-cups, listening to old tales.
And Alf and Bera feasted with the king
On the first night of Ingvi's home-coming,

Amid the flare of torches and the din
Of wassailers merry with the meat and mead.
In the high seat they sat and Ingvi told
The story of his battles and the run
Of the long ship through unknown stormy seas,
The taking of fenced towns, the deadly grip
Of open fields fierce-foughten foot to foot,
And how they captured a great stead at night
Once in the Frankland by a lonely firth,
And held it all a winter long, and fought
With many hosts, and harried near and far.
And so as Ingvi told his tale, the queen,
Who was the comeliest and far the best
And blithest of all women then on earth,
Leaned toward him, ever with flushed face and orbs
Shining and smiling lips intent; and Alf,
Silent and watchful, marked how Ingvi's eyes
Delighted with her beauty flashed and shone,
And how his voice, as the wild tale ran on,
Grew deeper for her ardent listening.

And Alf grew dark of face, and ill at ease,
And in a while he rose, and made excuse,
And left them, for it was his wont indeed
To rise by dawnlight and be soon abed;
And he bade Bera follow, but she heard
Or heeded not, and Alf lay long awake,
And anger and foreboding filled his soul.

Nor of the nights that followed was the tale
Other than this, for Alf abode not long
His brother's questings, but went soon to bed;

But Bera sat with Ingvi in the hall;
And they had kindly talk together, oft
Till the night waned and lightened, for the king,
Ingvi, was a wise man, and his stout heart
Was stored with thoughts, and he was quick of speech,
Nor ever in his lifetime had he chanced
On such a listener, so fair of face,
So witting, so intent; and Bera too
Loved well the talk of Ingvi and his saws,
His tales of wild sea-faring, and his lore
Of other lands and other ways of men,
And thereto was she weary of her life,
And the dull manor and the mirthless folk.

But always in his bed lay Alf, awake,
Eaten with thought, and ever before his mind,
A hateful picture.
He saw the two, Ingvi and Bera, set
In talk together; Ingvi's noble form
And comely face and sea-blue sparkling eyes,
And his blithe bearing, such as women love;
Bera he saw, balefully beautiful,
Alive and glowing with a terrible grace,
The cheek rose-lit, that ever at his side
Was pale and downcast, and the flashing eyes
That never flashed for him.   He seemed to hear
Their voices mingled in forbidden speech,
Or cruel laughter, and his doubting mind
Grew hot within him.   Like a fiery root
The fierce grief gathered at his heart and grew
Till it became a tree that veiled the world
In poisoned shadows.   Through the busy day,

In the long night time, wakeful, without rest,
Bera and Ingvi hung about his thoughts,
A ceaseless torment.   He became at last
So mad with brooding and so black with wrath
That life grew fearsome to him, and his will
A thing of terror.   Yet he held his peace,
And crushed his spirit under; for he thought:
"Perhaps her heart is guileless, and she does
"Only the promptings of a thoughtless mind,
"But in the inmost of it all she keeps
"Some fixed and dutiful care for me."   He feared
Lest he might lose even this cold regard,
Slain easily by a fierce or scornful word,
Were he not heedful.   He had clung so close
To Bera as his sole delight, so long
Had pored upon his jewel with dark pride
He could not bear that she should turn at last
To hate and loathe him.   Therefore in a mask
Of busy cares and blindness roughly feigned
He cloaked his anger; but the ardent queen
Marked well her husband's grim and growing gloom.
His presence chilled her.   Her quick spirit sank
Before him, and she met him helplessly
With dull constraint; and ever the more she clave
To Ingvi, not once thinking in her mind
A thought of evil, but because the gods
Had made her sunny-hearted like the flower
That gives its perfume only to the light,
That loveth the day, but closes to the dark.
One night, when Alf a weary while had lain
Alone and wakeful, Bera with light step
Entered, and in the flood of moonlight stood,
23

And loosed her robes, and as they fell, the sheen
Lay soft upon her curved cheek and side
Like marble; and her husband, grim with rage
And maddened by her beauty, cried aloud:
"A shameless woman art thou thus to scorn
"Thy duty and thy wedded husband's bed,
"To sit with strange and drunken men in hall.
"Art thou besotted? Dost thou never care
"For me, or for mine honour, or thine own?"
The moonlight shifted on the comely form,
Revealing in the tender cheek and neck
A haughtier curve; and, touched with angry pride,
Bera made answer: "Hast thou done thy part
"As husband then? or have I ever had
"Joy of thy presence? Nay, I think at times
"I am a stranger at thy board. Thy speech
"Is blither to the housecarles than to me.
"Men whose spirits are as dour as thine,
"As sullen and mistrustful, are not fit
"To wed with women, for their eager hearts
"Desire not duty and forbidding rule,
"But joy and fondness and free speech. See now
"How bountiful a man thy brother is,
"Frank and high-hearted. Happy were the wife
"Whose wedded mate were Ingvi rather than thou."
And Alf in silence turned him to the wall,
And his blood curdled, and his heart stood still,
But Bera slept, and haply it were well
There were no weapon at Alf's hand that hour,
For all his mind was full of murderous thoughts.

And Alf rose early with the dawn, and called
His wife, and set her wide awake, and said:
"Think of me even as thou wilt, and name
"Thy husband by the evilest of names, but this
"Remember, woman, thou art still my wife.
"Now mark! I bid thee sit no more anights
"With Ingvi in the hall apart from me
"Obey me, for I speak not twice nor thrice."
And Alf had passed the door, but suddenly
He turned.   His flesh was trembling, and his eyes
Were filled with tears; and he came back and cried,
Grasping her head between his hardy hands:
"I love thee, I do love thee!"   But the deed
Was sudden and sharp, and Bera shrank away,
Not in disfavour, but too roughly touched
And startled; and her husband, quick with doubt,
Mistook her; in a jealous rage he turned
And flung her fiercely from him, and rushed out,
A prey to madness; and, so tells the tale,
That was the end between them.

                    All that day
Much labour was amoving in the fields,
For it was harvest time; but Alf was spent,
As one half blind that scarcely sees the sun,
He wandered bootlessly about the stead,
And the thralls toiled or trifled as they would.
At nightfall, for his very flesh was sick
With care, and passion, and conflicting thought,
Alf laid him soon abed, and fell asleep.
When midnight was far gone he woke, disturbed,
Out of a bright and beautiful dream flung back

To hate and horror.   On the silent floor
The silvery moonlight shone, and from the yards
The cocks were crowing.   Alf sat up and stretched
His trembling hands abroad.   He was alone.
He rose and donned his cloak, and got his sword,
And hid it in the ample woollen folds.
A moment, as if doubtful of his mind,
He tarried with head sunken.   Then he turned
And came beneath the roof-tree of the hall,
And stood there in the glamour and the smoke,
And watched unseen.   Bera and Ingvi sat
In the high seat, and Ingvi had a sword
Across his knees; and Bera, leaning forth,
Was feeling with her fingers the smooth edge.
Then was the stricken mind of Alf aware
The end had come; and blackest deadliest rage
Rose up out of his empty heart, and stood
Behind his eyes, and like a demon glared
Out of his wide white orbs.   And up the hall
He strode, soft footed, all unmarked, for men
Were witless at that hour and blind with drink.
On Bera and his brother, ere they knew,
He came, and plucked the blade out from his cloak
And made a fearful thrust, and drave it clear
Through Ingvi's breast, but Ingvi with a cry
Piercing and wild, reeled up, and heaved his sword
And smote the head of Alf in twain, and both
On the grim floorway of the startled hall
Lay in their mingled blood together—dead.

DAVID AND ABIGAIL

A POEM IN DIALOGUE

PERSONS OF THE POEM

DAVID—Son of Jesse.
ABIMAEL—An old man of Judah.
JOAB—Son of Zeruiah.
NABAL—A sheep-owner of Carmel in Judah
CALEB—A youth.
ABIGAIL—Wife of Nabal.
MIRIAM—Cousin and companion of Abigail.
RACHEL—A handmaid.

SCENES

I. Near Nabal's place of sheep-shearing in Carmel.
II. In the court-yard of Nabal's house.
III. At the fountain near Carmel.

SCENE I

ABIGAIL

*David appears in conversation with Abimael, his armed
followers at his back.*

DAVID

Abimael, thou art my father's friend,
The friend of old and valiant men in Judah;
In many things I would receive thy counsel,
Following its glory, fearful of my youth,
But this last matter is beyond thy rule.
Nabal hath used me like a very dog!
I have borne much, but now my wrath is fixed,
Goaded beyond all measure of restraint;
No word of thine, nor any man's shall move me.

ABIMAEL

Methinks the sword of David should be kept
Sacred and stainless for the public foe;
This old man Nabal is an Israelite.

DAVID

So much the more my wrath! It maddens me
To find within, without, and everywhere
Enemies open or concealed.

ABIMAEL

O King;
Thus shall I call thee; for a king indeed
Thou art—and Israel's last remaining hope,
By Samuel's hand anointed, named, and blessed.
Be patient with me, hear me to the end.
The youthful reaper with unpracticed hands
Gathers the tares and binds them with the corn,
But he whose feet have trodden many fields,
The many fields that are the years of life,
More surely knows the false fruits from the true.
Young blood is dangerous, takes fire at little,
And one mad stroke hath made a life's regret.
The Sons of Israel are one house together,
Kin to us all, God's chosen, and know well
That neither prayer, nor fire of sacrifice,
Nor after deeds shall make his body clean
Nor his soul white in God's unswerving eyes,
Whose hands even for most black and bitter cause
Are dyed irrevocably with a brother's blood.

JOAB

If I were David, I would waste few words
In answer to the good Abimael.
These days are for the lion, not the lamb

And every hurt must draw a sudden stroke.
Let this old man but try to play the king,
And learn what profit he shall have of mercy!

DAVID

Abimael, thou art an old man now,
But still a man like me; thou wert, 'tis said,
A warrior prompt and valiant in thy youth,
And when I tell thee how these matters fell,
I think thou wilt not much reproach mine anger.
One winter, while a passing gleam of peace
Swept us like sunshine, ere the sons of Ziph
Had drawn upon us like shrill cackling birds
The restless rage of Saul, I and my men
Dwelt here with Nabal's shepherds in the hills,
And we were friends together, and my men
Touched not nor harmed one head of all his flock,
But rather were a guard and help to them.
We rescued many from the hands of thieves,
Aiding the shepherds often in their toils.
Now but a few days since there came to me
A word that Nabal's men were gathering here
In Carmel for the shearing of his sheep,
And I, being in a bitter strait, recalled
Our friendly deeds and former services,
And so chose out from all my strength of men
The goodliest ten and sent them up to Nabal.
I bade them kindle in the old man's mind
The strong remembrance of past courtesies,
And pray him send me swiftly by their hands
Some little help, some trifle easily spared,

Even whatever least accounted thing,
Might pass beneath the lifting of his eyes;
Thus I besought him, knowing not the man.
What answer had I, think ye?   This, but this,
"Who is this David, and this son of Jesse?
That I should take my water and my bread,
My meat preparèd for the shearer's mouths,
And give them to this upstart, this low dog,
This leader of rebellious servants, men
Houseless, unnamed, nor know ye whence they be."
That was mine answer!   Think'st thou I endure
That such a man should make of me, of David,
A jest and by-word to mine enemies!
As the Lord liveth, I will neither hear
Nor spare, but I will make of Nabal's house
A nouse of desolation and of silence,
And neither man, nor beast, nor living thing
Shall mine hand leave to call on Nabal's name!

ABIMAEL

O Son of Jesse, think not I am blind
To the sharp wrong that so inflames thy spirit,
An insult, hateful, hard to be endured,
Yet hath thy servant somewhat still to say.
Nabal, for all his spite, hath slain no life
And blood will weigh too heavy in the scales
Against a few rude words.   Think well, O King;
Put by thy purpose even for a day,
And tarry gently till thine even mind
Hath clearly seen the measure of his guilt.
Think well, O King, while yet the hour is thine,

That high of heart and noble shall he be,
Fair in God's sight and sweet in Israel's praise,
And neither time nor any power of change
Shall hide away his holy name for ever—
Who first in days of awful growth like these
Shall turn away his patient soul from wrath,
And yield his footsteps to the way of peace.

JOAB

Beyond the ridge yonder I hear a sound
That makes the spear shaft burn within my hand,
The innumerable bleatings and the shearers' cries.
Here where the noonday sears us like a brand,
And the earth cracks and breaks beneath our feet,
This old man's words are like the sting of gnats
Whetting my soul to uncontrollable fury.

DAVID

Old man, it is the privileged right of age
To talk of patience and the grace of mercy
With eloquent speech, but thou hast never known
What is the grief and madness of his heart
To whom the Lord hath said, "Take thou this people,
This nest of hornets, blind and reasonless,
Bring them to order, give them strength and peace.
These many years my people are bowed down,
A prey and scorn to every harrying hand,
Nor know they in their darkness which to dread
The most, their rulers or their enemies;
And I, whom God by Samuel's sacred hand
Gave for their shelter and protecting strength,

Am hunted like a fox from hill to hill,
An outlaw from the tents of Israel,
A butt and by-word to the high and proud.
Think'st thou to find in me, Abimael,
The quiet of age, the gladsomeness of youth:
My soul is like a fierce and smouldering fire
Even the harp within my hand hath grown
A shrieking shrew, and all its quivering strength
Can scarcely cry the anger of my soul.
Think'st thou that gentle words and gentle deeds
Shall break the proud and bow the oppressors' necks,
Nay, for the Lord hath chosen a surer way:
The strong right hand uplifted with the sword.
The strong shall fall by strength, even as of old.
And this old man, this son of Belial,
This truculent wine-bibber, vile of soul and speech,
Shall such as he find favour in God's sight,
Or aught of grace, or aught of pity in mine?
Nay, as the Lord liveth, he and all his house
Shall feel my strength, and know me who I am,
And his place be as a seared mark for ever
Of the Lord's might and David's heavy wrath.

ABIMAEL

O David, I have seen a caravan,
O'ertaken by the heat wind in the desert,
And the long line of helpless travellers,
Enveloped in the fierce and smouldering blast,
Bow down, huddled together, beast and driver;
So I, being old, and but a common man,
Cannot withstand the tempest of thy wrath;
But here comes one in whose victorious hands

Are stronger arms and surer spells than mine,
And I, the broken vanguard of the fight,
Gladly draw back to let his succours through.
'Tis Abigail, the noble wife of Nabal,
Famed for the power of her unusual beauty,
Whom every shepherd on these busy hills
Guards and reveres, and names with softened tongue.
The young men say that in her voice and mien
Are witcheries beyond the natural gift
Of all the loveliest of earthly women;
The sun-baked by-ways and the sterile rocks
Grow green beneath the treading of her feet.
The very air is perfumed with her presence.
Soft are her brows as roses, and her eyes
Deeper than midnight with its wreath of stars.
Her's is the gait of queens, and on her tongue
Language hath music softer than the flutes.
Yet is her beauty but the garb of truth,
The symbol of the wisdom of her soul,
The promise of the goodness of her hands
The poor, the sick, the blind, and they that suffer
From any hurt or any grief or madness
Have found in her the cure for every ill.
A storehouse of good deeds, whose generous doors
Are never shut, whose stalls are always full.
O David, I was afraid for thy youth;
Now I rejoice that thou art not grown old,
For youth is iron to a man's advice,
But soft as milk against a woman's beauty;
And I who gave my best of speech in vain
May see thy violence melt like snow in Hermon
Before the spring-tide charm of Abigail.

DAVID

Old man, my anger is but just, my cause
God's cause against the base and hard of heart;
This woman shall not turn me from my will,
And yet I think those honied words of thine
Have dealt but lamely with her outward virtues,
As she draws nearer with her maiden train,
And mute attendants following at her heels,
Beyond thine utmost promise I perceive
The potent beauty of a matchless woman.
Surely 'tis strange that this old thorny bramble,
This Nabal reared upon a plot of rocks,
Should be the shelter of so rich a rose.
But what is this to me?   What are these thoughts?
How have I steeled my mind that even thus soon
This woman goes about to master me,
And in the iron stronghold of my soul
Purpose hangs melting like a thing of wax,
Justice grows doubtful and the form of wrath
Stands like a warning ghost apart from me?
O! shall I be another Samson, bond
To every woman whose sheer beauty wears
The power of spells to weaken and besot us?
But no; what e'er she be, she shall not move me:
I'll shut my heart up like a very stone,
Press sharply on, and have no words with her.

Enter Abigail, accompanied by her women, preceded by
attendants, bringing asses laden with gifts.

ABIGAIL

O Son of Jesse, I am Abigail,
The wife of Nabal, who hath done thee hurt,
And I am come with gifts to make amends
For my lord's churlish and unnatural deed.
There is a gentle rumour gone abroad
That thou art kind and of a generous spirit,
Wilt thou not take these gifts, and grant to me,
To me, the present of this old man's life.

DAVID

Lady, I have already learned thine errand,
Know well that it is vain! I am not one
With honied words to argue out his causes
With everyone who meets him in the way.
O warriors, the hour is passing on;
The prey awaits us yonder at the ford:
Now with arms ready, running at full speed,
Let us pass round the shoulder of the hill,
And, ere the dogs take thought to fight or fly,
Fall on them with the sword!

ABIGAIL

                    O David, hear me;
On the hard earth I kneel to bar thy way.
Wilt thou not heed a woman, who with tears,
Seeking the gift of a few hapless lives,
        24

Humbles her forehead at thy very feet.
O, be not rash, and liken not thyself
To yon fierce Edomites, whose pitiless hands
Plunder our guarded flocks and slay our men,
Cold murderers, whose hearts are like the hills
Unknown to mercy. As for this old man,
This son of Belial, whose graceless speech
Thy violent anger would reward with death,
Regard not him. He is too far below
The thought or care of Israel's promised king.

DAVID

Thy husband was not wise but falsely prompted
When thus he sent to me his comely wife
With her fair locks and flow of wily words,
Laden with spurious hospitality,
Too lately tuned, the fruit of deadly fear!
Does Nabal think by such a sleight as this
To turn away the edge of David's wrath?

ABIGAIL

O David, surely that great heart of thine
Did never speak in those cold cruel words,
Or else my tongue indeed hath failed to utter
The simple meaning of thine handmaid's heart.
O hear me; not for Nabal's sake alone
Would I dissuade thee from unholy anger,
But for God's people's sake, O king, and thine!

ABIMAEL

O David, surely thou wilt not refuse

The touching prayer of this most noble woman;
For O, I think that even an old dead tree
Would draw new sap out of the chary earth
And, shooting life through all its mouldering limbs,
Reclothe itself with leaves to shelter her.

DAVID

Women have ever laboured to unnerve
The souls of men and turn their strength to weakness.
Have we not cause, then, to restrain our ears
From drinking of that smooth and pleasant poison
That wells so deftly from a woman's lips,
And shield our eyes, whose blindness cannot see
The chain that hangs within her fragrant tresses.

ABIGAIL

Again in this my lord is not himself,
But even as one that wills to hide his heart
He utters things, part truth, and partly false;
Nor will I strive to answer, calling up
The shapes of noble women from the past,
For these are readier to thy thought than mine.
Only one thing my heart would ask of thee:
O Son of Jesse, was there not one woman,
To thee above all earth's remembered names
Most dear; Micah, the lovely child of Saul,
Who set her own sweet life at naught for thee,
To save thine head out of her father's hand
As now I strive, if only God will aid,
To save thy soul from blood?   Wilt thou not hear?

DAVID

Were not my purpose fixed as adamant,
And set beyond all breaking by an oath,
Hardly could I, though strong in wrath, withstand
    thee;
Even now thou hast so far prevailed with me
That thou may'st speak and I will quietly hear thee;
Yet hope not I will lightly cast away
The purpose of my heart which is but justice.

ABIGAIL

O David, on the earth are many lives,
But each one deems that what his anger bids
Is justice, till the world is full of hate.
Men are become as beasts that hunt and kill,
And there is none, not one, to stay their hands.
Art thou not come by God's command to heal
The sickness of these days and not to feed it?
I know that thou hast suffered greater ills
By far than this and yet wert merciful,
At bare Engedi by the desolate sea,
To one not weak, the stern and treacherous Saul.
O David, though indeed I pity Nabal,
The poor old man, yet most I pity thee,
Whose goodness hath so suffered by this deed.
Ah, would that thou hadst sent thy young men up
To me for gifts, and not to Nabal's self
So had they not gone humbled from the folds,
Fraught with rude answers and with empty hands,
And in their hearts the unendurable sting
Of strange ingratitude.   But what is done

We cannot alter. What is planned we may;
Nor need my lord have any fear of me
That I will lead his mind at all astray
With any feint or cloakèd treachery;
Nor should his hand be slow to take these gifts,
Nabal knows nothing of them nor thy coming,
Nor am I here on any embassage,
But of mine own will solely, for I thought
That my lord's hot and impetuous spirit,
Bending a softened ear to my quiet words
Might stay to think, perchance might even learn
Some gentle good from me who am a woman,
Not light at all, nor foolish as some be,
But having many dreams and many thoughts.
O David, are the elder truths grown false?
Is life all changed, and pity but a word?
For I have heard the lips of old men say
That mercy even in the least of men
Is a high grace, but most of all in kings.
How shall a trembling people rest in peace
Beneath the wrathful hand that knows not mercy?
O Son of Jesse, thus a king should be:
Noble and valiant, to his country's foes
A memorable dread, but to his own
Patient and kind. And this I dreamed of thee;
For when I heard the rumours of that day,
To Azzah and Goliah dark indeed,
When Israel lifting up her voice in song
Advanced thy glory ten-fold more than Saul's.
I saw the coming of a man divine,
Greater than Barak or than Gideon,
Or Jephthah, whom the gates of Minneth saw,

On whom the Lord for some majestic plan
Had dowered the wonder of a two-fold gift,
The prophet's dream, the valour of a king.
Surely this gift of God, this sacred strength,
Was made to thee for holier use than this;
That thou shouldst war upon a weak old man,
Whose churlish spirit, like an angry bee,
Hath chanced to brush thee with its random sting.
O let my lord be patient, and think well;
Let not thine hand-maid come at last to know
That the great David of her burning thought
Is but a dream, and less than other men,
A like successor to the son of Kish,
Another Saul.

DAVID

            Nay, pause not in thy speech,
But let me hear thee to the very end,
For though thou may'st not tempt nor break my will,
Mine ears are greedy of thy voice; my soul
Drinketh the grace and music of thy words
More gladly than the sun-baked earth absorbs
The summer rain.

ABIGAIL

            Full well I know, O King,
That God hath put thee sharply to the test,
And tried thy spirit with unwonted fires,
And this he purposes not that thou should'st grow
Testy and dangerous like a baited bear,
Madly alive to every private hurt,

But that thine heart like Joseph's in his bondage
Out of the springs of fiery grief should draw
The nearer knowledge of this people's ill
With might of soul and strength of hand to save.
Yet though my Lord hath bent him to this fault,
I shall not deem that David's soul shall fail,
Nor in the end be wanting, fully weighed;
Lo! even now, most surely, though we see not,
The gradual winds of Time are bearing up,
Even as a little cloud out of the sea,
The promised day wherein delivered Judah
Shall cast away the sack-cloth from his limbs
And from the sadness of his hair shake out
The mournful ashes, having dried for ever
The fountain of his tears; and thou shalt stand,
The anointed of our God, a king indeed,
Girt with the radiant thousands of thy people,
The uprisen sons of mighty Israel;
And they shall be about thee for a guard,
Great as the sea for strength and as the sands for
    number;
On every tongue a song, in every heart
The light that shines between the cherubim,
The power invincible; and over all
The Shekinah, the glory of the Lord,
Shall find fit home on David's blessèd brow.
O David, hath my simple woman's speech
Touched thee indeed; so that thy cloudy brow
Lightens, and in the garden of thy heart,
A natural soil, the roses of God's goodness
Have overbloomed the poisonous weeds of wrath;
And now indeed I know that thou wilt take

These gifts, and spare me freely from thine heart
This old man's life, to me a priceless present,
To thee a fault o'ercome, a victory gained.

DAVID

My purpose melts away.   In all my soul
Only the magic of thy voice remains,
O radiant queen and milk-white rose of women;
Justice and wrath and the most fixèd wish,
And every fact, and every uttered oath
Gives way before thy beauty as the night
Gives way to morn.   Take thou the life of Nabal;
Let all his house and every living thing
Whereon the splendour of thy glance shall fall,
Be sacred from my touch and safe from fear,
And may thy days be full of praise and honour,
Encompassed with the valiant love of friends,
Nor any grief, nor shade of injury,
Approach thy soul, nor touch this plot of earth,
Made sacred by the usage of thy feet.
As for me, sooner shall mine eyes forget
The noon-day sun than from my soul shall pass
The vision and the voice of Abigail.

ABIGAIL

O David, wert thou come in peaceful times
With other thoughts, and had I met thee here,
So would I lead thee to my husband's house
With all thy men, and ye should rest a day,
And I would feast thee gladly like a king,
And serve thee of the best with mine own hand;

But now this cannot be; nay, it were well
That thou should'st leave this place and draw away
Yon dark-browed multitude of dangerous men,
In whom the fiery lust of blood and prey
Yet burns. I dread lest any horrid chance,
The approach of Nabal, or a passing flock,
Should prompt them to some sudden deed of pillage.

DAVID

The words of Abigail are wise and good,
And like the rushing cloud, whose sudden gloom
Hangs dark upon the valleys and is gone,
Our host shall vanish swiftly as it came.
I know not what the hidden hours shall bring:
The labours of my hands are void and vain:
My feet are compassed by the snares of foes:
My days are riddles that I cannot read.
Yes, when my soul is troubled most, my path
Most broken, most perplext, I will remember
Thy beauty and the goodness of thy words:
Thy name shall be as honey to my lips,
And like strong wine unto my fainting soul
Thy voice recalled and thy remembered presence.
And this much more, O beautiful, most wise;
Should'st thou be hurt by any evil change,
And need befall thee of the succouring hand,
Send thou to me, and whatsoever space
Should lie between us, whatsoever toil
Or want or sickness pin me to the earth,
Be it death's hour or even the battle's height,
I will arise and surely come to thee.
                    Exit David with his host.

ABIMAEL

So are they gone, and with a joyous heart
I see the gleam of their retreating spears
And the long cloud of dust that from their feet
Rises and hangs about the hillside yonder.
Lady, thou hast wrought well, and thy fair presence
And noble speech were potent as I hoped.

ABIGAIL

O now the word is spoken and the gift
Is won: the shadow of death is turned away
From witless Nabal and the peaceful folds;
O, I am happy, but withal undone!
My heart beats sharply; I am faint and sick;
Come hither, maiden; let me lean on thee;
There, thou art kind. · Abimael, 'tis strange
That we poor women oft in darkest hours
Have such quiet wills to battle with our hearts,
Even in the stormy face of manful passion,
Such settled skill to aim our shafts aright;
Yet when the foe hath fallen and the field
Rings with the cry of bloodless victory,
No longer calm, no longer strong we stand,
But helpless, thus, pale delicate conquerors,
Smitten with our own efforts nigh to death.
But this one thing, Abimael, I say
With joy: by no means hurtless or in vain
My mother bore me woman, weaker-limbed
And softer-thewed than men are, but more fair
To look upon, and with the woman's heart
By nature given to read the minds of men,

More quick than wind or water to give motion
With wingèd thoughts, and with the piercing skill
Of lips true-noted turned to flute-like use
Make music of them sweet and magical :
Nor more in vain was he that met me so
A true king's heart, the chosen of God's most high,
A man of men, from Heaven's treasury,
Coined in God's mint of kings, on the one side
The human stamp of testy wrathfulness,
But on the other the soft face of pity,
Between the two, the mass and weight of all,
Justice made lovely with the hue of gold,
As he made comely with fair face and stature.
O, blessèd be Jehovah's hand that formed
The son of Jesse more than common men,
Rearing in him the quick and malleable heart ;
And blessèd be His hand that He hath given
That gift of gifts, that woman's power, to me,
Who never wished to use it save for good.

MIRIAM

Still follow thy good fortune Abigail ;
Yon changeful lord and his tempestuous band
Have left this place no whit too soon, for here,
Down by the shady covert of the hill
Comes Nabal with uneven gait, nor knows
How close he trod to death.   Behold his eyes,
With what a wicked and revengeful fire
They dart from one to other of this group,
Like an old ram's that rove about the field,
Searching for some unguarded enemy !
How with his staff, as if it were a spear,

He thrusts and wounds the unoffending earth,
And grinds the sand beneath his furious heels!
On whom now will the man direct his wrath?
For well I see that both his hairy cheeks
Are blown and crimson with distending passion.

SCENE II

NABAL

In the courtyard of Nabal's house.

RACHEL

Last night's carousal was a merry one.
The floors, the courtyard, and the very air
Are soiled and bitter with the stale spilt wine
My brows ache still with all the noise and riot,
And thou art like a fresh-blown rose, my Miriam,
Blithe as the day.   Is Nabal yet astir?
Nabal! not he indeed! not he!   He lies
Heaped on his couch yonder, a shapeless load,
Fast anchored with a gallon weight of wine,
And moans and struggles in his bestial sleep.
Listen!   Dost thou not hear him from within,
Wheezing and snorting like an unstirred pudding?
Oh pleasure of the thick and wallowing slough!
Oh bliss of swine!   Oh joy of drunkenness!
What things have women for their wedded mates!
I would there were some dream so huge and black,
So monstrous and so loathing horrible,
Might sit upon his heart and with its bulk

Burst it in twain! And he will awake anon,
Saddled with aches, and lurching through the house
Mad and thick-voicèd like an uneasy bull,
Throw off the stupor of last night's debauch
In blows and curses.

RACHEL

Miriam! Miriam!

MIRIAM

                    Indeed I care not, I;
My tongue is like the wind that stays for no man.
I will not live and have my tongue tied up
Forbidden of its force and wholesome use.
What pleasure have we? Half the joy of life
Is in bold talk and pelting words about.
My cousin knows and loves me as I am,
Nor cares she for my tongue; and as for Nabal—
Nay listen then! I'll picture thee a scene.
Once in this very place his wrath took fire—
'Tis true I had done nothing worth a blow—
He raised his staff to strike me; she stood forth;
And oh! that look; I never saw before
That potent look in Abigail's soft eyes.
It was the queen that with a gaze of steel
Forbade the slave! He dropped his staff and quailed,
Bewildered as an ox whom the rough butcher
Smites full upon the forehead with his mallet.

RACHEL

Most blessèd Abigail! These walls are dead,
Or worse, denizened by an unclean spirit,
When she is not within. What cause, I wonder,
Draws her away thus early from her cares?

MIRIAM

I know not surely, but I think some trouble
Weighs sharply on her spirit, for at dawn
She took that well-worn wary staff of hers,
And walking with bent brow and hasty step
Made for the mountain paths. No doubt she hoped
In solitude and the keen upland air
To master and reclaim her scattered thoughts,
Seeking the source of their habitual calm.
Last night she slept not, her excited thoughts
Perchance brewed out of the day's adventure
Visions and dreams that, like unwholesome airs,
Menaced the health and safety of her soul.
This Abigail, whose gentle rectitude
Shines like a portent on our pettier lives,
Is no mere block of precept and of plan,
No shape of painted wood, but a real woman:
Think not because her eyes are like the stars
That ever look on men with equal gaze,
There is no fire or passion in her blood.
Because she is a true and steadfast wife,
With her own hands she binds her heart in chains:
But youth is quick and the o'ermastering blood
Tides up at times against the coldest will.
Oh, yesterday, I watched her as she stood

Calm, glowing, with that sovereign port of hers,
Before the royal David.   Never yet
Seemed she so beautiful, so warmly fair;
And as the warrior yielded and his eyes
Grew fixed upon her like two radiant stars,
There came a subtle yearning in her voice;
A mantling red glowed up in both her cheeks;
A light, as of a soul that sees unveiled
The distance of some unexplored joy,
Broke from her lifted lids.   I tell thee, Rachel,
That David's strength hath touched her to the heart,
And yonder on our well-loved mountain path
She walks alone, and strives to crush the flame.
Would that her lot were ordered otherwise—
A wondrous pair—David and Abigail—
And then to think of this old wine-skin, Nabal!
Ah! there I hear her voice.   She calls thee, Rachel,
Run girl!

Enter Abigail.

Good morrow, cousin; what strange whim
Takes thee abroad at this unwonted hour,
When all the house is crying for thy presence.

ABIGAIL

Last night I could not sleep, my Miriam;
A multitude of strange and wayward thoughts
Usurped my soul, and when I rose at dawn,
The house oppressed me with its cold gray walls.
My head ached and my hand had lost its skill,
And so, that I might conquer back myself,
I sought the hillside and the mountain path.

The fresh clear morning led me on and on,
Until I reached that last and loftiest spur
From which one looking from the windy north
Sees afar off, tender and white as wool,
The walls of Hebron and the tombs of Mamre;
And there I stayed, and there my peace returned.
Because we live these quiet and regular lives,
We think our soul firm poised, beyond the touch
Of passion or the fever of an hour;
Yet are our thoughts most often like the snows
That sleep upon the lofty mountain scaurs,
Yet once upon the silent depth there comes
A step, a shout, a sudden axe's stroke,
And like the magic loosening of a world,
Down from a hundred ledges light as wind,
Thunders and shoots the storming avalanche!

MIRIAM

My cousin is not wise to wander thus
Choosing the solitary paths, or wear
A countenance so grave and rapt in thought.
Soon through the countryside from mouth to mouth
The tale of David's coming will go forth,
And then it will be said that Abigail,
Who wanders in such sad and abstract moods,
Is eaten secretly with hopeless love,
And pines for David.   But how now, my lady;
The blood takes flame upon thy cheek like flax:
I almost think my words have hit the mark.

ABIGAIL

Ah! Miriam, I would not have thee speak so.
No! No!

MIRIAM

Forgive the word: I was but jesting.

ABIGAIL

Come hither, Miriam, give me thine hand.
By the quick ear and by the kindling eye
Intelligences flash from soul to soul;
But by the touch our very hearts are knit,
Rushing together like charged water-drops.
And I have often thought that if my mind
Were ever touched by any earthly care
Or common trouble, there were none but thee
Unto whose honest friendship I could bring it
Certain of comfort, sure of peaceful trust.
There is a common saying in these hills:
A sorrow poured into a faithful ear
Is half dispelled: and I have known it true.
O friend and cousin, she who deemed herself
The fair embodiment of lofty pride,
Secure and passionless, beyond a fault,
Is weak as air, unstable as the sand:
And I, who in my splendid confidence
Went forth to conquer an anointed king
Come back—not vanquished, God be thanked for it—
But touched, excited, sharply hurt at heart.
O, youth that is so dangerously quick
So quick and subtle! Must we bind and blind it?
25

MIRIAM

I saw the fiery contest of thine heart;
I saw it, and I loved thee dearlier for it.

ABIGAIL

Now it is gone, but I am happier,
Because thou shar'st in thy reflecting heart
The travail of my soul.   For one short hour
I struggled and cried out against my lot.
But life is straight and simple to the wise;
And I have learned already in my youth
An iron truth that most men never reach;
Our life is regular and bound by law,
For God hath given to each his changeless word,
Laid out his path and bade him walk therein.
Our only happiness, our final joy,
Is in persisting calmly to the goal,
And he who struggles from his ordered way,
How hard soe'er it be, even in thought,
Reaps in the end but bitterness and shame.
He only can be happy who is strong,
Who bears above the crying tides of passion
And movements of the blind and restless soul
A forehead smooth with purpose, and a will
Spacious and limpid as the cloudless morn.

MIRIAM

Here comes that—

ABIGAIL

We will speak no more of this.
The thought is dead and must awake no more.

Enter Nabal, rolling and heavy-eyed.

NABAL

Oh, what a noisome treacherous drug is wine—
I think mine eyes are full of heated sand—
And oh, my head is stuffed with wool, my tongue
Lies sapless as a chip in my dry gums;
I burn with fever, give me water, water!
Give me a panful, ah! the crystal stream;
I would I were a giant with my neck
Over the margin of some limpid sea;
I'd drink and drain until the world grew dry!
But yon great rocks, the hideous fearsome heights
And the huge gullies, and the gaping holes!—
What is the matter with my head? You girl,
Bring me a little wine to clear my wit—
I have upon my mind that cut-throat dog,
That David, who two mornings since, sent up
All lean and hungry from his mountain lair,
And at my very throat demanded alms.
Ah, how I cursed them! But I had a dream—
Methought I was a sheep—a vast great sheep,
All flounced and heavy with great clots of wool,
And after me a wolf with a black face,
Like unto the face of David, and I ran
Up into a steep mountain. 'Twas a place
Full of sharp rocks and thorns and horrible caves
Ah me! What fright I had! And as I ran,

How I cried out with doleful shrieks and cursed him
Even as I curse him now : may every blight—

ABIGAIL

Nabal, beware !   That blind and senseless rage
Hurries thee to the very brink of madness,
And robs thee of the semblance of a man ;
Beware !   For when the hour of danger falls,
Who that hath known thee in this wolfish mood
Will have regard or pity for thine age ;
And most of all this day, I counsel thee
To speak no evil of the son of Jesse,
For thou hast done him wrong, O blind insensate,
Thou art but a reed in David's hand !

NABAL

And dost thou take his part as against me?
Dost speak for him?   Dost thou?   Oh where are words
That I may tell how much I loathe and hate
And scorn, and flout, and spit upon his name,
The dog ! the foul hyæna ! the fanged viper !—

ABIGAIL

Nabal, I will no longer keep the tale,
For thou dost anger me beyond control !
From mine own tongue thou shalt be made aware
How terrible the Son of Jesse is,
How stern, yet merciful—and thou, how base !
Whilst thou wert strutting in thy petty rage

Above thy gray unconscious head hath hung
A hand that glittered with a sword, and mine
Hath turned it from thee.   Yesterday at noon
Came David hither with four hundred men,
Heated with wrath beyond all thought of mercy.
Swiftly and silently they marched, full armed,
Designing with a two-fold sudden movement
To take thee with the shearers at the ford
And slay both man and beast.   But I had learned
Already from the lips of one who knew thee
And knew also the fiery soul of David,
The story of thy base ingratitude.
I told thee nothing, for I pitied thee,
But took such presents as mine haste could find,
And laid them upon asses and went forth.
Already, when I met them, they had reached
With all their host the turning of the hill,
Four hundred spears that flamed against the sun
And from the neighbouring valley eastward rose
The mingled cries of shearers and of sheep,
Whetting their souls to yet more desperate wrath.
And there I stood and stayed the son of Jesse,
And stemmed his furious anger with my gifts,
And wrought upon him with my prayerful speech,
Yet only with great toil I turned at last
That fiery and inflexible soul, and drew
Out from between the very wings of death
Thy rude and thankless life.   Ah! thou art pale!
Poor man!   I would that thou might'st learn from
    this—
But what—Ah Nabal!—Speak to me! What ails thee?

NABAL

Oh, horrible! Be silent! Something strikes
Sharp at my very heart! Whither—O help me!

Falls.

ABIGAIL

O Nabal, husband! Ah, be merciful!
Forgive me! Oh, the cruel speech! The mad
Unthankful tongue! Indeed I never dreamed
My words had hurt thee so. Here! Miriam!

MIRIAM

His limbs are still and rigid! He is dead!

ABIGAIL

Ah, who shall say so, surely? Some slight spark
Like seed in the deep earth may yet be left,
Which we with careful tillage may rear up
Till the full stature of his life return.
Call me the servants hither, the strong men;
Then swiftly, gently we will bear his body
And lay him in the inner chamber yonder
Between warm coverlets, and chafe his limbs
With vigilant hands. Meanwhile between his lips
Two drops of this strong cordial may bear
God's respite to the sick and numbèd soul.

Exeunt Abigail and attendants, bearing Nabal.

MIRIAM

'Tis as my cousin said : the old man lives
But fitfully like an expiring candle,
The wick lies guttering in the blackened oil,
And soon it will be still.   Poor Abigail!
I cannot understand her passionate grief,
Yet do I see her tears and pity her.
So sweet and sacred is the bond of marriage,
We cannot part from anyone whose blood
Hath beat so near to us without some pang
And tearful wringing of the sundered soul.
For me 'tis but a ruffian brute the less
To make this life a bugbear and a plague :
And Miriam shall drop on Nabal's grave
Such glittering tears as the warm hillside sheds
When winter leaves his last rude breath and dies.
But here comes one will suit me for an errand.

Enter Caleb, a youth.

Hallo!   Boy!   What wise thought may bring thee
     hither?

CALEB

No more a boy, lady, but let that pass.
I heard a cry and tumult through the house,
And stayed to learn the cause.   Is't true Miriam,
That the old man is at the point of death?
Aye!   Then he falls in a most droughty season,
And weeping will be scanty even as rain.
'Twill be a merrier house when he is gone,
A place of better rest and better cheer.

MIRIAM

I understand ye, lad. What things are men!
The body is your dear delight; your God
Is not a golden but a roasted calf;
And all your prayer is for your body's ease;
Long slumber and a belly roundly stuffed.
Hark to me boy! I think this lady's rule
Will be short-lived. These passionate tears of hers
Will vanish southward like a gust of rain,
And leave the zenith brighter than before.
Husbands as many as midsummer leaves
Will woo the choice of one so young and fair.
And now the chancing of that word reminds me,
Dost thou know, lad, the way to David's camp?

CALEB

If Miriam bids, I shall be swift to find it.

MIRIAM

There is at least one virtue in a youth:
He's ever ready at a woman's bidding,
So she be young and not unfair; good lad,
Put all the vigour of thy legs to test,
And run to David wheresoe'er he be;
Tell him how God hath granted his revenge,
Yet kept him guiltless of this old man's blood.
Tell him that Nabal lies stone-still and speechless
At point of death; that Abigail now rules
The fruitful valleys and this rich domain,
And all the houses and all the flocks are hers.

O boy! I would the gift of subtle speech
Were thine, or that I were a man like thee.
Nay, I am almost tempted in my mind
To don men's clothes, and bear the news myself:
For with a shrewd addition of bold words
I would so fan within the soul of David
The kindled longing, that mere speed of feet
Would seem too tardy for his wingèd wishes.
But tell me, Caleb, with what joyous speech
Thou would'st present before the son of Jesse
The grace and goodness of our Abigail.

CALEB

Oh, I would say that, next to Miriam,
Our lady is the fairest among women;
That when she walks, for grace and majesty
She's like the slender daughter of a king;
And when she rests, there's not another living,
Save Miriam, that hath a whiter brow,
And eyes more dark, more melancholy sweet.
Her voice is vibrant as the deep-toned harp,
Though Miriam's is softer than the flute.
And oh, her hand! There's not another hand
Whose touch goes swifter to the beating heart,
Save only Miriam.

MIRIAM

O! brave lad!
A fine ambassador indeed! Go on!
Pray thee go on! I am not surfeited;
For when I drink, 'tis ever my delight

To drain the goblet to the very lees,
Even though the draught be only ass's milk.

CALEB

And I will tell him that our lady's mouth
Is like the gateway of some precious mint,
Whence only gold and silver issue forth,
A palace portal barred with ivory;
And yet those regal lips are not so fair
Nor half so sweet to touch as Miriam's.

MIRIAM

How now! Rash youth! Thy tongue hath hurried thee
Beyond the line of true experience.
What knowest thou forsooth of Miriam's lips?

CALEB

I'd tell thee, Miriam, if I only dared—
Aye! and I will sweet mistress, for I think
Some devil rides upon my tongue to-day.
One noon when thou wert fallen sound asleep
Under a tree yonder—thou'lt fancy when—
The half-wound distaff lying at thy feet,
I, by the guidance of some happy chance,
Taking the shadow of the golden wall,
Looked in.   Thou wert so near, so fair, so tempting.
With fear and creeping caution I approached,
And touched thy lips—the wind was not more light.
Once, twice, and thrice, and then I laughed and ran.
I was half mad for thinking of the deed.

There was a gentle fire upon my lips
That made me light of head and full of fancies
The shepherds jeered me as I passed, some saying
That I was moon-struck, some that I had found
A treasure hidden in the earth.   Methought
The very touch of food would soil my lips,
And so for many days I scarcely ate.

MIRIAM

I see the cause of all this flood of words,
The monstrous outgrowth of thy lips, sweet fool,
I would that I had wakened at that moment;
So hadst thou had a swelling of the ears,
And gone abroad among the shepherds, not
All lips a lover, but an ass all ears.

CALEB

Poor ass!   And yet the torment of his ears,
Had scarcely warmed the gladness of his lips.

MIRIAM

Nay, if thou be a very ass in sooth,
Thou'lt never serve my purpose, lad; but tell me,
What shall I do to make thee fleet and strong,
A runner surer than the mountain deer,
All legs and feet.

CALEB

Ah, but another touch—

MIRIAM

Nay, never, fool; away with thee.   Indeed,
I prize too much the sweetness of thy dream
To mar it with the flat reality;
A waking kiss upon thy waking lips
Would break the body's balance utterly.
Enough of jesting, boy, for I must go
To Abigail, who needs my hands; and thou
Speed thee away to David like a bird.

SCENE III

DAVID

The Fountain in Carmel.

MIRIAM

Here is the spot, our well-loved resting place,
The fountain and its easeful roof of trees,
The shrubs, the perfumes and the poppied grass.
Methinks it should be changed; so many things
Have fallen upon us, strange and unforeseen
Since last we rested in glad converse here.

ABIGAIL

And yet it changeth not.   Though yesterday
From dawn till eve and half the weary night
The air blew thick, the heated Khamsin blew
Full from the wide-mouthed furnace of the desert,

Yet is its heart not changed.   The cooling water
Comes gurgling from the deep and shadowy trough
A thinner stream, but sparkling as of old.

MIRIAM

So let it be with thee.   Sorrow and death
Have ruled thee like the Khamsin for a day,
And numbed thy spirit with their sickening stroke,
And now with glittering wand and golden key
The keeper of the palace of thy life
Shuts the grim doors of death and drives apart
The portals of the future.   Lo! the hills
Upon whose splintered crowns and sculptured sides
The sunlight and the violet shadows sleep,
Yon valley melted far in blue, and lo!
The spring, the morning, and this happy spot,
Sweet with the memories of pleasant hours.
This wind that bears upon its velvet wings
The cool and murmur of the middle sea
And mingles with our mountain balms the breath
Of Sharon's roses and her blossoming apricots.
Like the mad drunkard at his vat I stand,
And drain it with my nostrils and my lips,
And gladlier than a fond enamoured girl
Takes the first imprint of her lover's kiss,
Receive it in my bosom and my hair.

ABIGAIL

How grateful, even at this early hour
The solid shade of this huge terebinth,
Whose bole and round of leafage like a cloud

Seems moist and glistening with perpetual dew.
Already the fierce summer sun strikes down,
A white and pitiless edge. On either hand
The arid ridges burn like slacking lime.
Yonder already the spent winter stream
Shrinks in its meagre bottom of cracked clay,
And dwindles into little yellow pools
Adown the valley, and the pasture grows
An opiate lethargy, a drowsy calm,
And sound and motion cease: while far and near
From every cleft and hollow of these slopes
The heat spreads out upon the creeping air
The pungent scent of sage and lavender.

MIRIAM

I would I had the power of Joshua,
Who stayed the hour and made the sun stand still,
So would I lie here in the pleasant grass,
And hold this morning freshness for an age;
And I would water with mine hands each hour
Yon drooping fringe of yellow asphodels,
The poppies and soft-cheeked chrysanthemums
That spot the narrow sward with flame and gold.
But lo! the word of Miriam is weak,
Her hand is powerless and the sun moves on;
Yet, while the morning lingers, there is joy.
Beside thy Syrian fairness, I shall sit,
And laugh, and fret thee with my madman's talk,
And deck me with these poppies till I look
As wild and wicked as a desert queen;
Thou hast no need of flowers, my Abigail,

Who art more fair, more proudly beautiful
Among the flowers, than ever wearing them.

ABIMAEL

What limit is there to the reckless dance
Of thy mad tongue! Wert ever in thy life
Unhappy Miriam?

MIRIAM

                Aye, when a child,
But rather desperate than unhappy, mad
Than sad; for I was forced against the grain,
And curbed, and driven in all things till I grew
All fierce, and like a little wild thing fought
And bit at every touch. Who shall forget
The passion of our first momentous meeting.
Surely not I—I think not Abigail—
How, like a wild-cat in the snare, I shrank,
Half fierce, half frightened, then a little while
Stood sullen with my fixed forbidding gaze,
Till I had weighed and pondered and compared
Each note and shadow of thy speech and bearing,
And pierced and read thee to the heart:
How finally a sudden joy of faith
Possessed me, and I came, and touched thy hem
And grasped thy knees and sprang upon thy breast.
Since then like the wild rose-tree I have grown
And bloomed and climbed at will, and thou, my friend,
How little hast thou ever pruned or curbed me,
Too generous gardener, to whom I owe
That now I am as wild in happiness

As erst I was in grief. Sorrow and tears
In that mild measure that most women use
For me were pointless or impossible.
My joy is like a silver spouting stream
That dances in the sunshine—to be free,
To know no care, nor any doubting thoughts,
To dwell within thy presence like the sun,
And tread upon the natural earth at will,
These things are joy. And grief, I have forgotten grief,
But could I grieve—and life is wild with chances—
'Twould be no common touch of malady,
Or mood of woeful weeping, but a passion,
Frantic and terrible, a tempest stroke,
A bursting sea, a stream of hissing fire,
A storm that in the compass of a day
Would wreck my flesh, and leave me dead or mad.

ABIGAIL

How divers are our natures, Miriam,
And how distant, for I have seldom known
That buoyant life, that free and natural joy;
To me 'tis matter to be brooded on
Like something curious in a traveller's tale;
Nor have I been unhappy, but my joy
Has been a serious ordered thing,
The satisfaction bred of wifely thoughts
And well-planned labours studiously fulfilled,
To order thriftly my husband's house,
To keep myself a blameless wife, unstained
By evil thoughts, the nurse of evil deeds,
Single of heart, one-minded, dreamless, pure;

To tend with heartening speech and helpful hand
The dwellers on these waste laborious hills,
Making their life more easy; to be strong
Where men were weak, and in the frequent fall
Of times disastrous to be near to each
With needful counsel, were it stern or gentle;
Such was my task; to know it well fulfilled,
At first with effort, then as time went on
Its exercise became a lofty habit; that
My happiness.   A life so shaped and poised
To me was the supreme necessity,
To whom the restless and impassioned spirit,
Denied the choice and fancied lot of youth,
Must needs be curbed, and to this common earth
Fastened with wholesome and perpetual cares.
And yet with all my rule, rebellion, discontent,
The longing after things remote and large
Beyond the settled sphere of these quiet toils,
Have marred it, and in hours of lost command
Perplexed and tortured me.   Those lower wishes
That lawlessly disturb and haunt the young,
I scorned and easily cast from me; these
Were not my bane; but there were other longings,
Born of the very purpose of my heart,
I could not, and, meseemed, I dare not crush.
I thought of those great women praised of old
Whose presence mightier than rage and fear
Inured our fathers' hands to nobler deeds.
I dreamed that in mine own swift-visioned soul
Their spirit I discerned, a gift divine.
Fear fell upon me, dark perplexity,
Lest in my error I should waste unused
26

Some power appointed for our people's keep
Now most at need; I thought of Miriam
Who led her women in the dance of praise
With timbrels at the passage of the sea;
I dreamed myself another Deborah,
A spirit sharper than a two-edged sword
Whose word awoke in sleeping Israel
The might of Barak, when the northern plain
And all the fields of Kishon to the hills
Were darkened with the hosts of Sisera.
Such were my dreams, but in the end, with fear
And effort and the stroke of blind denial,
I rose and put them from me.   I attained
Not joy indeed nor young heart-happiness,
But quiet and the peace of proud content.
But now the order of that day is gone.
My system with its vanished sun dissolves,
And duty, the sad governess, whose wand
In former times to some undoubted path
Bade me inexorably, now veils her face,
And leaves me masterless, points me no way,
And yet through all the sadness of my heart,
The empty shadows that appal, perplex
And mock my strength, the old high dreams return
In fear and exultation.   Daring thoughts
That glow upon the future as with gold
A buoyant madness that I cannot name,
Possess my soul.   At hours a kind of joy
From the sheer dark flames out and dazzles me.
I seem to tread on wind.   Sorrow and death,
And all the story of the mournful past,
The shadows of remorseful memory,

Swirl back and leave me all alone
Like some strong traveller in the moon-lit desert:
The wonderous light, the silence and the stars
Absorb his thoughts and make within his soul
A solemn and mysterious joy; he stands
With arms uplifted on the gleaming waste.

MIRIAM

There comes a day, and, as I think, full soon
When Abigail shall find these thoughts and dreams
The premonition of some urgent truth.
Around us all at every hour unseen
The sleepless agencies that mould our lives
Are weaving with dark hands and glittering wit
From threads that have no end and no beginning
The tracery of our lives inwoven with all,
A shining web of unexpected things;
Even now methinks mine eyes behold a sign.
What say'st thou to yonder armèd shapes
That come so swiftly up our hillside path?
Could we, though many wild and busy years
Had crammed our memories, pass over or mistake
    them?
That outer one, with the long threatening staff,
The sinewy shoulders and the leopard stride—
Who knows not Joab?   In that supple form
The lean quick limbs, that dark and vigilant face,
There dwells an influence hardly to be named
The horrid magic of the circling snake.
What secret is there in that lip, that eye
That holds and pins you with its powerful gaze,
As soft and perilous as a bed of down

Whereon a tiger sleeps?   When he is near
I cannot choose but watch him; all my soul
Goes straightway to his black mysterious heart,
Striving to shape and picture forth its tale
Of bloody schemes and unhatched treacheries—
That one is Joab, cousin, and the other—
Mark the bold gait, the lofty head—is David.

ABIGAIL

It is indeed the form and gait of David.
What brings him hither?   Doth he know?
He cannot know!

MIRIAM

            To those whom love hath touched
And in the core of all their thoughts infixed
The strong desire of some belovèd woman
Tidings fly fast.

ABIGAIL

            Nay, Miriam, speak not so:
My heart already is o'erwrought.   Thy words
Will shake me from my little last control.
Talk to me rather of the birds and trees,
The house, the flocks, and common work-day things;
Or if thou hast some miracle of speech
To lay emotion and compose the soul,
O use it, Miriam, for now, now most
I would preserve my wifely dignity,
And arm me with the strength of two to meet
This stranger with an honourable front.

MIRIAM

David, I think, will look for sighs and tears
Rather than strength and austere majesty.
Doth Abigail not know what brings him hither?

ABIGAIL

I know not, yet his coming seems a thing
Familiar to me; I have dreamed it often.

MIRIAM

I'll tell thee Abigail—and in thine heart
Thou art assured of it as I.   He comes
To crown his life with Judah's best of gifts,
And rob these mountains of their priceless queen.
The vision of the wise, fair woman, tall
And glorious, of the potent flute-like speech,
Who turned his anger from the quest of blood,
Glows with a light unceasing, uneclipsed,
Set like a star within the heart of David.

ABIGAIL

O David, thou art coming; even now
I almost see thy features; were it so—

MIRIAM

And all that strange desire, that wild unrest,
That swayed thy spirit from its narrow path
Is but the force of David in thy soul,
The half-unconscious passionate love of him—

Aye let the rose mount up within thy cheek,
And thine eye kindle with that solemn fire!
Never hath man beheld thee yet so fair,
So beautiful, so queenly, so inspired!
Let all the magic of thy being rise
To make thee for the moment what it will,
The proudest and the best of Abigail.
That utmost grace shall not again return:
This is thine hour, thy one great hour of life!

Enter David.

DAVID

Changed is his heart, and changed are all his thoughts
Who seeks again thy presence, Abigail,
I came in anger with the sword and spear,
Athirst for vengeance, eager to destroy,
And found before my feet, a suppliant,
Mercy herself in very form of flesh.
I yielded, but I knew not even then
How deep the spell had touched, nor how that hour
Had bound me in the magic of thy beauty.
I come again, this time a suppliant,
Desiring pardon, if I jar thy grief,
With my rude haste and unregardful presence.
I come because the cold and prudent will
Hath lost all cunning to restrain my feet.
Thy vision and the music of thy voice
Possessed me and drave me; I could bear no more
The empty dream, the unassured desire.
Within my tent and on the barren hills,
By night, by day, the longing mastered me,

Haunted my sleep and maddened my awaking;
Till I became as a demented man,
The victim of some burning malady.
The heart of David yearns to Abigail,
And cannot rest but in her golden presence.
O Abigail, my ways are full of grief,
Shadowed by doubt, oppressed by enemies,
But I shall be a very king indeed,
The master of ten thousand palaces,
If thou canst give me of thy happy choice
The one great gift, the gift of Abigail.
I know not by what word to win thine heart!
But here the hands of David with his life
Go forth outstretched to thee.   Wilt thou not come?

ABIGAIL

One answer only have I for my lord:
My heart, my strength, and all my life are his:
And where he bids me, thither I will go.

THE STORY OF AN AFFINITY

THE STORY OF AN AFFINITY

PART I

Within the overlapping of two seas
There lies a golden land of fruit and flowers,
Stream barriered, and in that sunny tract
I know a corner at a green hill's foot
Where orchards cover up the spring-tide fields
Whitened with blossoms; and all summer long
The wind about the leafy mountain ridge
Purrs in the tops of forest hickories;
Where bees find richest harvest, and the peach
Puffs up its yellow juices till it cracks,
Splitting the stone; where in September days
The robins storm the vineyards, and the wasp
Punctures the swollen grapes and drains and drains
Till he goes heavily with freighted wings.

On this broad inland terrace lay two farms
Not far apart, and in the midst of them
The white farmhouses on whose lichened roofs
The towering pear-trees in October winds
Dropped golden fruit and whirling, golden leaves.
The one was Jacob Hawthorne's and the other
Was tilled by William Stahlberg and his sons.
The two were friends from boyhood, though unlike

In mood and aspect.   The monotonous life
Of those whose only care is with the earth
Had knit them into close companionship
Through daily habit.   They were next at hand.
Old Stahlberg had two sons, and Jacob Hawthorne
An only daughter; and the children played
Together, joining as their sires had done
Through all the mirthful years of early youth
In growing friendship.   This had end at last,
When Hawthorne, who had pictured for his child,
The lily-cheeked and dimpled Margaret,
A larger future than the farm could give,
Placed her at school; and thus another life
In the great city, other thoughts and ways,
New friendships with their fruitful sympathies
Absorbed the eager spirit of the girl;
And only at midsummer, when the terms
Were over, she returned a month or two
To join her old-time playmates; but a change
Fell with each year between them; the two boys,
Whose ways grew over-manful for the girl,
Heeded her visits less, till in the end
She came and went, her presence all unmarked.

Of William's sons the elder, as he grew
From youth to manhood, both in mind and limb
Fulfilled his father's utmost wish; a firm
Fair lad; no hand in all the neighbouring farms
Could turn so straight a furrow through the field;
Loving the tillage, grave and apt to learn,
He toiled with honour at the old man's side
A sinewy farmer, diligent and wise.

Not so the other, William's heart had dreamed
A different life for Richard.   He had hoped
To find in him the scholar of his house
Reared in some grave profession or skilled art ;
And Richard in his lisping boyhood gave
Rare flashes of a strange intelligence ;
But these with the full growth of years became
Less frequent, till his darkening mind took on
A sullen and impenetrable sloth.
Year after year, while the child's mind stood still,
Entangled in that strange infirmity,
In strength and stature he throve wondrously.
Vast shoulders with a broad and mighty head—
The fairer for its shower of yellow curls—
He towered above his fellows like a king,
A king whom some slow magic had dethroned.
Often there was a mood upon him, one
That fell at intervals, seeming to mark
A settled period in his cloudy life.
His eyes, whose wont was to be darkly dull,
Or bent in an unmeasuring fixedness,
Now with some trouble seemed possessed, as if
Disordered by an inly smouldering fire.
There was a fitful and ungoverned force
In his huge frame, a lawless energy
That yielded to no guidance, but stormed out
In passionate whim, and were it good or evil
Wrought each in desperate and titanic measure.
Sometimes a fiery eagerness of toil
Possessed him, and with silent diligence
He laboured with his brother in the fields,
And whether through the sere November light

With guided handles and slow running shares,
Keeping the glistening furrows all day long,
The ploughmen rolled the dark earth layer on layer,
Or whether in August in the fiercest heat
The yellow barley fell in toppling rows
Behind the clattering reapers, and the men
Following with red arms and dripping brows
Bound up the rustling sheaves; in either hour
Richard, a fitful giant, unperturbed,
Bent the wild vigour of his limbs to toil,
Labouring as no other three could labour
In all the friendly farms.   No man could turn
Or check his course, for as he willed he worked.
But sometimes when the toil was at its height,
And every hand was straining to the end,
He would cease suddenly, and straightening up,
As if in wrath with dark and ominous brow,
And eyes all strange with that disordered fire,
Hurl forth whatever thing was in his hand,
And stride away.   The rest without surprise
Glanced after him, but neither called nor dared
To follow, for no touch, nor any word
Had healing for his mood, or power to stem
The blind and witless passion of his soul.
Only his brother, whom perchance the toil
Pressed sore, or the white-haired and troubled man,
His father, with a sorrowful glance exchanged,
Bent them the sadlier to their task.   By day,
And night, perchance for many days and nights
He would be gone, wandering from farm to farm,
From village unto village, at some hours
Sullen and uncompanionable, at others,

Mingled with wayside groups at tavern doors,
Or where the country lads with halted teams
Gathered at eve about a blacksmith's forge,
Loudest in laughter, and when games were set
Supreme in his tremendous feats of strength.
He would return at last, perhaps at dawn,
Coming fresh-cheeked, or strolling in at dusk,
When hungry mouths were busy round the board;
And all would greet him smiling; but a voice,
His father's, would call joyfully out and bid
The women bring him of the daintiest fare ;
And yet their talk would flag, and they would sit
And watch him with mute kindness in their eyes,
Marking the mighty frame whose sinewy bulk
Seemed to have thriven in the soul's despite,
And the fair clouded face.

              So time passed on,
Till nineteen years were gone of Richard's life,
And the white locks that heaped his father's head,
Clustered like snow about his ruddy ears,
Were grown the whiter for that vanished hope.
The nineteen summers dawned with leaf and bloom,
With the light springing grain in many fields,
And dewy evenings when the pale clear west
Grew cool and distant round one lustrous star.
From many a darkening garden plot, unseen,
The vesper-sparrow, dreaming in the dusk,
Trilled forth his heart of love, his earth-pure song
Of passion and appealing tenderness ;
And so the beautiful days at length brought on
That tenderest, rosiest season of the year,

When roadsides whiten with anemones,
And the long grass, cool and waist-deep at noon,
Still flings the dew about the trudger's feet,
When corn-flowers gathering in neglected fields
Make all the wind-swayed spaces a surprise
With their bold gipsy splendour.

                              Now it chanced
One morning in that goodliest month of all
That Richard with blank eyes and dawdling feet
Passed on an errand to the neighbouring farm.
To-day the mood was on him, and his mind,
By feverous yearnings and blind powers distraught,
Seemed conscious of the weight that pressed it down.
He walked with sullen brow and earthward eyes.
Nor marked the Hebe loveliness of leaf
And flowers, the wind's soft touch, nor overhead
The limpid and interminable blue.
The meadow with its braid of marguerites,
That ran like glittering water in the wind
He passed unseen.   The tireless bob-o-link,
Poised on the topmost spray of some young elm,
Or fluttering far above the flowered grass,
Showered gaily on an unobservant ear
His motley music of swift flutes and bells.
Through an old vineyard full of trellised shoots
And reaching tendrils and thick twisted stems,
And tossing spaces, heaved with velvet leaves,
Gray-gleaming in the sudden gusts upturned
And past the bee-hives in the orchard plot,
A place to mid-day slumber consecrate,
He strode and came into a narrow lane,

That ran far forward hemmed with brier and bloom
Between the wheatfields and a towering wood.
And now a sudden frolic wind-rush came,
And smote the wood, and roared upon its tops,
And down across the level like a sea
Ran out in swift pale glimmering waves.   The sound
And moving majesty of wind and wood
Broke even the dull clasp of Richard's heart
And touched his spirit with a passionate thrill.
He started and stood still and stared abroad
A moment, like one suddenly awake,
With spreading nostrils and uplifted head,
And from his widening eyes there leaped and shone,
Like the blue strip beyond the thunder-cloud,
A single gleam of wild intelligence.
He turned this way and that with grasping hands
And moving lips, as if the astonished soul
Sought to expand its momentary fire
In the sheer strength of some tremendous word
Or violent deed; and as the gust died off,
He bent low down and seized in both his hands
The trunk of a young birch-tree, and with feet
And knees firm planted, stretching to the full
The corded muscles of his mighty back,
Tore it, root, stem and branches from the earth
And rising, hurled it, whirling, far apart
Into the centre of the wind-waved field.
The deed relieved him and he turned and closed
His hands on the black fence rails, with fixed gaze,
And stood with straightened neck and head thrown
     back
So standing he seemed rapt as if with thought
     27

The crimson flush ebbed slowly from his cheek,
And left a deadly pallor.   In his eyes
The remnant of that wild and startled flame
Died gradually away as embers die,
Shrouding with ash.   A little while he dreamed,
Then slowly turning down the sunny lane
Resumed his stride, but with a gentler tread
And brow less imminent and less disturbed.
Through a sagged gate whose hinges rough with rust
Yelled and cried out at every ruthless turn,
He swung, and by a winding footway came
Into an orchard old with gnarlèd trees.
Now in the orchard's midst on the warm grass
Under the goodliest of these fruitful trunks,
Close bowered in wooing shadows, flitted o'er
With multitudes of golden gleams, there stood
An old and curious rustic bench, contrived
Of boughs of cedar, interwoven and joined,
Still with the rough soft-smelling bark upon them.
Thither already ere the burning sun
Had robbed the shadowy dock-leaves of their pearls,
Old Hawthorne's daughter, pale-browed Margaret,
Had come with happy, gravely-gliding feet,
Swinging her wide-brimmed hat in one white hand,
And clasping in the other a small book
That pressed a slender finger shut between.
Across the humming orchard lawn she came,
Dappled with shadow and sharp light, a form
Tall with the slenderness of youth.
Her calm gray eyes, now earthward bent, and now
Fastened far off in unobservant gaze,
Seemed like clear fountains of divine content,

Fed by a crystal and perpetual stream
Of sunny meditation. With a smile
Upon soft parted lips, a little pale,
She reached the rustic bench, and nestling back
Into its softest corner, propped her head—
That sunny head with hair thick-coiled, not curled,
But tawny and soft-textured, smooth as silk—
On one white hand; and with the other turned
The slender pages of her book, and read.
Once and again she lifted her deep eyes,
And gazed before her long and absently,
Then pored on the white pages for a while,
With drooping lids, till they forgot to see;
And soon the warmth and luxury of the place,
And all the growing murmur of the noon,
Possessed her with their drowsy spell. The book
Slid from her loosened hand, and ere she knew
Her cheek had sunk against the cedar rest,
Soft-pillowed on her bended arm, and there,
With all the myriad patterns interlaced
Of sun and shadow floating on her breast
And nestling in her lap, she lay asleep.

Long years had gone since Margaret, as a child,
Had stirred the homely quiet of the farm
With her bright ways. Her seasons had been spent
In schools and cities; and in all that time
She had seen much and studied more. Her mind
A tireless gleaner in the field of books
Had skirted the world's ways with curious eyes,
And gathered knowledge with serene delight.
Her father on some learnèd life at first

Had set his plans for her, then as he grew
Older, had changed, and drifting to a sheer
Reversal of his former mind, resolved
To have her henceforth near him; for the dread
Of her long absences, and the delight
To feel her sun-like presence in the house,
Daily increased upon his narrowing heart.
This was the first great bitterness that fell
On Margaret's life; for she had built a dream
Of her own future, full of noble aims,
Traced out in many an ardour of bright thought,
A dream of onward and heroic toil,
Of growth in mind, enlargement for herself,
And generous labour for the common good.
At first she wept in anguish and plead hard
For her own way, but when the old man's will
Grew only firmer with the lapse of time,
Her smooth and buoyant spirit, as it bent,
Slowly inured to the inevitable,
Rebuilded in another lowlier shape
The ruined fabric of her hope.   To tread
The circuit of her home-kept days content—
Its tasks and quiet duties interwoven
With study and the loved companionship
Of books—or in the easeful intervals
Of labour with sweet ardour to cement
A loving friendship with all plants and birds
And creatures that inhabit earth or stream;
By gradual growth of knowledge and the gift
To others freely of her precious store,
By winsome bearing and persuasive speech,
To make her bountiful presence day by day

A help, a sweet refreshment, and a grace
To all about her : this was Margaret's dream,
The old dream smiling in a lowlier guise.

Only a day had gone since her return
When on the old warm-shadowed rustic seat
Thus with her fair and delicate head, so full
Of glowing dreams and golden purposes,
Soft sunk upon her slender arm—she lay,
Fixed in the rounded grace of innocent sleep,
Unconscious of her spiritual loveliness.
And now came Richard o'er the orchard lawn,
With plodding gait and wasteful eyes, wherein
The mindless grief and impotent hunger burned.
Along the little beaten path he came,
And reached the sweeping shade of Margaret's tree,
And saw the seat and her whose beauty made
The warmth and shadowy sweetness of the place
Warmer and sweeter still.   One wide swift look
He flung upon the scene, as if a blow
Had met him in the forehead from some hand
Invisible, he stopped and stood stone-still,
A statue of surprise with parted lips,
And eyes that for a moment only stared.
And then a wild light fluttered from them—joy
With terror mingled and an eddying sense
Of power unlocked ; for in a moment's space—
No longer than that single rapturous glance—
A vision rare and beautiful to him
As any by the Saint in Patmos seen,
Had slid beneath the cloud-bands of his soul,
And, flooded all with one enchanted gleam.

And as he stood, it seemed to him that all
His life had lacked of insight and of power
Came gathering in a great and welling tide.
With ever deepening pierce he saw the world
And his own life, and comprehended all.
And yet this light so rapturous, so divine,
Was like the terror of revealing dawn
To one who in the midnight wild had lost
The narrow path and wandered far astray:
For this fair creature, whose unconscious presence,
By its strange beauty and resistless grace,
Had burst the bolted prison of his soul,
Betrayed in every subtlest tint and line
Of form and feature, garb and attitude,
The impression of a life remote from his—
A life bred in a loftier air, and steeped
In pleasures of a daintier sense, distilled
From studious search and fine experience.
Slowly, like grasping poison, the cold truth
Spread over Richard's unresisting heart,
And filled him with a wild and helpless grief.
And now for the first time his wandering glance
Fell upon Margaret's little book.   It lay
Spread open in the grass, and almost touched
Her foot.   A sweet immeasurable desire
Possessed him, and he made a daring step
Forward, and took it softly up, and pored
Upon its slender pages with moist eyes.

With the sharp crackle of the fluttering leaves,
As Richard turned them in unskilful hands,
Margaret awoke, and started lightly up,

Wide-eyed, a little frightened and abashed.
But, as she looked at Richard, in a while
Returned the memory of him, and she rose,
And hastened towards him with delighted speed,
Smiling in welcome, and held forth her hand:
"Ah Richard, it is you; and you know me?
Why it is Margaret.   You don't forget
The games we had together in old days.
But you have grown so tall;" and Margaret stood
In all her subtle beauty and pale grace,
Arrested by a sudden bright surprise
A radiant wonder at his splendid height.
And Richard looked in silence a long while
Into her fair gray eyes—he was too full
Of grief and hurrying thought to be abashed—
But murmured inarticulately.   He held
Still in his hand the book.   It was a work
Printed in curious words and unknown type,
And Richard turned and closed the little book
With a despairing tenderness and said:
"You read this book before you fell asleep,
You, but a slight girl—so young—it seems
Only a fortnight since we played together,
And now you understand this print and thread
The mysteries of other tongues, while I
Whose idle body has grown great and tall,
I cannot even read my own, beyond
The simplest words.   How miserable to be
As mean and dull and ignorant as a clod!"
Then it was Margaret that with gentle stare
And wondering eyes looked full in Richard's face,
Discerning that the playmate, whom she knew

For his huge stature and unwritten mind,
Was changed, and with a lovely smile she said:
"Yes, it is bitter to look back and think
How many years have passed us and we know
So very little; to be far behind
When all the world is full of learned heads.
You think me a great scholar, but I've seen
Many whose knowledge is a thousand times
More great than mine.   I am more ignorant far
Compared with these, than you compared with me.
But, courage, Richard!   If you will to learn,
You may, for every port is possible
To him who stands unshaken at the helm,
And steers straight on!"   So speaking in a voice
That deepened with a tender earnestness,
A fleeting rose bloomed up in both her cheeks,
Leaving her pallor lovelier than before.
And Richard shrank a little as if bowed
By too great joy of that delicious word;
And as his eyes returned upon her face,
Enraptured to a passionate reverence,
A sweet and simple dignity possessed
This giant frame and fair large head upraised,
And his great face, and almost with a cry:
"I am resolved," he said, "to live my life anew
And follow manfully where your steps have gone,
Margaret; and this book shall be my guide—
The thing I prize beyond all else on earth—
If you will let me keep it for my own."
Again in sudden wonder Margaret turned
Her fair pale brows and beautiful eyes, and fixed
Their light on Richard's face, then let them fall,

As a bird veers before the wind, surprised
At his great earnestness, and half abashed.
Answering she told him he might have the book,
And some day in a future year they two
With wiser heads would read it through together.

Now at the farmhouse in a shadowy niche
Cut deep above the whitewashed kitchen door
Lay a great conche, a smooth and polished shell;
An echo at whose coilèd heart still cooled
Far off the listener's wave-enamoured ear,
That ancient inextinguishable sigh
And murmuring surge of the eternal sea.
The founder of the homestead, he who first
Made his axe echo in these wilds, and hewed
A circle in the frowning woods, and joined
Trunk upon trunk to house his little ones,
Had brought it from its pristine resting place,
Some sand-nook of the sea; and thrice each day
Since then, across the close-tilled summer fields
Its booming thunder launched by knowing lips
Had warned the hungry farmer and his hands
Of meal-time and the steaming board prepared.
And now as Margaret ended and her speech
Subsided in the sunlight of a smile,
There came one running toward the garden gate
A stout-armed girl, all ruddy from the fire,
And lifted the great shell with both her hands
And blew therein, till the slow roaring sound
Clave to the farthest limit of the fields,
And died in winding echoes on the hills.
And Margaret prayed Richard to return
With her and join them at the mid-day meal,

And he, whose brain was like a turbid sea
Of passion and fantastic purposes,
Swept and illumined with a reckless joy,
Turned gladly and went with her.   As they walked
A silence fell between them.   Richard's heart
Too busy with its stream of rapturous thought,
Encompassed with a wonder too divine,
A joy too sacred to be touched by speech;
And Margaret as she glanced in Richard's face,
Still studying with quick and curious eyes
His altered bearing and absorbèd mood,
Kept silence too, knowing not what to say.
So through the humming garden and between
The shadowy ranks of vines they took their way.

Now when the meal was finished and the men
Gone to their labours, tramping leisurely
Through the fresh fields, there woke in Richard's soul
A passionate eagerness to grasp at once
The clear beginnings of his altered life.
The dream lay wrapt in luminous mist as yet,
Confused, about his heart, but this he knew,
The plan, whatever in the end its shape,
Would bear him into long and distant toils
Far from his home and far from Margaret's face;
And so he rose and with a few soft words
Parted from all the kind and busy folk,
And Margaret went with him to the gate.
Then Richard turned and lifted his great eyes,
Striving for manful utterance and said:
"You do not know nor have I words to tell
The good that you have done me, Margaret;

But you have changed me, given me strength and will,
For you are beautiful, and wise and good,
And one may not be near you, and not learn
To be a man. I leave you. I am going,
Far off perhaps, to work and learn ; but now,
While I am gone this one thing more I ask,
That you will sometimes in your idle hours
Give me the priceless blessing of your thoughts.
They shall be borne to me, unseen, unheard,
And nerve me with fresh courage, when I fail."
But Richard spoke no more, for like a mist
His own unworthiness rose up and filled
At the last moment all his doubting heart
With a great choking grief.   He seized her hands
And pressed them in his own, and turned away :
And Margaret with down-dropped and troubled eyes,
Shrinking in wonder from the sudden storm
Of passion that she could not understand,
Murmured she knew not what of gentle speech,
Scared and surprised, yet fain to comfort him.
But Richard, ere he reached the homeward path,
Halted and turned aside into the fields,
Wandering he cared not whither, for a touch
Of his old truant mood was on him, not
The impulse of blind passion as of old
But a great need to be alone for thought.
The impulse of blind passion as of old
A measureless kingdom of content, shone down
On the still meadows and heat-drowsèd fields.
All the dividing woods twixt farm and farm
Stood motionless with pale and gleaming tops,
And distant banks of shadow, brushed with bloom.

By field and fallow Richard wandered on;
Now wading among timothy, waist high;
By fences in whose murmurous tangles shone
That symbol of the blazing heart of June,
The golden target of the corn-flowers, bossed
With purple, and lean stems of succory
Stretched, pale and shrunken, all their drooped
    rosettes
Hungering for midnight and its wreath of stars;
By silent copses in whose fragrant gloom
The quiet-eyed cattle knelt on folded knees;
And hayfields where the mowers wheeled and spun
Their drowsy clatter through the windless glare,
While the stooped labourers with dripping brows
And dusty hands spread out the new-mown hay;
Or halting by some deep and dreamy edge
Of restful woods, he heard the oven-bird
Assault the brooding fervour of the hour
With his increasing and accentuate note.
These things, although indeed he marked them not,
Distinctly yet upon his spirit breathed
A gentle influence, and the quieted will
Shaped gradually the tumult of his thoughts
Into an ordered counsel, bringing forth
A single stream of purpose large and clear.

And now the night had fallen and the moon
Rose large and golden in the sultry east,
When Richard to the tranquil farm returned.
There was a murmurous noise about the yard
Where the men stalled the cattle, and made fast
The pens and silent stables for the night;

But in the busy kitchen there was glow
And clatter, for the board was cleared away,
And Richard with a sudden tread appeared
In the broad doorway; and his mother heard
And met him with her fixed inquiring eyes.
So she was wont to do, when he returned
After long absence. 'Twas a lingering look,
Half of regret and pity for the past,
And half of expectation; for she said
Sometimes unto her husband in their talk
Together: "I can never see the lad
Without a haunting sense that I shall yet
Look upon Richard's face and see it changed."
When she had kept him for a moment thus
There came a wonder in her shrewd blue eyes,
And a bright smile upon her gentle lips,
And drawing near she laid her ruddy hands
On his great shoulders and looked up, and cried:
"What is it, Richard?   You are not the same!"
And Richard answered gravely, on her eyes
Fixing his own that now were deep with thought:
"Yes, I am changed mother, for something strange
And wonderful has happened to my soul.
I think I am a man now, but before
I was a brute; and I have got my mind,
And I can think and learn; I'm going forth
To make a new beginning of my life,
Where men are many and I may prove myself."
His mother, still regarding him with eyes
As gladly tranquil as the pale broad brow
Within its wavy arch of whitening hair,
Divined his heart and saw that he spoke truth.

Now when the labour of the night was done
In stall and kitchen, and the men came in,
Tired-eyed and heavy-booted, nigh asleep
With the day's weight of gathered weariness,
And the quiet women took their seats about,
Old Stahlberg, rising slowly from his chair,
Took from a shelf beside the ticking clock
The Bible and a slender book of prayer,
Whose parted covers and leaves browned and frayed
Spoke of the ancient custom of the house.
All rose and knelt and then the old man read
With a great voice that slowly rose and fell,
In rugged cadence stumbling now and then,
As daunted by some strange and difficult word,
Or plagued by slumber that unhinged his tongue.
Then prayers were said with many soft "Amens,"
The "Lord's Prayer" last with murmurous consonance
Of all the voices, and this duty done,
They rose, and with a low "Good-night" each passed
To his own bed, but Richard yet remained
Beside his mother, while the old man sat,
His forehead sinking heavier at each nod
On his tired hands, forgetful now of rain,
And withering drought, and everything but sleep.
But Richard roused him, and with a slow start,
He lifted up his snow-white head and stared,
Astonished at the look in Richard's eyes;
And Richard said, "My father you wished once
To make a scholar of me, and you found
Your purpose vain.   I could not do your will;
My brain was crushed and fettered; but to-day
A change has come upon me: I am free,

I know that I have power to think and learn.
It is not yet too late, and I have planned
To make a new beginning of my life;
To go to the great city, where the minds
Of men are busiest, and most alive.
There I will stay till I have proved my strength
And found my bent, and made myself a man."
Old Stahlberg gazed in silence on his son
For a long while, the wonder at his heart
Too great for any sign, too great for speech;
But slowly as he understood, the glow
Of a great gratitude suffused his face,
And he rose trembling to his feet, and cried:
"My son, an hour ago I would have given
My life and all I had to hear those words
And see you as I see you now. 'Tis fit
That we should thank Almighty God to-night
For this great mercy He hath shown to us!"
Then they began to talk of Richard's plan;
And the old man opposed it. He would fain
Have kept him with him at the farm a while
And sent him to the neighbouring country school.
He feared the treacherous city and its snares,
Its evils and temptations; but to this
Richard replied with softly kindling eyes:
"You need not fear for me, father; my way
Is watched and governed by a beautiful spirit,
Whose word shall be a surer guide to me
Than wisdom and the teaching of a life.
This beautiful guide has bidden me gain knowledge
And in the city where the great and wise
Are drawn together, I shall best succeed."

Only to hear the deep voice of his son,
Wondrous and sweet with resolute utterance,
Was joy to fill the old man's heart.
With a shrewd look and a contented smile
He gave consent.   Then for a little space
They sat communing with their own bright thoughts,
Till finally some common movement touched
All three together, and they rose; and then
His mother went apart with tender haste,
And brought a lighted candle for her son,
And as she held it high above his brows,
Peered into his bright eyes and questioned thus:
"Whom saw you Richard at the farm to-day?
Did you see Margaret?" and Richard looked
Back into his mother's kind and curious eyes,
Flushed and tongue-tied with tenderness and fear:
And so the loving woman read his heart,
And murmuring "God bless you Richard!" touched
His lips with hers, and when their eager hands
Had locked a moment, the two happy ones,
And Richard scarce less happy in that hour,
Took up their several ways and passed to sleep.

PART II

For half a day the rushing train held on
By meadow and quiet field and sleeping marsh,
Through stretches of dim woods, by gorge and rill,
Hammering the iron rails with rhythmic clang,
Or over piered and buttressed viaducts

And hollow bridges drawing with vast roar;
Halting at whiles with hiss and deafening scream
By crowded platforms in the busy towns;
Then on and on, leaving the flying miles
Behind, gloomed with its rolling wreath of smoke;
And Richard at a little window sat
And watched the world spin by him like a thread
Strung lightly as with darting beads of life;
He saw the dusty hoer rise and lean
A moment on the handle of his hoe
To watch the passing wonder with dazed eyes;
He saw the sleepy heron from the dreamy marsh
Lift heavily and over tuft and pool
Move off on cumbrous and deliberate wings.
He saw the unyoked horses, fierce and free
In lowland meadows wide with starry grass,
Career and scamper in affrighted joy;
Or at the crossing of some country road
He caught between the flashing of two fields
Glimpse of an anxious farmer holding in
His restive horses with tight-gathered reins.

So the hours passed until the slackening train
Stayed and began to move with mingling roars
Through legions of grimed cars and ranks
Of sooty walls, and past the reeking depths
Of ringing foundries, and the flaring gleams
Of smoke-veiled forges, piling din on din,
And the great city with its deafening press
Closed slowly round them.   At the window still
Sat Richard, stunned, bewildered at his heart,
Feeling this loud great world, a mountain weight,
28

Rolled over him, and yet with silent grasp
Preserving the mute purpose of his soul
In titan courage, blindly resolute.
The clanging station roof above them closed
In smoke and darkness and redoubled roar,
And Richard passed alone into the crowd.
A blind and simple impulse led him forth
Through crowded streets, where the dense multitude
Like a checked river, eddying and flowing on
In channels of vast fronts and glittering panes,
Moved, as he dreamed, for ever.   Forth and forth
He strode, not tarrying till the eager press
Grew thinner on the twilight walks, and now
The broad and stately thoroughfares were lined
With gardens and great stone-built palaces.
Still he kept on, and when at last the streets
Grew humbler with the little cottages
Of artisans, he slacked and stayed his feet
And wandered, peering with regardful eyes.

In vain!   He saw no welcoming eye, no hand
Outstretched to help or guide him, and despair
Rose like a black mist about his heart,
Fed by that sickening damp of loneliness
That no wild forest depth could breed so well
As this cold-eyed and unknown populace.
Now when the dusk was gathering and his feet
Were sore and weary, on a little lawn
He saw two friendly people, married folk,
The workman and his wife, who sat at rest
Before their open doorway after toil;
And hither and thither like a ray of light

A little child that scarcely yet had won
The safety of its feet, about them played,
A tender golden-curlèd, bright-eyed thing,
Now running with a headlong rash delight,
Now tottering with its dimpled hands outspread;
And all the while upon those happy ears
Pouring with laughing lips and busy tongue,
Soft as the gurgle of a summer brook,
The inarticulate silver of its talk.
And when the workman lifting up his eyes
Saw Richard's towering form without the gate,
And marked his earnest face and wistful gaze,
He rose, and coming toward him with a voice
Of honest salutation, round and bluff,
Asked if he could do him aught of service.
And when our friend had told him what he could
And how he sought some humble place to lodge,
The other mused a moment, and then called
His wife to him.   She, catching up the child,
And brushing swiftly back some wayward curls
From off her happy cheeks, obeyed the call.
The two communed together softly, now
Glancing at Richard, as with settled eyes,
And now as if some worrying doubt arose
Deepening their speech. But while they still conferred
The little child whose clear and tranquil orbs
Had never moved from Richard's honest face,
Stretched out her small round arms and pursed her lips
And uttered forth a tender cry, and made
As she would kiss him, and the workman laughed
And turned upon his wife a merry look
And cried: "The child decides, her will is law

And if it please you, you shall lodge with us."
And so they struck a bargain, and the wife
Went in, and spread the table, and brewed tea
For Richard, who was hungry and footsore.
Then when the hunger was allayed and rest
Had loosed his limbs, and something of sweet talk
Had passed between them, a more hopeful heart
Came to our friend, as the spent mariner,
Whom some long billow of the wreckful sea
Hath flung far up upon a sunny strand,
Crawls out of reach, and basks and is content,
So Richard rested, thankful and secure.
And now the little child, because the hours
Grew long, and it was hard to keep her feet
For tottering weariness, when all were kissed,
And the soft night-robe clothed her rosy limbs,
Was carried with drooped head and sinking lids
To sleep; and Richard too not long delayed
But sought his attic chamber and with thoughts
That two long days' unwonted sights and sounds
Had goaded to wide-eyed intensity,
Lay patient in his bed and courted sleep;
And still the thunderous jar of passing wheels,
The tramp upon the pavement, the slow sound
Of bells that at monotonous intervals
Intoned the midnight hours, and farther off
The roar and shout of trains, possessed his ear,
And made a lonely strangeness in his soul.
But sleep defeated oft and baffled back
By some strange sound or starting up of thought,
Conquered at last, and not till morn was high
And the wide city rattled at full din,

Richard awoke, and like a sudden blow
Dealt by remembrance on his sinking heart,
The newness of his altered life returned.

That very day Richard began his work.
The schools had closed; but for our friend, whose soul
Was fierce with hope and wild with eagerness,
The seasons were but forms and empty names.
He found a teacher, one whom strenuous ties
Kept through the long midsummer months at watch
Bound to the city, though reluctantly.
Wondering at Richard's kingly height and touched
By the rough strength and sweetness of his speech,
He took him to his heart, became his friend
And guided his first steps for many weeks
With love and patient care; and when the schools
Re-opened in the soft September days,
Nerved and relieved him with continual help.
All through the autumn in the busy school
Richard among small children sat and wrought,
A humble giant at their petty tasks.
The mount of knowledge seemed a giant height
With neither ledge nor path, attainable
Only to patient and eternal toil,
Cutting each foothold in the granite stone.
But he, the milder titan, neither paused
Nor quailed, but with a spirit sternly strung,
Wrought onward, step by step; above, beyond,
Perceiving on the summits proudly bright
The gleam of his neglected heritage;
And so for many weary months, by day
Among the children in the humming school,

Or in his attic chamber half the night
He pored upon his books, or strove to store
The crumbs that fell about him.   Then at last
By little and little the desirèd light
Dawned and increased; the slow reward began.
'Twas given gradually to his soul to know
The joy of mastery.   The clearing brain
Grew nimbler in its movements, more secure
In sight and thought and memory,
Throve and expanded.   With a grave delight
He passed from grade to grade, from task to task.
The heads grew taller round him; step by step
He rose among the scholars, pressing on
Happy, and restless, and insatiable,
Filling the compass of his days and nights
With larger and more loved activities.

In Richard's attic room a little shelf
Stood high above the table where he read,
And on the shelf as in a sacred niche
There lay apart in honoured singleness—
The guide and symbol of his hope—the book
That Margaret's hand had given him.   His eyes
Falling upon it often in dark hours,
When toil seemed fruitless, and the goal far off,
Brightened anew, and his strong heart revived.
Again he saw the orchard and the trees,
The sunny shadows and the rustic seat,
And her whose beauty and serene regard
Half gloomed, half lit the abysses of his soul
With passionate wonder and religious awe.
And so the winter passed, and roaring March

Thundered upon the city roofs, and drove
The soft cloud-masses, over deepening heights
Of laughter-glimmering and diaphanous blue;
And April came, and charged the running drains
With the last knots of the discoloured snow,
From sunny street and tinkling alleys poured
In dancing rivulets.   With dawning May
The blossoms of the maples broke and fell,
Reddening the pavements with their rosy wreck.
The willows turned to golden green.   The birds
Came flocking in full chorus with the flame
Of crocuses in teeming garden beds.
A golden oriole with midnight wings
Dreamed in the city's topmost elm and sang
Of endless summer and undying joy.
Months came and went, and with the mid-most heat
The schools broke up, but Richard still remained
In the great city resolute at his tasks;
For neither to his home, nor Margaret's face
Would he return till strength was in his hands,
And the full purpose of his life fulfilled.
And ever day by day, in his strong heart
The thirst of knowledge grew—all knowledge, not
The love of books alone; he yearned to know
And penetrate the meaning and the ends
Of all the interlinking toils of men.
Often, when study had grown wearisome
Through too long service at the printed page,
He roamed the crowded streets, haunted the shops,
Or lingered by the bridges or the wharves,
Watching with rapt insatiable eyes
The maze of life, a tireless questioner.

He loved the central roar, and made his way
Into the workshops and all haunts of skill
Where men were busy at their various crafts.
His simple speech and friendly bearing pleased
The workmen, and they fed his curious mind
With endless learnings of the ways of trade,
The wonders of their mightiest and subtlest arts
And all the mysteries of machinery.

Another year and yet another passed
And Richard, restlessly persistent, saw
His mind's clear volume like a river grow
Supported by increasing tributaries.
His labours waxed and multiplied; he laid
Fresh hold on every side, and wrought at all
With love and mastery and perpetual gain.
The subtleties of figures caught at first
His mind with keenest fascination; then
The feats and beauties of geometry;
The lore of language in the common speech;
The story of the races of mankind,
In turn absorbed his brain.   In the fourth year
He mounted to a higher range, and there
With ardour and renewed delight, began
The study of the old and learnèd tongues,
The Roman and the Greek; and year by year,
With the keen growth of easeful memory
And opening of new springs of radiant thought,
The masters of old beauty set apart
Their charmèd doors and inmost haunts for him
The Mantuan with his firm and stately flow,
Now tender-touched and sorrowfully sweet

With Dido's love and beautiful despair,
Now ringing with the city's fall, and now
Loud with the rush of armèd men, the clash
And tramp of battle on the Latian plain :
He too, the smiling master of the lyre,
Whose light and delicate hand so long ago,
In that old, shadowy, half-forgotten world,
Drew from its strings so many human chords,
Whose days were filled with fancy and content,
The wondrous tenant of the Sabine farm.
The song of Homer rapt him.   He beheld
The leaguer of the Greeks, the ten years' toil
Around the fated walls of Troy, and heard
The stormy words of heroes ring and roll
In thunder from the sweet and eloquent verse.
He saw the wise Odysseus wandering far
Through many outer lands of monstrous men,
And shadowy tracts and many friendless seas,
And then for all his subtle craft at last
Led back, world-weary and companionless,
An old man, to his home in Ithaca.
He followed in the drama of the Greek
The doom of Œdipus, the storied deed
Of stern and beautiful Antigone,
The blood-stained destinies of Pelop's line
Old symbols of the linkèd fates of men.
He mused on Plato's vast and golden dream,
And drank the old-world histories of strife,
Of golden deeds, and freedom lost or won.
These things and many more he understood
After long labour ; and a rich new life
Grew up, and decked as with an artist's care

The erewhile formless chambers of his soul.
Its floors and hidden depths became alive
With moving figures, lovely or sublime.
Its barren walls were hung by viewless hands
With tapestries of magic workmanship,
Fabrics of beauty beyond human skill.
Through all its cells and haunted corridors
Went echoes of immortal music set
To words dropped from forgotten lips and left
Long since to the maturing care of age.

And now with these enlarging studies rose
In Richard's soul a new and curious sense
Of the world's life about him, a desire
To pierce the surface of its outer shows
And read as by the light of things untaught
The simpler heart within.   Because his soul,
Sprung suddenly into power, had not obeyed
A custom-moulded youth, he learned at once
To meditate the words and ways of men.
Weighing their motives and the forms of life
In the fine balance of impartial truth.
He saw how fair and beautiful a thing
The movement of the busy world might be,
Were men but just and gentle, but how hard,
How full of doubt and pitiless life is,
Seeing that ceaseless warfare is man's rule
And all his laws and customs but thin lies
To veil the pride and hatred of his heart.
And utterances of spiritual beauty passed
Between the babbling lips of men whose souls
Remained as blind and impotent as before.

He sat in the great churches and amid
The grandeur of their silken ceremonies
Heard the vaults thunder with the solemn chants
And sacred hymns immeasurably sad,
Wherein the universal human heart
Had voiced the quietude of its vast despair,
And all the awful weariness of life.
He heard the pastor with impassioned tongue
Preach the great love and brotherhood of man,
While round him, silent in the velvet stalls,
The rich and proud, the masters of this world,
Sat moveless as the ever-living gods,
While all that wordy thunder rolled and rang
About their heads and pitiless ears in vain.
He saw rude multitudes in wild despair
Wear out their days in labour for small gain
And sink care-weary into unknown graves,
And how the strong, by chance and sleight made
        great,
Fattened and throve upon the general need,
Hiding their cruel and remorseless hands
Behind a mist of custom and the law,
Huge offspring of a boundless anarchy!
He saw the public leaders in whose charge
Was given the chiefship and the common weal,
Gulling men openly with fulsome lies;
And on the trustful ignorance of the just
And the blind greed and hatred of the base
Building the edifice of their own power.
All this because his soul was like a child's
Simple and keen; he saw, while most men dreamed
And passed it by, or seeing, did not care.

Yet also because his soul was fresh and stout
And of a natural birth, he lost not faith,
Nor grew distempered, as the weaker may
Amid this forceful fraudulent air of life;
For he found many that in heart and head
Were of the better world and the securer path,
Men, wholesome, tolerant, temperate and sincere,
And women who are the safeguard and the hope
Of human destiny, the pioneers
Of man's advancement and the larger life,
Generous and gentle as his utmost dream.

Now, too, our friend had entered on fresh paths
Of studious labour.   Through her magic doors
Science received him to intenser thought,
And led him to her silent mountain heads
Of vaster vision.   He explored the round
Of glittering space, the heavenly chart, and saw
The giant order of immenser worlds,
The wheeling planets and our galaxy;
And far beyond them in the outer void
Cluster succeeding cluster of strange suns
Through spaces awful and immeasurable,
Dark systems and mysterious energies,
And nebulous creations without end—
The people of the hollow round of heaven
In trackless myriads dwelling beyond search
Or count of man—beneath his feet this earth
A dust mote spinning round a little star,
Not known, nor named in the immensity.
He probed the secrets of the rocks, and learned

The texture of our planet's outer rind,
And the strange tale of her tremendous youth.
He touched the endless lore of living things,
Of plant, of beast, of bird, and not alone
In the mere greed of knowledge, but as one
Whom beauty kindled with a poet's fire.
The old desire of wandering, the delight
In solitude, and hunger for the wilds
Returned upon him, and at times impelled
By such impetuous stress, he left his books,
And far beyond the city's wearying roar
Cooled his hot brain amid the blossoming fields
Or salved his spirit in the peaceful woods.
And many a day at noon, or fall of dusk,
Found him half-hid in towering meadow grass
Or seated by some gurgling forest brook
In still communion with all forms of life,
The sense of kinship filling his wide heart
With dim mysterious joy; and now he knew
That the old wildness of his darkened youth
Was not a meaningless power, but the same charm
And sympathy of earth, the blind desire
Of Beauty, more restrained, less desperate now,
Because illumined by the conscious mind.

One day in the first break of busy spring,
As Richard leaned across a broken fence,
Receiving with strange pleasure in his ears
The murmurs of a shallow reedy pool,
A voice rang at his elbow with a note
Of gentle salutation.   Turning round,
He saw a young man, slight, and somewhat tall,

With thin clear cheeks, bright eyes and lofty brow,
Whose presence like the grass and budding trees
Seemed part of the still sweetness of the place.
"Already" said the full sonorous voice,
"Mine eyes have marked you often in these fields,
I being an oaf and wanderer like yourself,
And, if you be, as I surmise, a friend
To Beauty and the wisdom drawn from earth,
I pray your friendship and I long to hear
Your speech."   Richard had often seen this man
In the dense city streets and reverenced him
At awestruck, wondering distance, for he bore
The poet's golden fame; and now thus met,
He answered, half-delighted, half-abashed,
A few blunt words.   The poet's swift reply
Embarked them on a steady stream of talk,
And, as they kept the long way homeward, far
Into the April evening, with its crown
Of pallid emerald and purple gloom,
High wreathed with tremulous and eloquent stars,
Made solemn with the full antiphonal cry
Of soft Pandean voices, the two friends
Drew into close communion, and reviewed
Their several dreams of life, illumining each
With many a glowing fancy and swift flight
Of uttered vision; and when Richard saw
How the wise poet opened his full heart
Spreading before him with unstinting hand
His stores of joy and knowledge, he too rose
To a new height and potency of mind,
And, tremulous with delight, his tongue took on

A sureness and impetuous eloquence
Unknown before. The poet as each thought
Flashed up before them, capped it with some strain
Or proverb from the famous lords of rhyme,
Pouring the cadences in Richard's ear
In strange and passionate chant. So ere the two
Had plunged again into the city's roar
Richard had seen fresh worlds, and a new day
Dawned on his eager and awakened soul.

He pored upon the pages of old rhyme,
Until a music, hitherto half-heard,
Or wholly undivined, possessed his ear,
And made him in the day-break of its joy
A winged and bodiless spirit loosed from Time,
Floating in golden fire 'twixt earth and heaven.
He lived in Shakespeare's venturous world and passed
That eloquent multitude of living shapes,
Lovely or terrible; and Milton's line
Bore him upon its volume vast and stern
In august cadences to the sheer height
Of earthly vision; Wordsworth, Keats and Gray,
The spell of Coleridge in his magic mood
Opened his soul to every mystery
And heavenly likeness of the things of earth.
And now between the poet and our friend
Meeting together often, there grew up,
A strong and sacred friendship. Richard's mind
Gained from the touch of a creative soul
Guidance and clews to many novel paths;
The poet found in Richard a sound heart,
An eager ear, an understanding brain.

Meanwhile through all the learning of the schools
Richard had toiled his way from grade to grade,
And filled his brain with many sciences,
The long-stored fruits of old philosophies,
And all the harvest of the modern light:
And so, passing beyond the scholar's rank,
Replete with honours, he became
Himself a teacher, first in lowlier sort,
And then ere many busy months had passed,
A lecturer in a famous college hall.
And all the while in his small upper room,
He kept the little book within its niche,
And in the deep seclusion of his heart
One delicate image sacred and unchanged.
Through all the toilsome channels of his life
The beautiful guide had made his path secure
Pointing him on in grave serenity,
And Margaret was his strength, his hope, his goal.
Ten years had passed: the season's work was done;
The long midsummer rest was near at hand;
And Richard rising from his table took
The little volume in his dreaming hands:
"Now I have reached the very end," he said
"My task is done, and I shall see the face,
And touch the very hand of her whose power
Clings to thine every page, belovèd book."

PART III

So had our Richard, through triumphant toil
And steadfast will, and prospering fortunes, grown
To his soul's spreading stature, and fulfilled
His being's purpose; but for Margaret,
Secluded in her country home, and far
Removed from the magnetic touch of life,
The years had brought a different destiny.
Little by little the monotonous round
Of duties and incessant petty cares
Absorbed her, slowly deadening at the heart
The joyous fervour of her early dreams.
The neighbouring life—the life of struggling souls—
Bound in its narrow range of earthly needs,
A mist of melancholy industry,
O'ertopped her spirit with its sober pall.
At first she battled with it, throwing off
The imprisoned force and passion of her soul
In wayward and unusual deeds, and storms
Of secret weeping.   Often she surprised
The quiet country folk with her strange moods,
Of bitter scoffing and her wild discourse,
But not for long; this passed and gradually
The gentler will, the store of helpful love,
That formed her spirit's mainstay in the end,
Rose paramount, and daily broadening
Enwrapt her in its sweet and luminous calm.
In the third year, a bitter grief befell:
She wept upon her mother's new-made grave.
And though still heavier about her thoughts
29

The bondage of the quiet household grew—
For Margaret and her father were alone—
She grieved not, nor complained; her father's touch
Was dear to her, and she had grown to love,
Already, with a homely sympathy
The silent house, the stolid country ways,
The gentle service, the unruffled peace,
The freshness and the beauty of the fields.

But ever as her motive-core of life,
Deep-hidden, far within, there lingered still,
Unquenchable, the sense of lost desire,
Of cramped and fettered capability,
The adventurous yearning for the freer sway:
Nor did the outward habit of her days
Lack heat or lustre from that inner fire:
Through all their slow routine with watchful eye
Finding in every smallest chance some food
Or sport for the unconquerable mind,
She kept a certain amplitude of thought,
And sleepless movement of the nimble wit.
Through all the countryside her name was known
And honoured.   By her keen and gracious ways,
Her bright activity and speech so full
Of kindling laughter, and of grave discourse,
She drew the best about her, and, as time
Went on, planted in many a genial soil
The seeds of knowledge and divine desire.
Among the neighbouring women she became,
With her soft touch and ever ready ear,
A priestess and a confidante to all

Who strove with any dark perplexity,
Or grief, or any sickness of the soul.
But most she loved to gather at her side
The children on their sunny holidays,
And tell them stories of the birds and flowers,
The grasses and the lofty forest trees,
Weaving a web of tender allegories,
Wherein some core of spiritual beauty shone.
Or she would read to them from books, or round
The doorsteps on the murmurous summer nights
Unveil to them in simple sweet replies,
Fraught with such knowledge as their minds could
      take,
The wonder and the mysteries of the stars.
So with perpetual movement and the use
Of all the simple functions of the soul
Margaret maintained a sturdy happiness.
Only at moments, rare and quickly healed,
Of sharpened consciousness and lost repose,
Perceiving underneath its cloak of ash
That dim and secret smouldering at her heart
Of formless yearning and unnamed regret.

Long years passed on without event or change;
And then another gradual influence
Began to shape the current of her life.
One day—'twas in the midmost noise and heat
Of a fierce-fought electoral campaign–
A lawyer from a busy neighbouring town,
Searching the country here and there for votes
Tied up his horse at Jacob Hawthorne's farm.
An hour was spent in earnest talk at first

With Hawthorne, then with Margaret, for in her
He found a mind as quick as wind to catch
The wider drift and purpose of his speech,
A nobler and a juster listener.
When all his end was gained, and from the shy
Close farmer a plain promise had been won,
For a long while the lawyer still talked on,
Fastened by Margaret's bright and kindling grace,
Her beauty, and the music of her voice.
Parting reluctantly at last he bore,
Through the long remnant of that busy day
With all its chaff and chatter, a heart full
Of mellow meditations mixed and pricked
With strange uneasiness and soft regrets.
Before a week was over, he had found
Some pretext for another call, and still
Another followed, till at length he grew
A frequent figure at the lonely farm.

This lawyer, John Vantassel, was a man
Of mark and value in the neighbouring town,
Honoured by most, and feared by some,
Proud, generous, quick to think and do,
Given to anger in tempestuous gusts,
But easily placable, a man full-framed,
And of a keen and ruddy countenance;
And Margaret liked him, valuing at its worth
The honest strength that gave him worth with all.
On many a summer evening ere the dusk
Had fallen, by a short and private path,
Striding at will across the cooling fields,
He came, with his light heart and merry tongue;

Or far upon the lonely country roads,
The two would stroll, filling the careless hours
With endless and contented talk.   So years
Passed by, and Margaret grew to like
The bright companion of her easiest hours,
The goodness of his soul, his buoyant ways;
She liked him; but her heart remained untouched.
Even from the first Vantassel well divined
His suit must be a long and difficult one;
And so, being a wise and resolute man,
He laid his siege with slow and patient care,
Until by gradual stages there grew up
In Margaret's heart such friendship as not love
Could have made truer, albeit passion-free;
The friendship which in woman is more rare,
More self-forgetful and of finer touch
Than that of man for man.   At times indeed
She questioned of the future, knowing well
That he who sought her friendship with such zeal
Must needs be suitor to her in the end;
And once or twice when he had somehow dared
To tremble on the edge of love-making,
She warned and checked him with a sudden chill
Or rapid altering of her mood that feigned
A blindness to the meaning of his speech.
As time went on, even this thought became
Less strange, less fearful to her; she would fain
Have utterly forgot her former dreams,
And banished from the woman's settled life
The lingering aspirations of the girl.

One night when Margaret and her friend had paced
For a long while the dewy orchard path
In talk, that somehow deepened to a note
More sharply from the heart than ever before,
Vantassel, lingering by the orchard bars,
Forgot the long-kept passion and poured forth
The fiery volume of his hoarded love:
And Margaret standing with the silent night
Above her, and around her feet, sharp-thrown
The dark and motionless shadows of the trees,
Stirred not, nor spoke for a long thoughtful while,
Looking far out across the murmurous fields.
And then she turned, and with a gaze of fear,
And passionate trouble, and perplexity,
Full on Vantassel's set and pallid face:
"O do not ask me now," she cried, "not now;
Leave me a little while—a day, a week;
Give me a week, and I will answer you;"
And, when Vantassel, bending to her will,
Had passed the meadows and the farthest fields,
And vanished by the looming mountain side
In vasty shadows, Margaret still remained,
Gazing far forth across the shadowy slopes,
Surcharged with passionate thought. She scarcely
      knew
The countless voices of primeval life.
That round her in the deep and dewy dark
Haunted the motionless trees and thronged the grass;
Nor saw the moon, the golden harvest moon,
Rise from the woodland, shedding slowly down
On all the silvery meadows of the world
Her magic of old memories and dreams.

With hands light-clasped upon the topmost bar
She stood, and in her busy mind reviewed
All the past course and movement of her life,
That life so simple in its outward marks,
But inwardly so complex and so full
Of doubt and struggle.   With the clearest eyes
She saw the narrowed current of her days
Flow forward in the groove the years had made.
Her destiny was named and fixed, and now
Rebellion seemed a vain and hopeless thing.
Her life with John Vantassel would be still
The same long round of plain activities,
Performed upon a little larger field;
And he was dear to her as a close friend;
She knew him kindly, faithful and sincere;
And she could trust him.   When she turned at last
Into the homeward path between the trees,
Walking with gently bended head, she gave
The lawyer's longed-for answer in her heart,
And sealed it solemnly with sacred vows.

One morning to the Hawthorne folk there came
The word that Richard Stahlberg had returned,
And that he would be with them ere that day
Had come to end.   Margaret was well pleased
At thought of Richard's visit, and her mind
Kept running all day long upon it, touched
With curious excitement; Richard's fame
Had rung so often in her ears, the talk
Of every household in the neighbouring farms,
A sort of mythic splendour wrapt it round.
The story of these long and arduous years,

His patient labour and his rare success,
Had grown familiar to her thoughts, retold
Again and yet again with eloquent joy
By Richard's mother, sometimes at the glow
Of the red firelight in the winter nights,
The rapid needles glistening in their hands;
Or sometimes on long summer afternoons
When apples were selected, peeled and cored,
And quartered, and with busy care spread out
On boards to tan and shrivel in the sun.
And Margaret had been flattered by the tale,
Remembering with a subtle sense of power
That curious meeting by the orchard tree,
The boy's wild bearing and the violent change,
And his strange burst of crude and passionate speech.
And now the sense that she should face once more
That powerful man, to whom perchance some touch
Of her own soul had given the need to grow,
Thrilled her with vague and indefinable thoughts.

When Richard passed that evening through the lanes,
And up the well-remembered orchard path,
He had the sense of one that went with power
To claim a fortune given by destiny.
He could not think that that mysterious spell—
He deemed its source to be affinity—
Whose touch had spurred his clouded soul to life,
Would miss its fated goal and not demand
Reaction on the heart from which it sprung.
He trod the dim-lit gravelly path, and reached
The grass plot and the garden beds that made
An odorous round before the farmhouse door,

A many-hued ellipse of lawn and flowers,
And just as he had pictured in his dreams,
Margaret rose smiling from the gallery steps
And came to meet him, bearing in her eyes
And gracious tread the welcome long desired.

Margaret was less slender than of yore,
Her figure firmlier set, her face less pale.
To her gray eyes the kindling ardours sprang
Less often, with a graver brilliancy:
Yet was she in all more nobly beautiful
Than when she talked with Richard years ago.
Her gentle poise of head, her fearless grace
Of mien and movement, and her candid look
So full of sunny thought and sovereign strength,
The music of her voice made mellower
With deeper chords and tenderer cadences,
Her smile that some rare knowledge seemed to haunt
With glimmers of mysterious tenderness;
All this combined to heighten and endow
The presence of her perfect womanhood
With charm and influence gracious and supreme;
To Richard, as he met her with rapt gaze,
Her beauty, with its ardour manifest
Of truth and gentleness, awoke at once
The glorious vision of that earlier youth,
And loosed the long-locked flood-gates of his heart.
In passion, for a moment uncontrolled,
He looked upon her with such fervid eyes
As never yet had dared to meet her own,
And, taking both her hands between his two,
Murmured with lips, half trembling "Margaret!"

And Margaret's eyes fell, stricken and abashed,
And her cheeks reddened, but her helpless hands
Remained in Richard's, having no power to move;
And a strange light broke in upon her soul,
A rushing thought, so sudden, so enforced,
It robbed her of control, and made her sense
A trembling tumult, whereof joy and pain
Were equal parts; for at a single look
She saw, not the pale student lured at last
Back to old scenes and former friends, from books
And charmèd studies drawn reluctantly,
But the strong lover, here at last to lay
In hope and anxious triumph at her feet
The fruit of giant toils for her sake borne,
And claim the dreamed reward.   This too she saw
In his great stature, noble and erect,
By the swift heart-stroke of intuitive sense
That he had gone beyond her, and stood now
Her spiritual master, large and armed with power.
She felt rather than saw the beauty that abode
In the large head still clustered with its curls,
The broad brow, pale and open, and made full
With study and the gathered weight of mind,
The bright blue eyes with dreams and passion charged
The mouth, not dull, nor frenzied as of old,
But lightly set, supremely sensitive.
She knew, as by a passionate gift of sight,
That this man was her soul's repository
Of strength and trust, her spirit's answering type,
The man that she could dream of; so it fell
That for a moment like a girl she stood
Flushed and tongue-tied, but Richard marking this

Released her hands, and turning to her side
Went forward with her up the quiet walk;
And both regaining in a moment's space
Command of thought and speech, their tongues were
      loosed
In talk about the farm, the country life,
The playmates of their childhood, of the times
Gone by and of the present. Richard drew
From Margaret in her full and mellow voice,
Touched with soft flashes of all-loving wit,
The scanty annals of her own quiet years;
And then led by her questioning sympathy,
Sketched out his own more varied story, not as yet
Daring to link the motive of his toil
With thought of her, nor ever bearing back
Her memory to that sacred turning point
And magic moment of the past. His soul
Filled with her presence, her delicious speech,
The brightness of her eyes, rested content
In dreamlike joy and glowing quietude;
And Margaret too, so captured, so surprised,
All other thoughts forgotten and cast by,
Gave herself wholly to the wondrous spell,
The deep excitement that she dared not name.
And so 'twas almost midnight, and above
At the sheer purple zenith and beside
The midmost ridge and milky wreath of heaven
Shone Vega like a pulsing star of love
When Richard to his triter sense recalled,
Parted from Margaret by the garden beds,
And strode, flame-footed, homeward through the
      fields.

And Margaret, slowly gathering up her thoughts
Out of the mist of blind emotion, sat
In the broad porch, a dim and odorous bower,
Framed and built up of honeysuckle bloom,
And strove to read her heart.   One thing she knew
That Richard's presence like the stinging draught
Of some unknown elixir, hot with youth,
Had stripped her soul and robbed it utterly
Of all its guarded vesture of content,
Its gathered veils and careful barriers
Of stoic, crystal-clear philosophy.
Ten years had vanished like a midnight mist
And all the old unrest, the spiritual strife,
The nameless yearning, kindled and rerisen,
Possessed her heart with ten-fold passionate power.
Like a bright herald from the outer world,
Whose pride and splendour always had for her
A fascination, pregnant with revolt,
Richard had come and with his radiant touch
His earnest eyes, and voice of ardour filled
With limitless suggestions to her soul,
Laid open the old dreamed-of path, so lit
And gladdened with emotion new and sweet,
She dared not yet regard it with full gaze.
And now upon her startled heart returned
The memory of the recent days, the thought
Of John Vantassel and his patient love,
Of the strong, faithful and so generous man,
Whose friendship she had valued and found sweet.
She knew that by an inward vow, as clear
As any outward, she had given herself
To him, yet saw that the slow-ripened thought

Sprang from a life that was not hers at all,
Nor was the offspring of her natural being.
A storm of struggle rose within her soul.
In marriage with Vantassel she beheld
The certain failure of one-half her life,
And yet their friendship had been close and sweet.
To set aside his love, to break the troth
So consciously heart-given, the cold thought
Filled her with horror, and her spirit shrank
In dread and agony.

                      Hour after hour
That night upon her racked and sleepless bed
Margaret lay watching with wide eyes.   She saw
Beyond her open window with its frame
Of vines, the moving stars, the silver gleam
Of branches hung with peach leaves in the moon,
The glimmering hillside and the silent trees.
Her thoughts rushed ever crowding back and forth
Too full of questioning, too madly swift,
For tears.   The sleep that came at last with dreams
Héld her enchanted in a luminous land
With vivid journeys and fantastic flights
Of feverish joy.   With the first streaming gold
That crossed her window from the rising sun,
She woke in anguish, weary and heart-sore.
That evening, when the common tasks were done,
And all the tea-things washed and laid away,
And everything made spotless for the night,
Margaret grave-eyed amid the falling dusk
Was busy with her flowers.   Her troubled heart
Had worn itself to rest, the sluggish rest

Of very weariness, and when the clack
Of the closed gate and jar of Richard's feet
On the sharp gravel, broke upon her ear,
She hushed her spirit with an inward word
And rose to meet him, blindly purposing
To keep her heart in check.   She dared not now
Look full in Richard's fixèd eyes, too bright,
Too dangerously potent with the sense
Of worship and possession.   Richard marked
Her charier smile, her pallor, her tired eyes.
He strove to read them, and a pang of doubt
Startled his thoughts and made them less secure.
Long in the lingering twilight up and down
The dewy walks and by the orchard path
They strolled and talked, and Richard gathered heart;
And Margaret, under the reviving spell,
Yielding little by little to its power,
Grew well nigh reckless.   Richard told at length
The story of his life, and sketched his plans
For the great future, things that fired her thoughts
And roused the old deep-hidden enthusiasm,
And drew her to him with mysterious arms
Of pride and yearning.   They had come at last
Down to the very spot, the rustic seat.
The well-known tree, whose every feature fixed
In Richard's memory, now again beheld,
Under the silent sanction of the stars,
Spurred him beyond control of doubt or fear.
He had talked long, and Margaret had replied,
With a wan touch of hunger in her voice:
"You have toiled so bravely and so well,
Have learned so much and gained so much from life,

Must you not think me weak and slight indeed,
Me who have lost what little light I had.
Who have gone backward in the march of mind,
And let the sacred fire decline and die,
Grown over with neglect and petty cares?"
And Richard turned upon her with grand eyes.
His voice shaken with passion: "Margaret!
'Tis that that I have dreamed of all these years,
That I, grown to the utmost of myself,
Might someday thankfully bring back to you
The life you gave to me. Do you not know
That that which broke the fetters from my soul
Was love, the love of you; and that alone
Has nerved my heart and made me what I am.
This light, I know, could never have flashed forth
With such quick charm, such fruitful potency,
Unless our answering spirits had been charged
With a like force, and fated sympathy.
I dreamed it always, and these final hours
Have made me sure of it. Henceforth as one
Let us take up the way together, each
Made stronger by the other's loving touch.
Shall it not be so, Margaret, beloved?"

And Margaret looked full in Richard's face
With eyes wherein a terrible brightness shone,
And her hands clenched with effort and her face
Grew whiter than white lilies to the lips;
For all was now so simple, could she waive
The word of every teacher but the hour.
Could she but let the golden moment rule,
Forgetful of all else; but through her heart

Still reigned the guardian spirit of her life,
Relentless with a stern and silent power,
The queenly honour that she must not soil.
And Richard, with outstretched and eager arms,
Drew near her murmuring still her name; but she
Drew back, and striving with herself at last
Found strength to speak: "Oh I have been unwise
Not to have warned you at the first, and yet
I was not sure you loved me. You are true
And know that faith and honour must be kept.
You would not deem me worthy if I broke
My solemn troth. What you would ask of me
Another has already claimed and won."
Thus Margaret, bravely with half-broken speech,
And Richard answered, filled with fierce despair:
"O Margaret, you love me; in your heart
You love me, and before this sacred love
All other cold resolves are swept away.
Remember what awaits us; it is law,
A law so deep and sacred that our hearts
Must yield and follow its command, or break.
How can you think of any bond, but this?"
And all the woman rose in Margaret's breast,
The yearning and the yielding tenderness;
And the wild power that tugged at both their hearts
A moment kept her spell-bound. Richard's arms
Had almost wound her in their reckless grasp,
When she sprang from him, and, "No! No!" she
        cried,
"I cannot; you, if you are brave and kind,
Go now, and leave me, think no more of me;
I must be true!" and Margaret, very pale,

Turned from him, and with swift and steady steps
Went up between the dark and silent trees,
And through the garden and the dreaming porch.
With her last strength she climbed the narrow stair,
And found her room, and sank beside the bed,
And laid her head between her hands and wept.

For a long time, like one blinded and stunned,
Richard stood moveless on the orchard path;
And then, little by little like a cloud
That spreading brings the tempest, the mute maze
Impending over all his soul, dissolved
In madness and immeasurable grief.
He sought the house and lingered at the porch,
And roamed the garden, calling "Margaret!"
And then he strode away and walked for hours
About the midnight fields, and through the woods,
Till once again, not knowing how it fell,
He found himself beneath the silent walls
Of the dark-eaved and dreaming house, and knew
The porch and the belovèd garden beds;
And a great fear possessed him, for he seemed
To feel the gathering of a heavy mist
About his soul, and with it came the thought
That as the hope of Margaret from the first
Had given him power, so now the dream destroyed,
The former impotent cloud-life might return.
30

The sleepless night passed over Margaret's head,
And fanning forth in crimson from the east
The summer morning brought the happy sun
Golden and glowing; but to Margaret's heart
The anguish of the thing that she had done
Rose in its naked horror palpable.
She had beat down the true and perfect love,
And dashed away the sparkling cup of life,
Wounding the hand that held it.   Not alone
Of her own grief she thought, but Richard's face,
With its wild stare of blight and agony,
Stood fixed before her, an accusing ghost.
To Richard with his years of toil and hope
Ruin was written in the shattered dream.
All day she wandered through the house and strove
To gain the freedom of her wonted tasks;
In vain; and all was blind before her, will
And purpose shifting idly in the toss
Of thought made weak and masterless by grief.

That day across the fields, so often trod
With easier heart, Vantassel came to seek
His answer, wearing in his handsome face
Care-furrows and unwonted wistfulness.
Margaret had marshalled all her strength and tried
To meet him brightly; but he read her face;
He saw its weary pallor, and the lines
Of strife and suffering, and he marked the change
To effort in her once so gracious speech,
The dull embarrassment that clogged her smile,
And made it piteous.   When the evening meal

Was over, and the two were now alone,
Vantassel standing in the arboured porch
With all his nerves in governance, tightly strung,
Spoke softly, with a gentle hand on hers :
"You know why I have come to-night, my friend ;
My week is over, and it seemed a year—
Each day so full of doubt, and clinging hope.
Can you not give me now the one bright word
Whose music shall ennoble all my life?"

So Margaret with pale lips and fixèd eyes
Stood silent, face to face with destiny.
The blind resolve discarded and remade
To give the fateful answer and have done
Struggled a moment at her heart, and then
She could not say the words; her lips refused
To utter what she willed; but other words,
Reckless and wild, surged up upon her lips,
And broke in utterance, she knew not how.
"I cannot be your wife ; you do not know,
You could not know, you could not understand
The longing of my heart; my inmost soul
Forbids ! I cannot, dare not!"   Then she turned
Smitten with wild compassion and bent down,
And seized his hands and pressed them to her lips,
And kissed them.   "Do not grieve" she cried "at all ;
Indeed I am not fit to be your wife.
You do not know me; no, for all these years
You do not know me !   She whom you should wed
Should be a leal and trusty woman, not
Like me, faithless !" and with a wringing look

Out of great eyes, woe-widened, charged with tears,
She dashed into the house and left him there,
Standing perplexed and dazed. A sudden voice,
Half-friendly and half-mocking at his side,
Woke him out of his dreams. 'Twas Hawthorne's
    tone,
The old man watching him with curious eyes:
"You are too late," he said, "a month ago
Your case was sure; you have heard tell, I guess,
Of Richard Stahlberg, our next neighbour's son,
The college prodigy. He has returned,
And brought a sort of magic in his tongue.
A single day sufficed him to undo
Your work with Margaret. He has turned her head,
Bewitched her utterly!" The old man stopped,
Marking the other's stricken face, and changed
His note, and strove to comfort him; and then
The loosening current of Vantassel's grief
Turned to a wrathful hunger to be told
All that the old man knew of Richard's life,
The make and inward fashion of the man
He deemed his enemy. When night had fallen
And he could hope no more for sight or sound
Of Margaret, Vantassel took once more
His bitter way across the moonlit fields.

Now in the active spirit of the man,
Loving the concrete, too thick-nerved and bluff
For vague emotion, wrath and the desire
Of vengeance almost swallowed up his grief.
The form of Richard towered above his soul,

A thing that he could strike at.   As he strode,
Scarce marking how he chose or kept the paths,
His heart brewed out of the strong fierce blood
A tempest blast with thunder and with fire.

Beyond the fields there lay a scattered wood,
And in the midst thereof a quiet glade,
Tenanted only by the silver moon
And the sharp shadows.   As Vantassel came
Into the open space, a giant form
Loomed out before him from the dusky trunks,
Brow-bent, bare-headed, and the brooding face,
As of one startled by his sweeping step,
Turned into the full moonlight, and grew clear.
Vantassel knew the face, and knew the form,
And his hands clenched and with a rushing stride
He fronted Richard.   In a terrible voice,
Broken and hoarse and reasonless with rage:
"You are the man who robbed me of my love!
Who came at the last hour when all was well,
And ruined both our lives!   You are a thief!
A mean and treacherous thief!   There is a law
To punish them that rob us of our goods,
But how shall we be safe from such as you,
Traitors who creep about us in the dark,
And tempt and steal away our happiness!"

Richard had scarcely time to ward the blow
So sudden was the other's wild attack,
But he gave ground, and in a gentle voice
Cried out, "There is no need to strike, my friend;

Put by your anger for a moment now,
And let me speak, and I will tell you all.
You do not know the matter as it is;
Be patient!" But the other neither heard
Nor heeded, but bore in on Richard's guard
With reckless fury. Then in Richard's soul
The old berserker passion of his youth
Rose for a trice, and putting forth at last
The sudden volume of his mountainous strength,
He seized Vantassel's body round the midst,
Lifted him high in air and thrust him down,
And pinned him like a feather to the earth:
"See! you shall hear me, whether you will or no!"
He said, "Will you be governed now?" He drew
His hands away; and, humbled, and half-stunned,
Vantassel sitting with averted eyes,
Turned sullenly to listen. Richard stood,
Looming above him like a tower, and told
The story of his labour and his love,
Dashing it forth in short and trenchant phrase,
And as he spoke the lawyer locked his arms
About his knees; nor did he break at all
The silence, when the eloquent tongue had ceased;
But Richard in a moment, not yet salved,
Forth leaning with a deep and passionate cry,
Continued: "Now you know how all my life
Is linked with Margaret's, how I draw from her
All that I am, and all I hope to be!
Do you think then, that I can give her up?
There is a bond between us, sacred and inherent,
She too has felt it now, and turns to me

With the one love that cannot be gainsaid,
For the first time discovering her own heart;
If you should break this bond you would not win
The happiness you seek.   Your life and hers
Would find the fate of all unmated things,
The incurable curse of blight and emptiness."

And both were silent, in their stormy hearts
Revolving things beyond the reach of words,
Till in the end the lawyer slowly rose,
And, "You have conquered, both by force of hands,"
He murmured, "and by force of soul.   I yield;
Do as you will.   I read her heart to-day,
And know that I am hopeless.   May the fates
Be good to her, for I have been her friend.
I will release her from all debt to me
By word or letter."   Then he turned away,
And Richard would have touched him with his hand
Or said some gentle word, but he was gone,
Striding with heavy steps and bended head.

The murmurous stillness of the summer night
Was gathering round the silent orchard trees;
The shadowy grass was thick and cool with dew;
And Margaret, hungering much to be alone,
Along the darkening pathway toward the fields
Had come, and reached the bars and lingered there.
The mountain, in the silvery radiance
Of the full moon, stood large and sombre-flanked
Above her with its glittering crest of leaves.
Her heart, like weary water after storm,

Lay spent with care and passion. It seemed now
There was no room for her to think or do,
But just to follow with obedient steps
The beck of destiny. Upon her bed
In the dark farmhouse yonder she had left
The final sad memorial of her strife,
A letter soiled and blotted with her tears.

She laid her arms upon the silent rails
And stood gazing into the darkness, full
Only of love and limitless regret.
For a long time, until her limbs were tired,
Thus rapt and unregardful, she remained
In dreamland quietude ; and then at last,
Without surprise, as if it were the next
And final stroke of some impersonal fate,
The form of Richard, coming with slow steps
Out of the mountain shadows near at hand,
As half irresolute, seized and absorbed
Her sense, and gathered in one noiseless stream
All the dim drifts and currents of her soul.

Richard drew near, with blanched and fixèd eyes.
He saw the form, the beautiful pale face,
Set like a shadowy statue in the dusk
Of spiritual enchantment. He stood still,
Half fearing : "Am I right to come?" he cried,
"I dreamed that I might come to you to-night,
That something might be changed, and I might dare :"
And Margaret did not answer, but her eyes,
The signals of the mute and shining soul,

Gave themselves utterly to his—one look
Of silent full surrenderment. Her lips,
Melting into a strange and speechless smile,
Became a flower, whose poignant loveliness
An age of dearth and hunger had made pale,
Lingering the sweeter from its hidden root
Of shame and agony. Without a word
They took each other's hands, and turned and passed
Up the cool path between the orchard trees,
Wrapt in such thoughts as only they can know
Whose hearts through tears and effort have attained
The portals of the perfect fields of life,
And thence, half dazzled by the glow, perceive
The endless road before them, clear and free.

The undersigned in completing this memorial edition of Archibald Lampman's poems desire to express their thanks to the anonymous donor of an amount sufficient to cover the whole cost of the book, to Messrs. Copeland & Day, 69 Cornhill, Boston, Mass., who courteously presented their copyright in "Lyrics of Earth," and to the Linotype Company of Montreal for having gratuitously set the type of the whole book. Thanks are also sincerely tendered to the many who, throughout Canada, the United States and England, ensured the success of the volume by their personal interest and effort and to those who contributed by their subscriptions to the total amount realized for the family of the author.

S. E. DAWSON,
W. D. LeSUEUR,
DUNCAN C. SCOTT.

CONTENTS

Contents

AT THE LONG SAULT: MAY, 1660

UNDER the day-long sun there is life and mirth
  In the working earth,
And the wonderful moon shines bright
  Through the soft spring night,
The innocent flowers in the limitless woods are springing
  Far and away
  With the sound and the perfume of May,
And ever up from the south the happy birds are winging,
  The waters glitter and leap and play
  While the grey hawk soars.

But far in an open glade of the forest set
  Where the rapid plunges and roars,
Is a ruined fort with a name that men forget,—
  A shelterless pen
  With its broken palisade,
  Behind it, musket in hand,
  Beyond message or aid
  In this savage heart of the wild,
  Mere youngsters, grown in a moment to men,
  Grim and alert and arrayed,
  The comrades of Daulac stand.
  Ever before them, night and day,
  The rush and skulk and cry
  Of foes, not men but devils, panting for prey;
  Behind them the sleepless dream
Of the little frail-walled town, far away by the plunging
      stream,
  Of maiden and matron and child,
With ruin and murder impending, and none but they
To beat back the gathering horror
Deal death while they may,
  And then die.

1

At the Long Sault

Day and night they have watched while the little plain
Grew dark with the rush of the foe, but their host
Broke ever and melted away, with no boast
But to number their slain;
And now as the days renew
Hunger and thirst and care
Were they never so stout, so true,
Press at their hearts; but none
Falters or shrinks or utters a coward word,
Though each setting sun
Brings from the pitiless wild new hands to the Iroquois
      horde,
And only to them despair.

Silent, white-faced, again and again
Charged and hemmed round by furious hands,
Each for a moment faces them all and stands
In his little desperate ring; like a tired bull moose
Whom scores of sleepless wolves, a ravening pack,
Have chased all night, all day
Through the snow-laden woods, like famine let loose;
And he turns at last in his track
Against a wall of rock and stands at bay;
Round him with terrible sinews and teeth of steel
They charge and recharge; but with many a furious
      plunge and wheel,
Hither and thither over the trampled snow,
He tosses them bleeding and torn;
Till, driven, and ever to and fro
Harried, wounded and weary grown,
His mighty strength gives way
And all together they fasten upon him and drag him
      down.

At the Long Sault

So Daulac turned him anew
With a ringing cry to his men
In the little raging forest glen,
And his terrible sword in the twilight whistled and slew.
And all his comrades stood
With their backs to the pales, and fought
Till their strength was done;
The thews that were only mortal flagged and broke
Each struck his last wild stroke,
And they fell one by one,
And the world that had seemed so good
Passed like a dream and was naught.

And then the great night came
With the triumph-songs of the foe and the flame
Of the camp-fires.
Out of the dark the soft wind woke,
The song of the rapid rose alway
And came to the spot where the comrades lay,
Beyond help or care,
With none but the red men round them
To gnash their teeth and stare.

All night by the foot of the mountain
    The little town lieth at rest,
The sentries are peacefully pacing;
    And neither from East nor from West

Is there rumour of death or of danger;
    None dreameth tonight in his bed
That ruin was near and the heroes
    That met it and stemmed it are dead.

3

At the Long Sault

But afar in the ring of the forest,
    Where the air is so tender with May
And the waters are wild in the moonlight,
    They lie in their silence of clay.

The numberless stars out of heaven
    Look down with a pitiful glance;
And the lilies asleep in the forest
    Are closed like the lilies of France.

1898

THE FROST ELVES

I FELL into a sleep at midnight, while the frost
Spotted my window hoar with crystal stars, and crossed
The panes with garlands gathered at the night's noon
By fairies in some mystic meadow of the moon.

And when I woke methought I saw two strange large
    eyes
That watched me through the icy wreathes and
    imageries;
Two eyes alone, and if it were a dream or no
I could not guess, for they were fixed upon me so,
With such intent regard and such immovable peer
So misty pale and yet so mystically clear.

I rose and quickly as two rain drops from hot stone
The shadowy thing had fled, the curious eyes were gone.
But on my window in a small and intricate hand,
Written in elfin symbols hard to understand
I found some occult sayings; as it seemed to me
A poem in quaint rhythm rhymed fantastically.
All that night of reverie I dreamed and pored
Upon them till their meaning opened word by word;
And in the starshine while the crimson dawn was young
I made this transcript of them in our common tongue:

In the land of the frost elves under the pole,
    Azure and gold and rose,
Where the crystal tides of the north wind roll
    Through the valley of perfect repose,

The Frost Elves

A city of amber stands withdrawn
  On the opaline edge of the west,
And noonday and even, darkness and dawn
  Are like one at the core of its rest.

Its domes and parapets clear and still
  Their nebulous heights uphold,
There's a wind at a street's end up on a hill,
  But it bloweth a dust of gold.

'Tis half a year and a day tonight,
  As I passed that city and sped
By its frost sealed gates in the emerald light
  I saw through the deep half-red,

Where the battlements nick their notch upon notch
  And the surge of the daybreak falls,
A million shadows of ghosts at watch
  On the crystalline length of its walls.

Peasants and emperors, old and young,
  They fronted the low sunrise,
They sat with no sound; and the hoar frost hung
  In the width of their passionless eyes.

From the depth of the violet zenith there fell
  On that pallid impalpable line
The grasp of an infinite silence, the spell
  Of one vision auroral, divine:

The Frost Elves

These were the spirits of men who came
  To the marvellous moment of birth,
With a body of flax and a spirit of flame
  Who could never find rest upon earth;

Who lived at the uttermost tension of life
  In the power of its pitiless need,
Whose night was of dreams and their day was of strife
  But now they have peace indeed;

They lean from their emerald battlements there
  Where only the frost flower grows,
And dawn-tide and even are perfectly fair
  In the realm of eternal repose;

With never the breath of desire, without will
  On the common of Time they endure,
And the mood of Allfather enwraps them as still
  As eternity, boundless, frost-pure.

January 3, 1893

A VISION OF APRIL

IN my dream I saw a meadow
   And a group of leafless trees,
With a net of lucid shadow
   Delicatest traceries
Fallen in a purple mass
On the warm grey matted grass.

And beyond the meadow blowing
   Down a narrow slope of wood
I could see the trilliums glowing
   And the dog-tooth golden-hued;
All the maples blossoming
Made their branches red with spring.

There a little brook grey-sedgèd
   In an earthy channel crept;
And a single cloud white-edgèd,
   That in heaven beamed and slept,
From the deep blue-bosomed tide
Turned a purple underside.

Where the farther bank was shady
   With that net of tangled boughs
Stood a slender grey-eyed lady
   With pale cheeks and pure pale brows;
Brown her hair was, soft of hue
And her dress was tender blue.

8

A Vision of April

Like an angel slipped from heaven
   Or a dryad from the tree,
Something wide as life was given
   To her fixèd reverie,
Something noble, something bright,
Leagues of summer, leagues of light.

All the small birds sang around her
   And the sunshine seemed to cling
At the narrow zone that bound her
   And about her feet, and Spring,
Like a new world from the South,
Dawned and dreamed upon her mouth.

Was it April then I wondered
   In an earthly girlish guise
With that glowing hair soft-sundered
   And those pure and cloudless eyes?
April fashioned by a spell
Like a Lady I love well?

Passion seized me beyond measure,
   And I leaped the brook and cried
" 'Tis the hour of perfect pleasure;
   Like a lover by his bride
In this plot of light shall stand
I and April hand in hand."

A Vision of April

But the vision broke and vanished
  And this little mead was rolled
Wood and brook together, banished
  In a curling mist of gold;
Doubtful glooms began to weave
And I woke at last to grieve.

For I heard the high roof rocking
  And the forest clash and roar
With the wailing wind, that mocking
  Howled and whistled at my door;
April was too sweet a boon
I and autumn came full soon.

December 28, 1895

THE EMPEROR'S TRUE-LOVE

I AM the emperor's true-love
  And mine this moated tower;
Far away are the camps and the cities
  But they have known my power.

I rise with the lark at morning
  To make me fresh and fair,
And the warm blood laughs within me
  As I bind my golden hair.

There is witchcraft in my beauty,
  There is magic in my mien;
I am the Emperor's true-love
  And I would not be his queen.

He takes my hands as he enters
  And he bends to kiss them so;
His are as brown as walnuts
  And mine are as white as snow.

I lie on his breast at even
  With never a boon to crave,
Like the mote in the wind, or the seaweed
  On the breadth of the long sea-wave.

The hurry of men and their travail
  They tell me is bitter to see;
But here there are night and day-dreams
  And love is enough for me.

The Emperor's True-Love

I hate the stir and the tumult
  The coarse great world and its lies;
But I love the meeting in silence
  And the light of my conqueror's eyes.

There is silence and bloom in my garden
  With only the hush of the trees,
And the lingering note of the thrushes,
  And the day-long murmur of bees.

January 17, 1893

MAN AND NATURE

I STOOD in yonder city streets today
  And saw the crowd pass by me young and old,
A medley of strange masks, some sad, some gay,
  Some foul and fierce, some pitiless and cold,
A few were fair and sweet to look upon;
But perfect beauty could I find in none.

Some passed whose footsteps made a stately sound,
  Whose eyes were like armed gateways barred and bare,
Sweeping the world as 'twere a battleground
  That neither love nor truth might enter there;
And others wore smooth faces but their eyes
Proclaimed their masks so many bitter lies.

And when I thought of what good men have done,
  Heroes' bright hopes that darkened in distress,
Of the vast world and all the race to run,
  And nature in her easeful loveliness,
A burden of great sorrow swelled and lay
Hard at my heart and so I turned away.

But here in these wide fields touched by no skill
  Save nature's only, perfect and unstained,
All men may surfeit to their utmost will
  The thirst of beauty, yet leave half undrained;
For here the old seems always strange and new,
All shapes are fair and every touch is true.

Man and Nature

That only which is nature's friend shall find
    Beauty's firm law and follow it aright;
But long ago the children of mankind
    Abandoned nature and sought other light,
Made their own Gods, endowed with other power,
And beauty left them at the self-same hour.

These marguerites whose bright and innocent heads
    Nod at the wind and smile about my knees,
How fair are they; and that great elm that spreads
    Its level fleece and pendent draperies
O'er the drowsed head, it hath not soul; but see
What grace, what strength, what generous dignity!

1889-1890

YONDER through the darkness surging
   Gather to the drums of Fate,
All the dreams of life converging,
   Joy and sorrow, love and hate.
Thou canst hear the voices calling
   Faintly from Eternity,
Rising in the void and falling
            Deo confitemini.

Rolling doors are opening slowly
   In the ghostly house of Time,
With a murmur mild and holy,
   To the cloudly portal climb:
Trains of fates and memories bearing
   On a vast and shadowy bier,
To the dim gray silence faring,
     One more dead and crownless year.

And they lay the old year grimly
   In a great and lidless tomb,
Under vaulted depths that dimly
   Only mists and stars illume:
There no word is ever spoken,
   And no sound the silence stirs:
There the ages sleep unbroken
     Over endless sepulchres.

New Year's Eve

But afar beneath the arches
  Of the midnight, outward bound,
Moves the host of Fate, and marches
  With a faint and spectral sound;
All the realms of Time invading—
  Only holiest eyes shall see—
Farther yet and farther, fading:
                    Deo confitemini.

THE CHOICE

THE world goes by me an unfathomed stream
   Too bright with flame, too dark with mystery,
A shadowy glory and an ancient dream;
   Its conflict and its pomp are not for me.
By others let great epics be compiled,
   Let others' songs in stormier measures flow:
   I sit me in the windy grass and grow
As wise as age, as joyous as a child.

1895

THE USURER

WHERE the streets are most astir
Sits a bright-eyed usurer,
Like a crinkled spider set
In the centre of his net.

1884

18

EPITAPH ON A RICH MAN

HE made himself a great name in his day,
A glittering fellow on the world's hard way,
He tilled and seeded and reaped plentifully
From the black soil of human misery;
He won great riches, and they buried him
With splendour that the people's want makes grim;
But some day he shall not be called to mind
Save as the curse and pestilence of his kind.

December 18, 1893

OTTAWA

A CITY set like a star
  Of stone on a soft grey hill,
A river that shineth afar,
  A serpent silver still.

An endless sun-stretched plain
  With forests in dim blue shrouds,
And little wisps of rain
  Falling from far-off clouds.

These are my friends today,
  I have come to their shrine again
By the lonely well-loved way
  From the fiery haunts of men.

To my troubled soul they call
  In a language large and sweet,
And the rede of the deathless all
  To my shaken heart repeat.

1894

WINTER-SOLITUDE

I SAW the city's towers on a luminous pale-grey sky;
Beyond them a hill of the softest mistiest green,
With naught but frost and the coming of night between,
And a long thin cloud above it the colour of August rye.

I sat in the midst of a plain on my snowshoes with
        bended knee
Where the thin wind stung my cheeks,
And the hard snow ran in little ripples and peaks,
Like the fretted floor of a white and petrified sea.

And a strange peace gathered about my soul and shone,
As I sat reflecting there,
In a world so mystically fair,
So deathly silent—I so utterly alone.

February, 1893

21

ESTRANGEMENT

TWO noble trees together stand
Silent in an autumn land,
   One is dead and bare;
But the winds have stripped the other
Brooding by its sapless brother
   In a grey despair.

Two hearts that once were bound together
Sit apart with broken tether,
   Thoughts that blindly grope,
Between the two no word is said;
Love in the one is dead
   And in the other hope.

1887-1888

PERSISTENCE

TO those who ever march with faith unbent,
Preserving in its fervid prime
A single purpose clear and plain,
Ready, although the twentieth time
To strike and fall, and strike again,—
Fate changes and the Gods relent.

1898

FATE

BY gift of some mysterious law
  I cannot fathom or divine,
Thy spirit hath the power to draw
  And master mine.

Thou art the wind and I the tree,
  The aspen trembling and distressed,
The prairie bloom, the broken sea
  That cannot rest.

September, 1893

CLOUD AND SUN

WITH those cold eyes, my dear,
Those cold grey eyes,
You cover all the blossoming earth with cloud
And leaden skies,
You dim the stars and make the daylight sere;
And wind me in a wintry shroud
With those cold eyes, my dear.

But if you smile, my dear,—
Ah! if you smile—
I care not if the mighty sun in heaven
Be quenched the while,
Or if the moon, or if the stars appear;
For light enough to me is given,
If you but smile, my dear.

October 18, 1895

LONELINESS

SO it is with us all; we have our friends
 Who keep the outer chambers, and guard well
Our common path; but there their service ends,
 For far within us lies an iron cell
 Soundless and secret, where we laugh or moan
 Beyond all succour, terribly alone.

1894

EVEN BEYOND MUSIC

TOUCH not the ivory keys again
    No music tonight, my dear,
The rhythmic sound is too full of pain
    I cannot bear to hear.

For the music out of a golden air
    Sings only of peace and joy,
Of the ever great and the ever fair
    And love without alloy;

And points us here in a world of pain
    To joy and all its cost,
To the beautiful things we sought in vain
    And the things we loved and lost.

Then touch the ivory keys no more,
    Nay, let them be, I cried,
For my heart tonight is bleeding and sore
    And all its wounds are wide.

1898-1899

LIBERTY

JUST a hundred years ago
All the nations were a-ring
With the shout of freedom—Woe
To the hated fetich—King!

Freedom, Ah! the cry
Was a sword to conquer by
Hate, injustice, tyranny
Beneath the word would cease:
Plenty, brotherhood, and peace
Like a heaven for the free!

But the tyrant kings are gone—
Word, or substance, like a dream—
And the nations rule supreme.
Teeming millions grow
And the anxious world rolls on;
Brilliant cities tall and wide
Boast their numbers and their pride.
But the justice comes not, woe
Harvests still her field: and fate
With as blind and dark a weight,
Unproportioned now as then,
Presses on the souls of men.

Still the ancient curse survives
Making wreck of human lives;
Pride and slavery and shame
Prosper in the people's name.

Liberty

Lo! the master still
From his palace gate commands,
And the toiler works his will
With his worn and bleeding hands.
Golden ladies sigh
From their cushions and their lace,
While the stricken trull goes by
With her wild and haunted face.

Was it for this—for this? we cry
That you made the peoples free,
That your vessels plough the sea,
And your buildings climb the sky;—
For this that one should hold
All that kings possessed of old
And be laid in balm and gold;
While the other, just a clown,
Should have service for his lot,
Be a bondman, and go down
To the soulless pit and rot?

This! my Masters, Nay!
For there comes at last the day
When the meanest and most poor
Having scanned the ages' flow
Probed his hurt, and guessed the cure
Shall rise up and answer—No!

January 1, 1898

29

CRETE *

I

ABOUT the fields of Ida, now no more
The happy choristers at autumn throng;
No longer by the bright and storied shore
The harvest echoes with old Dorian song;
Now only the fierce fronts of crag maintain
Unblanched the ancient unforgotten trust,
And grim with centuries of pride and pain
Defy the foul barbarian and his lust.

Have ye no pity, Nations, and no shame,—
Remembering the great deeds and songs of old,—
No shame, no pity in your armèd might,
That so ye stand cold-eyed, and watch the night
Of helpless ruin and despair enfold
The last bright remnant of the Dorian name?

II

This remnant of old Hellas, this fair isle,
That gave long since the laws to newer lands,
Whose scattered stones with sweet mementoes smile
Still of old glories and Hellenic hands!
Have ye forgotten the old tongue whose sound
Still lingers in your softest syllables,
Forgotten the fair founts on sacred ground
Where the pure river of all knowledge dwells?
And thou, O England, must thou shrink indeed
Thou at the shadow of a nameless fear,
Nor dare alone, alone to rise and heed
A fate so tragic and a cry so clear;
Shalt thou not strike, sole-handed though it be,
A blow for pity and for liberty?

*These Sonnets were inspired by the rebellion of Crete against Turkish rule which, after years of conflict, ended in the union of Crete with Greece.

Crete

III

Through all the world, in every natural heart
That beats for truth and beauty, rings and thrills
Above the selfish clangor of the mart
That cry for succour from the Cretan hills.
The soul of Italy awakes and warms,
Touched by her own immortal memories;
And Sparta for her famished sister arms;
Athens remembers Epimenides;
And thou, America, whose busy hands
Long since have sheathed and laid aside the sword,
Not yet to other and less happy lands
Canst thou be blinded wholly, such a word
Must blot the sunshine of thy peaceful world
Till thou too stand with starry flags unfurled.

October 14, 1896

THE POWER OF MUSIC

MOST beautiful because thou canst not die,
Changeless, eternal as the perfect sphere,
Lonely and strong because thou canst not fear
But winnest to thine end unfalteringly,
Glorious and sweet thy touch because thereby
This life's great width and splendour are made clear,
Yet strangely sad in that thou bringest near
The knowledge of life's frail inadequacy.
Music which art the inarticulate speech
That beauty uses when she fain would reach
The very heart, her spirit listening
Beside the gates of life with passionate ears,
And thence to us with power interpreting
The meaning of all growth, and time, and tears.

1887

ON THE DEATH OF TENNYSON

TONIGHT while the grey wings of storm are spread
So wide and deep about the unquiet world
And yonder where our spring-loved flowers uncurled
Lie withered ferns and crimson leaves instead,
Passes, sad-lipped from bended head to head,
On every English land, mixed with the blind
And fevered surge and tumult of mankind
The word that Alfred Tennyson is dead.
Aye, he is dead!   Even as those great ones die,
Who leave their sacred bodies to the dust—
Lest Death himself, even Death, should suffer wrong,
Being robbed of his just due—yet deathlessly
Leave us their essence in eternal trust
The word, the power, the passion and the song.

October 6, 1892

MAN'S FUTURE

YON elm-tree towering at its perfect ease
With level fleece and pendent draperies,
What man with all the gifts of all his lands
Can match its clean perfection as it stands?
None, for that noble and harmonious tree
Fulfils its law of being utterly:

What nature meant the elm for from of yore
Even now it is, and time can do no more.
But man is still unfinished: many an age
Must bear him slowly onward stage by stage
In long adjustment,—mind and flesh and soul
Finally balanced to a rhythmic whole,
Installed at last in his appointed place,
Divine in beauty and undreamed of grace.

May 1, 1898

THE TRUE LIFE

THIS life is a depressing compromise
Between the soul and what it wills to do
And what your careful neighbours plan for you,
Often the thing most odious in your eyes,
A makeshift truce, whereby the soul denies
The birthright of a being bright and new
Puts on a mask and crushes down the true,
And lolls behind a fence of courteous lies.
O, world of little men, how sweet a thing
The true life is, what strength and joy it hath,
What grandeur and what beauty it might bring,
Could we but sweep forever from our path
Your cant rules and detested casuistries,
Your clap-trap, and your damned hypocrisies.

March 2, 1894

FAIR SPEECH

THE sword is laid aside; when shall we feel
   The cruelty of careless speech; the sneer,
   The idle taunt, the unconsidered jeer,
The volley of fierce answers that like steel
Straight to the soul cut stabs we cannot heal,
   Cold speeches that with lingering bitterness
   Deal unknown curses where we ought to bless;
Think not because thine inmost heart means well.
   Thou hast the freedom of rude speech; sweet words
   Are like the voices of returning birds
   Filling the soul with summer; or a bell
   That calls the weary and the sick to prayer:
   Even as thy manners let thy speech be fair.

September, 1889

THE GROWTH OF LOVE

I

YEARNING upon the faint rose-curves that flit
About her child-sweet mouth and innocent cheek,
And in her eyes watching with eyes all meek
The light and shadow of laughter, I would sit
Mute, knowing our two souls might never knit;
As if a pale proud lily flower should seek
The love of some red rose, but could not speak
One word of her blithe tongue to tell of it.
For oh, my love was sunny-lipped and stirred
With all swift light and sound and gloom not long
Retained: I with dreams weighed, that ever heard
Sad burdens echoing through the loudest throng,
She, the wild song of some May-merry bird;
I, but the listening maker of a song.

II

My Lady is not learned in many books
Nor hath much love for grave discourses, strung
With gaudy ornament; for she is young
And full of many pranks and laughing looks;
And yet her heart hath many tender nooks
Of fervour and sweet charity; her tongue,
For all its laughter, yet is often wrung
With soft compassion for Life's painful crooks.
I love my Lady for her lovely face
And for her mouth and for her eyes and hair;
More still I love her for her laughing grace
And for her wayward ways and changeful air;
But most of all Love gaineth ground apace,
Because my Lady's heart is pure and fair.

37

III

Oft gazing on her fairness I would fall
Into a dream beholding unaware
The daughter of old Hengist blithely fair
To her new master, once in his loud hall,
Tread queenly with the golden cup, and call
To him soft wassail, loud as she might dare,
For shame of peering eyes and the red flare
And middle stream of ringing festival.
For like a saint's her yellow hair doth shine
Most lovely when the soft locks fall amiss,
And I would call her mouth one perfect bliss
Of glimmering dimple and pale laughter-line,
Enough to make a man's heart faint and pine
To take them all up with one blinding kiss.

IV

"Sweet trees," I cried, in plaining dreams astray,
Through mead and woodland dolefully ylad,*
Where all the leaves and fretless flowers were glad
With the sweet fervour of full-bosomed May,
And the birds sang soft marriage-hymns alway;
"Sweet trees and flowers," I dearly would ye had
Some little note somewhere of tired and sad,
For I go heavy-hearted all this day.
When I would woo my love, she turns aside,
And shakes her head and smiles and is at ease;
"Ah me, why doth my Lady so?" I cried,
"Sweet trees and flowers"; but they did never heed;
There was no answer in the shining mead,
Or in the flowers, or any in the trees.

* Obsolete form, meaning "led."

38

V

Where many changes fall of gloom and light,
And many shades of sad and sweet have place,
In fast and vigil for my Lady's grace
Kneeleth my soul in corded raiment dight,
And evermore a murmuring anchorite
With sleepless hands, and love-bright passionate face
Counting his golden rosary apace
In prayer and praise divides the day and night.
And diverse answers to my suppliant drouth
Giveth that love in diverse moods to me;
But, good or ill, my heart would count them sweet
For all my life is at my Lady's feet
And joy and peace and biting agony
Are in the keeping of her soft sweet mouth.

VI

PRAISE AND PRAYER

1

Her cheeks are softer than small clouds that lie
Touched with the rose at even, and her eyes
Are blue, and broad, and honest, and so sweet,
For their sake deeper are the May-time skies,
And the green grasses, as she passes by,
Are greener for the treading of her feet.
Sweeter than Spring, new risen from the south
The smiles that dwell upon her maiden mouth,
The curvèd lips were made to bear the rain
Of happy kisses, that are laid away
In shadow of much longing, and sweet pain,
Waiting the dawning of a holy day.

2

Ah, God were very good to me, I said,
If this, this only, he would grant for alms,
That one day I might hold her yellow head,
With all its locks between my worshipping palms,
And bend and kiss the innocent lips upheld;
And the fair cheeks caress from youth to eld.
Ah me; I would have toiled, as no man did
Ever on earth, or with a strength divine
Have braved the whole hard world, if she did bid;
Only to touch her glorious lips and twine
Thrice-blessèd her two yielded hands in mine,
And tell her all that in my heart lay hid.

VII

I saw a distant ballroom loudly fair
And how my Lady with her child-soft face
And firm sweet shoulders laden with the grace
And curlèd richness of her yellow hair
Sat laughing in some softly cushioned lair,
Or in among the dancers whirled and sped
With dainty feet, and in my dream I said,
Among them all my Lady's rich and rare.
My Lady's rich and rare, and tenfold sweet:
Ah, well I wonder if the sound and glee,
The maze and talk, the rush of spinning feet
The only masters of her feet may be,
Or if her heart doth ever fall abeat
With any sudden nestling dream of me.

The Growth of Love

VIII

Long days and months my Lady did not know
What weary longing for her love I had,
Or how the days to me were dark or glad
With every change of her sweet face, and oh,
I dared not tell her that I loved her so,
But dreaming on her fairness thought me mad,
And the long nights to me were sharp and sad
With so sore longing, sick with many a woe.
But now, O Heaven, the world is all divine;
For she hath let me touch her lips and twine
Both arms about her beauty; even now
With so sweet dreams my face is lying meek
Upon my Lady's heart, and lo, her cheek
Like a great rose, is soft against my brow.

IX

One hour we have, sweet love, to kiss and say
Soft winning words, and kindle soft replies;
The small sweet mouth, touching my shoulder lies,
So near to mine it cannot say me nay.
Dear Lady, hear me, many times this day
My eyes adream were kindled with thine eyes,
Thy lips touched mine in kisses crowned with sighs,
And the dear heart was never far away.
Dear Lady sweetheart, Oh that Time were dead,
And we might live and love forever here
Mingle soft murmuring talk and no more thread
The shifting mazes of swift faith and fear;
Like honeyed minutes feel the years fall by,
And in a dream forever kiss and sigh.

41

X

Or whether sad or joyous be her hours,
Yet ever is she good and ever fair.
If she be glad, 'tis like a child's wild air,
Who claps her hands above a heap of flowers;
And if she's sad, it is no cloud that lowers,
Rather a saint's pale grace, whose golden hair
Gleams like a crown, whose eyes are like a prayer
From some quiet window under minster towers.
But ah, Belovèd, how shall I be taught
To tell this truth in any rhymèd line?
For words and woven phrases fall to naught
Lost in the silence of one dream divine.
Wrapped in the beating wonder of this thought:
Even thou, who art so precious, thou art mine!

XI

Belovèd, those who moan of love's brief day
Shall find but little grace with me, I guess,
Who know too well this passion's tenderness
To deem that it shall lightly pass away,
A moment's interlude in life's dull play;
Though many loves have lingered to distress,
So shall not ours, sweet Lady, ne'ertheless,
But deepen with us till both heads be grey.
For perfect love is like a fair green plant,
That fades not with its blossoms, but lives on,
And gentle lovers shall not come to want,
Though fancy with its first mad dream be gone;
Sweet is the flower, whose radiant glory flies,
But sweeter still the green that never dies.

1884-1885

A PORTRAIT IN SIX SONNETS

I

TALL is my friend, for Nature would have marred
Her breadth of vision with a meaner height:
Full-browed, for at her bidding are unbarred
The gates of Beauty and the inward sight:
And slender, for her eager soul denies
A needless burden to the delicate frame:
Grey-eyed, for grey is wisdom—yet with eyes,
Mobile and deep, and quick for thought or flame
A voice of many notes that breaks and changes
And fits each meaning with its vital chord,
A speech, true to the heart, that lightly ranges
From jocund laughter to the serious word,
And over all a bearing proud and free,
A noble grace, a conscious dignity.

II

Light-footed and light-handed, quick to feel,
And sensitive as water—life to her
Its sweetest and its bitterest shall reveal,
Yet leave her a secure philosopher.
The spirit's inward hunger and thought's care,
Strange birthgift of our dark witch mother, Truth,
Have only given her what is tenfold fair,
The grace of knowledge with the grace of youth.
Impulsive, yet clear-minded, nature's stress
Keeps her too human for the stoic's part,
And wisdom hath she for her lord no less,
A wary helmsman to the generous heart.
Her friendship—'tis for them that know the worth
Of all things subtlest and most rare on earth.

A Portrait in Six Sonnets

III

She laughs with all, but none hath seen her weep;
A tender stoic, beautiful and wise;   ·
What sorrow or what passion she may keep
Behind that full pale brow, those veiled grey eyes,
I know not, none shall know; but all the tide
Of all her being softly set to truth
In brow and breast and dainty foot abide
The strength of woman's years, the grace of youth.
What gentle power I wonder in her moods
Sustains her, what unvexed philosophy;
For when I think of her I seem to see
April herself among the sunny woods
With laughing brooks and little clouds that pass;
I dream of bluebirds and hepaticas.

IV

You talk of age, my friend, to whom youth's prime
Is hardly past, whom Beauty's slow eclipse
Hath not yet neared: I see no mark of Time
In the bright eyes, quick step and laughing lips;
A wrinkle—'tis the sign whereby we know
The laughter habit of a kindly face;
A few grey hairs mixed with the brown to show
A rarer wisdom added to your grace.
And when age comes in truth it will but give
Discovery of some greater way to live.
How lovely you will be when you are old
I fancy the smooth brow, the snow-white hair;
Years cannot mar you ever for you hold
That potent grace of soul that time must spare.

V

There is no single hour for me, no place
Unhallowed by her presence nobly sweet,
The slender form so deftly made for grace,
From the pure forehead to the wingèd feet,
The beautiful broad brow so soft and full
Above the tender eye-lids and veiled eyes,
Where gleams of lovely laughter break and lull,
And sparkling tears and such deep mysteries
Of mind and spirit as the kind sweet lips
Leave speechless for the sense of love to learn.
To her forever like storm-stainèd ships
To the old havens, all my thoughts return—
Return and lie close moored—to rest a while
By some stored look or some long-treasured smile.

VI

To hold for a possession in the mind,
In every hour of life, in every place,
A noble spirit's influence, pure and kind,
The image of an honoured form and face,—
Better than any soundest article
Of any creed is this; and this to me,
This image and this faith unchangeable,
This pattern of the fairest dignity,
Is present ever in my friend,—my friend,—
Whom only shall high thoughts and deeds attend,
The gentlest and the wisest.   Touched by her,
A world of finer vision I have found;
Less heedful of the common fret and stir,
I tread, grave-hearted, upon loftier ground.

1895-1899

45

DATE DUE

GAYLORD			PRINTED IN U.S.A.